A Scotsman of advancing years, resident in the west of Ireland, the author has fished since he was a child. He started out working in a mill sweeping the floor and descended from that to senior management and consultancy, all the time finding relaxation and contemplation on Ireland's loughs and rivers. Inherently mean, he ties his own flies, uses dilapidated tackle and drives old wrecks of cars but is generous with his time and advice. How his beautiful and talented partner puts up with him will forever remain one of life's great mysteries.

To my fellow anglers

Colin McLean

ANGLING AROUND IRELAND

AUSTIN MACAULEY PUBLISHERS™
LONDON * CAMBRIDGE * NEW YORK * SHARJAH

Copyright © Colin McLean 2023

The right of Colin McLean to be identified as author of this work has been asserted by the author in accordance with sections 77 and 78 of the Copyright, Designs and Patents Act 1988.

All rights reserved. No part of this publication may be reproduced, stored in a retrieval system, or transmitted in any form or by any means, electronic, mechanical, photocopying, recording, or otherwise, without the prior permission of the publishers.

Any person who commits any unauthorised act in relation to this publication may be liable to criminal prosecution and civil claims for damages.

The story, experiences, and words are the author's alone.

A CIP catalogue record for this title is available from the British Library.

ISBN 9781528954402 (Paperback)
ISBN 9781528956321 (ePub e-book)

www.austinmacauley.com

First Published 2023
Austin Macauley Publishers Ltd®
1 Canada Square
Canary Wharf
London
E14 5AA

Where to even start! My parents for buying me my first fishing rod and constantly encouraging me to stand on my own two feet. Helen, my partner, for her patience and positivity no matter how badly I mess things up. My fishing buddies (you know who you are) who put up with my nonsense and humour my idiosyncrasies. The readers of my blog who gave me the confidence to try my hand at writing a book. And you, dear readers, for buying and (hopefully) enjoying this diary of fishing exploits.

Table of Contents

Foreword	11
What Is It All About?	13
About the Writer	19
Chapter 1: Sligo	23
Chapter 2: Roscommon	32
Chapter 3: Leitrim	40
Chapter 4: Clare	47
Chapter 5: Cavan	55
Chapter 6: Offaly	63
Chapter 7: Longford	71
Chapter 8: Westmeath	79
Chapter 9: Mayo	87
Chapter 10: Galway	95
Chapter 11: Armagh	103
Chapter 12: Fermanagh	111
Chapter 13: Meath	119
Chapter 14: Laois	127
Chapter 15: Dublin	135
Chapter 16: Monaghan	146
Chapter 17: Antrim	155

Chapter 18: Carlow	164
Chapter 19: Kildare	172
Chapter 20: Louth	180
Chapter 21: Down	188
Chapter 22: Wexford	197
Chapter 23: Kilkenny	204
Chapter 24: Derry	212
Chapter 25: Tyrone	220
Chapter 26: Cork	229
Chapter 27: Kerry	237
Chapter 28: Tipperary	245
Chapter 29: Waterford	253
Chapter 30: Wicklow	261
Chapter 31: Limerick	269
Chapter 32: Donegal	277
Reflections	286

Foreword

Thank you for picking up this book. I'm guessing you are interested in angling so here is the lowdown on the contents. This is a chronicle of 32 individual fishing trips, one to each of the thirty-two counties on the island of Ireland. Just me driving around in an old beat-up car trying to catch a fish, any fish, using whatever legal methods and my experience permit. What was supposed to be a breezy jaunt around Ireland with a fishing rod over the course of one season turned into something very different when Covid struck in 2020. Along with everyone else all my plans turned to dust and the ensuing lockdowns and restrictions turned my pet project into a drawn-out plod instead of a brisk sprint.

    I am a fly fisher, have been for almost all of my life. While planning this project it soon became clear that to give myself a better chance of success I had to learn about coarse fishing. This book therefore documents my painfully slow progress learning that discipline too. So there you have it, one old fella with a few rods and reels chasing about the Irish countryside trying to outwit a variety of fish. I hope you enjoy reading it as much as I did when fishing.

    Colin McLean
    September 2022

What Is It All About?

Ideas churn around in my mind as if stirred in some kind of witch's cauldron. Most are flights of fancy which never get off the ground but sometimes, just occasionally, an idea grows roots and turns into actions. '32' is one of those few notions which became a reality. I want to take a bit of time to describe to you this bold new idea of mine and how exactly I turned my thoughts into actions.

So what is 32? It is not the answer to all life's questions nor is it indeed anything to do with maths or arithmetic. Those of you who are familiar with Ireland will instantly recognise it as the number of counties on the island of Ireland. A small history lesson may help to make things a bit clearer for those not well versed in the machinations of Irish history. When the Irish Free State was formed in December 1922, the English government wanted to hang on to the 6 counties which make up modern day Northern Ireland (please note this is not Ulster as it comprises of 9 counties, 6 in the North and 3 in the South).

That left 26 counties in what would become the Republic of Ireland. So 26 counties in the south, 6 counties in the north makes a total of 32 counties. Are you with me so far? The 6 counties in Northern Ireland are part of the United Kingdom and the other 26 together form the Republic of Ireland.

My great idea is to set out to catch a fish in each one of the 32 counties on the island of Ireland and document the highs and lows in the process. Why bother you may well ask? By the early winter of 2019 I came to the conclusion that the previous couple of fishing seasons had been a disappointment for me with repeated blanks and poor catches from my local waters. At the same time, I could recall some brilliant fishing in other parts of the country from my past. Spinning for bass in Kerry as the sun rose in the east, catching feisty little brown trout from a tiny lochan on a hillside Donegal, rainbows leaping as they felt the hook on a put-and-take in Tyrone—the list goes on and on. It all seems in such sharp contrast to the endless blank days on lough Conn I had endured over the past 2 seasons. Mulling over these past successes and recent failures I came to the conclusion that I needed to spread my piscatorial wings somewhat and try new venues. From there, it was but a short hop to the need to give these wanderings some structure. That was when the concept of the 32 counties came me. There was no 'Eureka' moment, just a slow, plodding thought process which gradually took shape and found some structure as I sat making flies at home one winter's night.

Sat at the vice on that December evening the idea of catching a fish in each county infiltrated my train of thought to the point where I stopped making the Sooty Olives which were so sadly lacking in my fly box. I logged on to my battered laptop, made myself a coffee and sat down to see who else had done this before. In all probability, many anglers have done but none of them seemed to have written anything of their wanderings. Over dinner that night I excitedly told Helen about my latest idea. Strangely, she seems less enthusiastic than I was and changed the subject, 'Have you seen the news about that new 'flu in China?'

Refining the structure of the project took me a bit of time. Exactly what was I trying to achieve? What were the self-imposed rules of this venture going to be? My initial thoughts were to aim to catch a trout (any species of trout) in each of the counties but upon further examination this seemed to be a bit restrictive. The notion of encompassing all legal forms of angling fitted in better as I enjoy a wide variety of fishing experiences. In the end, I settled on a rather broad-based structure, 'to catch at least one freshwater species of fish from each of the 32 counties on the island of Ireland'.

As for the timescale I initially felt it was important to set a firm start and end date. The obvious choice is 1st January to 31st December 2020 but I wouldn't be able to commit to cramming all 32 into one calendar year. So, I decided to stretch the project over an elastic timeframe, starting on the first day of 2020 and just running on with no firm date for completion. Then Covid-19 struck! Travel was banned here in Ireland and the years of 2020 and 2021 were a patchwork of restrictions being imposed, lifted, reimposed and so on. Work dried up for me as a direct result of the pandemic which meant I had time on my hands but was not allowed to go anywhere. With the easing of restrictions in the summer of 2021, I was able to tick off a few more counties but the notion of completing the project within 12 months had been firmly knocked on the head by then. Instead, I just accepted the timescale was open ended.

I need to be honest here, I was not planning on spending a small fortune on this project. Cheap and cheerful was always going to be my approach. Expensive beats on salmon rivers were definitely out for a start. I'd make do with day-ticket waters when chasing silver. Here in Ireland we are blessed with lots of inexpensive fishing so there should not be any need to overspend.

Then there is the obvious lack of technical knowledge on my part. I am OK when fly fishing and spinning but all forms of coarse fishing were black arts to me at the start. Using feeders, ground baiting, float selection and shotting patterns, where and how to fish for the different species of coarse fish were all going to have to be learned and learned quickly. I didn't have the luxury of an extended apprenticeship in coarse angling, catching a few perch and pike on spinners in Scotland or tiny roach by accident on the fly were the sum total of my experience. I had a lot to learn!

Now we come to the question of my health. I suffer from arthritis in my feet, ankles and knees which curtails much of my fishing. I also suffer with vertigo and until recently took medication to keep it under control. A flare up of either condition was going be a big problem. The arthritis is there more or less constantly, giving me a lot of pain in my feet and ankles and reducing my mobility considerably.

I have learned to live with it and put up with the pain. My vertigo is a different beast and an attack in 2018 left my sense of balance severely compromised and the need for daily medication after a five day stay in hospital. Until you lose your sense of balance it is impossible to realise just how important it is to your everyday life. Tackling the 32 counties would certainly mean taking my physical limitations into reckoning.

One of the great attractions of this venture was the sheer variety of locations out there for me to sample. I've always enjoyed the challenges of fishing new places so the mix of previously untried venues and methods of angling, all set against the backdrop of the Irish countryside seemed like a heady brew to this tired and jaded angler. I am well aware this is the exact opposite of the most efficient way of catching a few fish. Learning one water over an extended period allows an angler to really get to know the venue in such detail that they can catch fish on a regular basis. Jumping from one place to another does not allow you to learn this level of detail and means each new fishery must be quickly analysed and tactics adjusted based solely on one's experience on other waters. I happen to really enjoy this process and was quite willing to accept reduced catches as a result.

Reaching the furthest corner of the Emerald Isle can be a bit of a trek from my base in Mayo. Antrim and Derry for example are 4–5 hours from home. The same goes for Wexford/Waterford area in the South-east. Although traffic can be heavy in the cities, rural driving is largely a pleasurable experience once you have grown used to the Irish style of driving. I drive very old cars so allowance would have to made for the possibilities of breakdowns too.

Tackle would not be an issue for the game angling as I own a range of rods and reels in good condition. Apart for small bits and bobs of end gear I didn't anticipate buying any new tackle for trout fishing. Coarse fishing was a different story and I am shocked at the volume and expense of coarse angling equipment which the top anglers use on a regular basis. I own a pair of float rods, a couple of leger rods and some old, fixed spool reels to match. These would have to do for now. A selection of end gear and some new lines had to be bought though, as well as bait and ground bait. eBay yielded some floats, feeders and the like at a reasonable cost.

My plan was to visit local tackle shops which would provide me with permits, bait and ground bait and hopefully some advice as well. At the outset, I guessed the coarse fishing areas would present my biggest challenges and so the local tackle shops in those counties would definitely be visited and consulted. Irish tackle dealers are the same as those the world over, only too keen to help out anglers with advice as well as selling them gear.

I had to consider what happens if, despite all my planning, I failed to catch a fish at my selected venue. I was in no doubt that this was going to happen and possibly happen quite often. A blank would mean me visiting that county again and again until I caught a fish so blanks in Antrim or Wexford were going to be expensive and time-consuming failures! I decided the best approach was to give myself the maximum chance to catch fish at each venue, meaning I needed to do a lot of research into each place beforehand.

I also required backup plans for when things are going wrong. For example, finding a river in flood may rule out the chances of catching anything there but if I had a "plan B" in the shape of a second or even third choice of venue it could negate the loss of the first venue. I couldn't just turn on my heel and drive all the way back home just because one river is out of ply. I figured that I needed varying locations and target species in light of any blanks, there being no point in going back to the same spot and hoping for a better result! There was a huge element of "suck it and see" with the whole of this adventure and making adjustment and changes as I was going along was part of its very fabric.

I wanted to try to vary species and methods as much as possible without tying myself to impossible dreams. My disturbing lack of knowledge about all forms of coarse fishing meant I would be taking some calculated risks but taking along a small spinning rod to cast worms or small spinners for perch should go some way to providing a back-up in many places. But I didn't want this to end up as me simply fishing for the lowest common denominator. It would make for dull reading indeed if all I did was worm for perch. Hence the different types of venues and methods of fishing.

I read somewhere recently that a 'good' days fishing happens to competent anglers on average every fourth trip. I know my own average of good days is well below that level, leading me to conclude that I am far from a competent angler! Then again, what actually constitutes a good day? Long ago I abandoned all hopes of catching lots of big fish on a regular basis. Too often I have blanked on good waters while those around me hauled out their share (and mine too). As long as there is some faint hope of catching something I am a happy angler.

Once that hope dies, I pack up and head for home or the pub. Flogging empty water is a thoroughly depressing business and one to be avoided at all costs in my book. Attempting to catch a fish in each county in this land was going to test my resolve and willingness to keep going even through tough situations. Any stretch of a trout river is going to be a joy to fish and I'm comfortable casting small flies for wild trout, meaning these venues were going to be the jewels in the crown for me. What to do when Bream or Tench refuse my cunningly presented feeder was going cause me much more difficulty.

Density of loose feeding, castor versus maggots, boilies or minis? As a complete novice, these and a hundred more coarse fishing conundrums awaited me. It proved to be a steep learning curve but one I am really enjoyed. I beg forgiveness in advance from those of you coarse experts who are reading this, all I can say is that we all had to start somewhere. My mentality is simply to catch one fish at each venue, not attempt to secure large bags. For me, one bream would constitute a good day's bream fishing whereas an experienced match angler would consider that a disaster.

Planning with near military precision was going to be required and I spent many, many hours poring over maps and reading fishing reports. I intended being flexible and taking advantage of any opportunities which presented themselves as the months passed. No point in turning up at the other end of the country to find my chosen spot has not fished for a month or that it produces good catches in August but I am stood there in my waders in December! In these days of the internet it is relatively easy to glean sufficient information to make informed decisions but I had to accept that sometimes I simply got it wrong and be in the wrong place at the wrong time. Such is angling!

So what did I hope to achieve by all this dashing across Ireland, waving rods at fish I had never caught before in places I have never even visited previously? I guess I wanted to address my jaded approach to angling, to re-invigorate my fishing so that I get more enjoyment out of it. Seeing new rivers and loughs, pitting my wits against fish in new waters and seeing more of the Irish countryside were all integral parts of the challenge. Isn't a change as good as a rest?

At the same time I hoped to show you, the readers, some new and interesting places as I travelled the highways and byways of this lovely country. Ireland has the capacity to confuse, irritate and disturb you at times but alongside that there is a beauty and charm which is hard to match. I hope you enjoy reading about my travels, the successes and inevitable failures, the people I meet and the stunning locations I fish.

So, there you have it. I planned, over the period of a couple of years or so years, to catch a fish in every county on the island of Ireland. Would I succeed gloriously or fail miserably?

About the Writer

Let's start with a confession—despite this book being entirely about fishing in Ireland I am not Irish. I am in fact 'a blow in', born a raised in Aberdeen, Scotland. The locals kindly put up with me because I have been hanging around this neck of the woods in the west of the country for many years now. By way of an introduction to me and my fishing here are some scribblings on how I arrived at this point in my life. It may go some way to explaining why I undertook this odyssey.

Born into a working-class family in the granite city of Aberdeen at the fag end of the 1950s, I was fortunate to be brought up in a loving environment. An absolute tearaway as a small child, always in some sort of trouble, I did poorly at school despite being of reasonable intelligence. I left at 17 years old one Friday afternoon and started working in a local papermill at 6am the following Monday. I can still recall being led by Stevie Alexander, the supervisor, into what seemed to be the very bowels of hell. Hissing steam, the clanking of old machines and men clad in little more than rags were all cloaked in dank darkness.

My employers saw something in me and promptly packed me off to the local Technical College where I did well, excelling in the technical subjects. So I worked hard, met a lovely girl and we got married. Like many couples we bought a tiny flat on the very edge of the city. After a few years, I took a job in Ayrshire and flew out to Finland for an extended period of training. Dawn and I left Aberdeen, never to return. From there, it was a role as Production Manager in another mill and we moved to Dunfermline, again working long hours and under near constant pressure.

Almost inevitably, my wife left me and I threw myself into work and my passions for climbing, hillwalking and fishing. I was living in an old house at the time which I decided to refurbish, pouring myself into rebuilding the place in the evenings after work. Weekends were spent on the razzle in Glasgow or Edinburgh. Looking back, I was leading an unsustainable lifestyle based around long hours of hugely stressful work interspersed with a chaotic social life, it could not go on like this!

All this time a big part of my life had been annual holidays in Ireland. I had visited the country first in 1977, hitching lifts or catching trains/buses to reach the town of Westport in Mayo. I loved it there, the fishing was good and the friendliness of the locals intoxicating. Over the next couple of decades I returned frequently, visiting the west coast mainly but venturing to many other parts as well. The hitchhiking gave way to manic motorbike trips and then four wheeled transportations. Sometimes I camped, other times I used B&B accommodation depending on my circumstances at the time.

A kind of a plan to retire to Ireland had been fermenting in my head over the years but those half-baked thoughts coalesced into something more immediate when I fell for a pretty girl in the town of Castlebar on one particular trip. My life then pivoted on to a completely new axis, one that still had many twists and turns to make. In November 1997, I boarded a Stena ferry in Stranraer and left the land of my birth, heading for who knew what in Connaught.

The next few years were unremittingly tough. Periods of unemployment, manual work when I could pick it up, a marriage which never really worked and, on reflection, the disappointment my life in Ireland was not the idyll I had imagined. I split up from my second wife, sold a lot of my personal belongings including my boat, then moved back to the UK, eventually finding myself in an equally small flat on the outskirts of Glasgow.

The year was 2005, I was 46 years old, unemployed and living alone. I guess this was a real low point but it did not feel like it, instead I sensed new opportunities were ahead of me if I made the effort. I applied for an MBA course at Cranfield University and, amazingly, was accepted. My scant worldly belongings went into storage in my mate's shed and I headed off down the M1 to Bedfordshire.

Cranfield was bliss. I loved the learning, the challenges and my fellow students. All too soon I had to return to reality though and I found a well-paid job in London. The job kept me very busy and I made some money but life in the city was a torture to me. So I started to drift back to Ireland whenever I could wangle time off, meeting up with old mates and doing some fishing. When the job in London came to a sudden end, I decided to move back to Mayo in the late spring of 2008. Pitching up in Ballinrobe, I bought an old boat and fished Lough Mask, the river Robe and further afield.

During this time I was fortunate enough to bump into Helen and we quickly became inseparable. Moving to Castlebar was the next logical step and I have remained here ever since. To make ends meet I became an Interim Manager, working hard in high pressure roles on short term contracts. Those different roles took me to far flung places and I travelled widely during the early 21st century. The middle east, Africa and India were just some of the places I worked and the chance to experience different cultures made a big impact on me. I suppose for many people this sounds like an ideal existence and in many ways it was. I consider myself to be extremely fortunate to have lived the life I have and to be here in the west.

So what about my fishing experience? My angling apprenticeship was on the rivers Dee, Don and Ythan in Aberdeenshire in the company of some excellent fishermen, many of whom are sadly no longer with us. In those far off days, salmon and sea trout were present in good numbers and big baskets were not uncommon. Spring salmon are now rare and the huge runs of summer grilse are but a memory. Here in Ireland the ecology of the great western lakes has altered and the massive hatches of flies and accompanying rise of trout are also a thing of the past. I fish hard for meagre returns, as do those expert anglers I am lucky enough to fish with. Despite all these problems, I still get out as much as I can and enjoy the Irish countryside.

Fishing in Ireland is much more than just going out with a rod and catching a few fish. The challenges are great and the results sometimes leave a lot to be desired but the 'craic' is a huge part of the whole angling scene. In modern Irish culture, 'the craic' is good enough reason to do just about anything and fishing is an extension of that devil-may-care attitude to life which I think goes a long way to defining the Irish.

In addition to the actual angling, I also tie a few flies, both copies of existing patterns or more often my own designs or derivations. Many are the tales of the ones which worked and the ones which didn't (many more of the latter than the former I am afraid). Dark winter evenings are often spent at the vice, churning out flies for myself or for other anglers. These days I get as much pleasure from hearing a fellow fisher landed a good trout or a salmon on one of my flies as I do catching a fish myself.

My apologies in advance to all you coarse anglers who are reading this book. Having never been a coarse fisher before starting this project it has been a steep learning curve and my woeful lack of experience means that my early forays with the float and feeder were amateurish in the extreme. In between the '32' outings, I was busy learning the basics of coarse fishing and spent many hours on the banks of loughs and canals getting to grips with the technical aspects of the sport. To say I have a lot yet to learn is an understatement but I am a willing learner and absolutely love fishing for roach and tench. My only regret is not taking it up earlier.

I am not a tackle tart who invests huge sums in the latest hi-tech angling equipment. Instead I try to maintain my gear so it lasts as long as possible and view the tackle industry through a jaundiced eye—it looks like a marketing managers dream and we anglers are the suckers who rush to buy the latest new-fangled gadgets. Most of my gear is over 20 years old and some of it dates back to my teens. A few rods and reels were bought new but over the years I have purchased a lot of second-hand gear.

It fits in with my views of over consumption and the reckless consumerism which blights western society. I'd rather reuse something which is adequate for the job than buy a new one. I accept that many people would view my collection of rods and reels as little more than junk but it works for me and I catch the odd fish here and there on it so I am happy out.

The same views on over consumption and waste apply to my personal transport. I have owned relatively few cars during my life. Instead of swapping them every couple of years for the latest gadget laden model I hang on to my cars, running up huge mileages on them by maintaining them well. To me, this is sensible and means less of a drain on our planets limited resources. It also means I am a laughingstock, noted by many for the old rust buckets I habitually drive around in.

I could go on and on about myself but I think this is sufficient for you to get a basic idea of who I am. I've led a full and very happy life, been lucky enough to travel and see many exotic places, meet amazingly gifted and talented people and reside in a safe, friendly society here in Ireland. My idea of catching a fish in every Irish county brought me to places I had never been before as well as catching lots of fish. I hope these scribblings may inspire you to try out the fishing here in Ireland for yourself.

Colin McLean

AKA the Claretbumbler

Chapter 1
Sligo

County number 1

Thursday 6th August 2020

    Making a start

    Some projects start exactly on time, the first steps of a meticulously planned operation where all the little cogs and wheels start to spin in synchronisation. My 32 project was the exact opposite, it commenced almost by accident and I was totally unprepared bar some cursory checking of a wrinkled OS map and a visit to one website. This level of ineptitude would not sustain me going forward but it did get the ball rolling so I am not going to be overly self-critical. My planning would improve over time as more distant counties were tackled but as Sligo was almost next door, I got away with my slovenly approach this time.

    So in early August 2020, I finally was making a start to this odyssey by visiting Lough Talt in the neighbouring county of Sligo. My vague plans to start the 32 project early in 2020 were dashed by the pandemic. We were all of us plunged into a welter initial fears and apprehension but for me this dread was superseded by feelings of injustice as I was not allowed to travel more than 5 kilometres from home for many months.

    I found being banned from just going out in my boat far from any other human being insufferable. The virus waxed and waned, the fluctuations wrong footing the powers who run Ireland at every turn. Finally, now, in the summer of 2020, restrictions on travel eased somewhat, presenting me with a window of opportunity to start the project at last. I needed to pick my first county so I plumped for Sligo. Let's not get overly adventurous to start with I thought.

    I was out of work, again. What I euphemistically referred to as 'resting' between the short terms assignments which made up my working life those days. Interim management is not for everyone and those breaks between jobs would be intolerable for many people. It's an odd sort of existence which swings violently between busy beyond belief to what borders on idleness. I liked it that way, humdrum is bad for people like me. So that summer, while awaiting the next call to go and fix some issues for a company somewhere, I began my little vanity.

As this little venture progressed and grew it would throw up a whole series of challenges for me. The most obvious was a lack of local knowledge for the vast majority of the venues I would be fishing. I know my own 'patch' around Mayo reasonably well but beyond that I would be pretty much in the lap of the gods. Even though Sligo is very close, I had virtually no local knowledge to fall back on. I'd wing it!

It was a low-key start to the project, no fanfare or tickertape. I informed nobody that I was kicking off the project on that day, it just sort of happened. Now, as Ireland appeared in the sunlight of rediscovered freedoms it felt right to make a start. The threat of further travel restrictions hung over us all so I was well aware this could be a false dawn but the need to get out and about exerted a huge pull on me. August is a funny month to be starting any sort of a fishing expedition. Our game fishing season closes at the end of September so I knew I was not going to get much done but the need to be on the water was too strong to be ignored. Putting off action any longer felt wrong, maybe the lockdowns had made us more aware of the need to live for today.

Why Sligo? Firstly, it is close by for me, just a few miles to the north of my home in Mayo. Driving to one of the distant counties felt like taking on too much for my first foray. I have never fished in Sligo before so it still retained that element of challenge but without a long road trip it would be less demanding on me than most other counties. I'd ease myself into this, a summer afternoon jaunt just up the road instead of a full-blown adventure visiting the other end of the country. By selecting a venue where I would be fly fishing for trout, I felt I was also reducing the risk of a blank on my very first outing.

I am a dyed-in-the-wool fly fisher, ten feet of carbon fibre seems to grow naturally out of my right hand. It has been my lifelong passion. Natural baits suspended under floats and other similar black arts would need to be learned but for now I'd stick to what I know.

Sligo is an amazingly beautiful county with a rich history. The county town is a bustling hub for business and culture, miles of beaches face the Atlantic ocean and pretty little villages dot the green fields of this western county. The bones of William Butler Yeats lie under the shadow of Ben Bulbain while the pubs are filled with Irish traditional music.

Lough Talt sits in a glen amid the Ox Mountains just inside the Sligo border. Those of you unfamiliar with the west of Ireland will be amused to know the Ox Mountains are a range of low hills a few hundred feet high. There are no towering crags, steep slopes of loose scree or hanging corries, only mist shrouded rounded hills clad in heather and sheep nibbled grass. It may lack alpine grandeur but it is still a very scenic area much loved by walkers and hikers. Indeed, on this day the path would be busy with family groups and dog walkers out enjoying the fresh air.

I reached the lough after a quiet drive via Ballina and the little village of Buniconlon. The road twists and turns as it gains height then drops again as the lake comes into view. A short, narrow road leads to good parking at the south end of the lake with room for a dozen or so cars. Shutting off the engine, I dragged my stiff frame out of the car and opened up the boot. Unsure of the terrain ahead of me I pulled on a pair of thigh boots and a waterproof jacket then turned my attention to rod and flies.

My elderly eleven foot, six weight Hardy with a floating line would do. I missed a ring when threading the line, a near constant error these days for me. Failing eyesight is another of those gifts bestowed upon us aging fishers. Tackling up with a three fly cast I tied on the ubiquitous Bibio on the bob, a Jungle Wickhams in the middle and a small Claret Bumble on the tail then I set off crunching along the gravel track around the lough. The stretch of shoreline near the car park was uninspiring so I plodded on in waders.

I was not sure what the shore would be like so I had donned a pair of thigh waders to cope with any potential stream crossings or to get out past any weed beds. This choice of footwear proved to be a bit of overkill and my hiking boots would have been a much better option as the banks were firm and the path along the shore was well maintained. I will know for the next time.

Walking is a slow and often painful business for me, the result of arthritis and a knee joint which never really recovered after shattering it in a motorbike crash. I hobble along like a man twenty years older, sometimes just stiff but more often fighting back against the bolts of pain each step generates in knees and ankles. The medical profession have plied me with drugs in the past but all to no avail. In an effort to increase my mobility, I long ago stopped eating meat and that simple change had a dramatic effect in terms of reducing pain to a tolerable level. I kept going as the path wound around the edge of the rippled lough.

Weather wise it was just about ideal for fishing this lough, a good strong south wind was whipping up the length of the lake and cloud cover was not too low, at least when I was fishing. 'Low skies' are anathema to trout fishers in Ireland. When the clouds reach down to the land, the fish become dour and very hard to catch. I suspect this is closely linked to air pressure but that begs the question how are fish swimming in the water affected by the tiny changes of air pressure above them?

I confess that pondering stuff like this takes up an inordinate amount of my time. Long ago I stopped trying to figure out the details of why the natural world works in certain ways, looking for exact answers to questions so large and complex they make my head spin. I do look for clues though, the minutia which we anglers become immersed in when fishing.

Eventually I reached a spot on the shore which looked fishy to me so I set about my business in the strong cross wind. Casting up to about 15 yards was fairly comfortable, after that the wind gave me some issues so I stuck to the medium length of line all day. No offers for the first while as I slowly worked my way along the maze of rocks and tussocks. Experience has taught me to try different retrieves, fast, slow, steady or jigged, the fish might prefer one over the others so I think it pays to experiment. Out of the blue, a lightning fast take startled me but I only lightly hooked a small trout which promptly fell off. Bugger!

A few casts later and I rose another trout but felt no contact. Was I going to have one of those days? Lough trout can be funny and come 'short' to the flies on occasions for reasons known only to themselves. I eyed the flies on the leader with some doubt, especially that Claret Bumble on the tail. Tied on a size 14 hook, might it be a bit too small for today I pondered? It is the standard dressing with tippets for a tail, maybe my version with a yellow wool tail would be better? What the hell, I will leave it there for now. For all the flies I carry with me, I am always loath to swap flies too often. I fish with some guys who spend more time changing the flies than they do actually fishing but I am the opposite. Maybe I would catch more if I wasn't so lazy! Reeling in, I crunched along the loose gravel path a bit further and around a small rocky headland where I found another likely looking spot.

Out shot the line, steady retrieve back to about 5 yards out then lift off and cast again. I was getting into the rhythm now and concentrating hard so that I was diligently covering the water. Twenty casts, then thirty, each one requiring close attention and tiny adjustments to cope with the wind. A splash followed by a tug and I was into a fish at last. It twisted and turned but being only a small trout there was little to trouble me when bringing it in. Not the biggest fish I have ever hooked but he was very welcome indeed. Of course he had taken the wee Claret Bumble I had so little faith in!

A quick pic then he was popped back into the water. Two casts later and the exercise was repeated with a slightly larger specimen. Then it went quiet again so I wound in. I'm not sure what to take from my lack of faith in the Bumble which then caught fish. Usually I find if I lack confidence in a fly it will not work for me on that day. Maybe there was a deeper, hidden belief inside me that the small claret was a good choice.

I moved once more and landed another trout then lost one too from a few yards further up the bank. The same pattern was repeated as I picked my way along the shore with only one or two offers at any one place. The trout seemed to be spread out with nothing of any note to keep them in one spot. My theory is that lough trout like these need a couple of square yards of space when they are feeding and are loathe to move beyond that area. An angler needs to keep moving and covering new water all the time to show his flies to the fish.

Of course that is easy when you are in a boat and the wind does all the work for you but the bank angler needs to be mindful to keep on the move. Eventually I did find a large sunken rock about ten yards out from the shore and by carefully placing my flies just in front of it I lured the best trout of the session. By then, I had removed the Bibio which had unusually failed to register a single offer. In its place I had tied on a Welsh Partridge, a fly that I have not used in many a long year. The Wickham also failed to attract any interest either so I substituted it with a small Soldier Palmer. In the end, the Welsh Partridge, Claret Bumble and Soldier Palmer shared the honours with each of them catching about the same number of trout. Size 14 turned out to be the fishes preferred size on the day.

The water looked 'fishier' further towards the north end the lough. Occasional large rocks now jutted out of the water and fish were to be found near to them. The wind made casting accurately more difficult but mastering the elements is all part of the enjoyment of days like this. I ended up with about a dozen brownies ranging in size from tiddlers to respectable three-quarter pounders. I guess I fished for about three hours before turning and retracing my steps back along the well-made path. I got to the car and stowed the gear way just minutes before the heavens opened and a heavy mist descended. Perfect timing for once!

Driving home through the heavy rain meant a slow journey, Irish roads can be dangerous in poor driving conditions and it pays to take your time in less than optimal weather. The old car struggled up the hills, panting asthmatically and slowing down at every incline but she got me home safely. With only the bare minimum of gear to unpack at home, I was soon relaxing and contemplating the day's events. Herein lies another joy of this form of fly fishing, the simplicity and minimal equipment. No engines or other heavy gear to be lugged around, just a rod and reel.

For me, fly fishing on the smaller Irish loughs for wild trout is a lovely way to spend a day. There is an intimacy which you don't get out on the big waters and the trout tend to be willing takers. These smaller loughs are also easier for a visiting angler to read. Cast afloat on Corrib or Mask in a small boat with the vast open area of water to find fish in can be daunting to say the least for those unfamiliar with the big lakes. A small lough consists of features any experienced angler will recognise as potential fish holding zones. Rocks, either on the shore or in the water, weeds, reed beds and drop offs are all places the fish like to patrol. The fish will be smaller but on scaled down tackle these spotted beauties still provide great sport.

I fished from the bank on lough Talt but many small loughs have a boat or two on them. These are typically owned by someone who lives on the shore and asking around locally will usually lead you to the owner who may rent their boat to you for the day. Sometimes these are advertised but mostly they are not, so a bit of detective work is often required. An enquiry at the local shop/petrol station or B&B can point you in the right direction. €20 is about the normal fee for the use of a boat for a day, without an engine. Remember to always wear a life jacket when out on a small boat, accidents happen and no jacket can turn an uncomfortable soaking into a life lost.

You may have noticed that I returned all the trout I caught so let's address the tricky question of C&R. I habitually return most of the fish I catch, keeping only a few for the pot. I don't eat much brown trout so virtually all of them are returned. Further down the line I may keep a few rainbows I suppose if I catch them from stocked fisheries. Any sea trout I am lucky enough to catch will be returned as they are under so much pressure these days from the disgusting fish farming business.

I usually keep one salmon each season but put any others back. There will likely be some coarse angling coming up and in the Republic you can retain up to four coarse fish per session. I personally think this is sheer nonsense and all coarse species caught should be safely returned to the water. I know I will be doing that. Don't start me on 'cultural' reasons for killing coarse fish, each one is precious and should be released. I abhor waste, especially wasting fish which could otherwise have been released.

I can heartily recommend Lough Talt to you for a few hours gentle fishing in lovely scenery. The trout may not be large but that to me is insignificant. Flies tied in small sizes seemed to do best and claret or red were the colours which got a reaction today. Anything small and dark should do the job though. There was a wind there today and that was a bonus both for the ripple on the water which is always a help and, probably more importantly, it kept the midges at bay. It looks like a place where you would be eaten alive on a calm day. Don't expect solitude on this water, there were many walkers on the path all the time I was there.

So I am up and running at last and I can tick Sligo off my list of counties. It was a thoroughly enjoyable few hours amid glorious scenery, archetypal Irish trout fishing you could say. It was interesting how the 'need' to catch a fish added and edge to the day. Once I had caught the first fish I could feel the self-imposed pressure come off and I relaxed more into the remainder of the day. A bit like the relief a competition angler feels as they net their first fish. The ever present need to avoid a blank is certainly heightened by setting myself this challenge. One down, thirty one to go!

The flies.

1. Claret Bumble I used today was the standard dressing but tied on a smaller hook than most anglers use. I find a size 14 can be a good choice on smaller loughs and also on difficult days on Conn or Cullin.
2. Jungle Wickhams is simply the standard pattern with a pair of tiny jungle cock cheeks added. An 'all-or-nothing' fly, this one is either lethal or useless. Today it was the latter.
3. Soldier Palmer is a particular favourite of mine and the dressing I used and was successful on Lough Talt was the standard one.
4. Welsh Partridge is a lovely fly which I have used since I was a lad. The tail is made from fibres from a brown partridge hackle, the body is half claret fur and half bronze peacock herl ribbed with fine gold or copper wire. At the neck tie in a claret hackle with a brown partridge in front. Smaller sizes seem to work best.
5. I use all kinds of Bibios but the one I tried today was the standard pattern with a black cock hackle palmered down the black/red/black fur body and a black hen hackle at the head.

Chapter 2
Roscommon

County number 2

Friday 14th August 2020

The day dawned fine and fair as promised by the forecasters. An easterly breeze blew across the garden as I surveyed the flowers and pulled up the odd weed. Where shall I fish today? The eternal question needed a swift answer and looking at the thin clouds I plumped for lough Conn. Out came the outboard engine and fuel tank, the fishing bag and rods to be stowed in the car. But wait! The thin cloud cover had broken already and blue sky was filling the heavens above me. That wind seemed to have dropped to a mere zephyr too in the short time it had taken to load up the car. Conn would be terribly hard work in a flat calm and brilliant sunshine. Maybe I needed to re-think my plans. It was a few minutes work to empty the car of the trout tackle and fill it again with my coarse gear. I would go to County Roscommon for the day and try to chalk off another of the 32 counties.

In the townland of Creeve, some miles to the north of Strokestown, there is a lake with excellent access called Lough Cloonahee. It is apparently home to Bream, Rudd and Hybrids so it sounded like a good place for a novice like me. My local filling station provided a shot of diesel for the car and a couple of loaves of bread for bait then I hit the road. As always, actually finding the lough was harder than it should be. This being rural Ireland the brown signposts pointing out the fishing lakes were either missing or facing in the wrong direction but I managed to figure it out.

In the end I found the lough without too much hassle, the final few yards requiring the old Golf to slither down a gloriously unkempt track. In the small, rough carpark I got chatting to the local farmer about this and that, as you do. What with the Covid he had seen virtually no anglers this year so he had no idea how the lake was fishing. We talked cattle and GAA for a while before he took his leave. A quick look at the water revealed the good folks of Roscommon had seen a lot of rain recently as the fine wooden walkway which stretches for 30 metres along the shore was partially submerged. I tackled up and found a dry spot off to the right to commence operations.

I am still getting used to my coarse fishing gear, even though it is old, second-hand stuff it still feels 'new' to me. Threading the thin running line through tiny standoff rings takes me ages as I often miss a ring in my haste to get fishing. The sliding reel fittings just feel odd to me, why don't they fit locking fittings? Why use a loop to loop connection when a tiny swivel could arguably do a better job? Never mind, just get on with it. Plumbing the depth I found 15 feet of water close in so I set up the float rod with 3 pound straight through and a size 14 hook adorned with a single ear of sweetcorn. My other rod (also old, this time it is a Shakespeare) and venerable Cardinal reel full of 6 pound mono was rigged with an open cage feeder and a size 10 hook tied to 9 inches of 3 pound. 3 ears of bright yellow sweetcorn were pushed on to this hook and I lobbed it out a few yards.

This process was repeated a few times so the feeder full of bread and corn could unload in the same area to try and attract the fish to me. I also loose fed corn into the swim as I fished. All the while I tried to convince myself I knew what I was doing. I guess that I do know the basics but it is the detail which is tripping me up. Bait is my biggest concern but I have read that corn is a great bait for virtually all coarse fish so that is why I am fishing it today.

I know that I am pushing it trying to fish the float in such deep water and I have a few tangles. Somewhere in my box there is a sliding float and I toy with the idea of setting that up but in the end laziness gets the better of me and I stick with the normal crystal waggler. I bulk shot at the float with some small shot above the loop to loop connection to the hook link. This seems to work OK from a casting point of view but with no bites forthcoming it is highly debatable if it is the right choice. All those YouTube videos are rerun in my mind as I try to make sensible decisions to improve my chances.

Time flew by as I made small adjustments to the rigs and re-baited frequently. It is a lovely day to be out in the fresh air so the fact I am not catching is not a disaster. About an hour into the session though I lifted the feeder rod to recast and felt a sharp tug. There had been no discernible bite as far as I could see. Striking, I met fierce resistance and I was obviously into a good fish. What was this now? It felt heavy so it might be a bream and images of slab-sided bronze fish filled my head. Off on another run went the fish, so it definitely was not a bream!

Still unseen, she hugged the bottom shaking her head and making lunges in different directions. Maybe it was a huge Rudd, there were supposed to be some big 'uns in here. No, Rudd would be higher up in the water column. What about a Hybrid? After all they are supposed to be great scrappers. I applied as much pressure as I dare with the 3 pound breaking strain tippet foremost in my thoughts. Up came the beast and she broke the surface—it was a blooming Pike! The battle raged for a while longer but I admit I could scarcely care less if the fish broke free. She didn't and at the second attempt she slipped into the meshes and was lifted out. I thought it must surely be foul hooked but no, the pike had taken the sweetcorn fair and square with the hook nicely placed in the scissors.

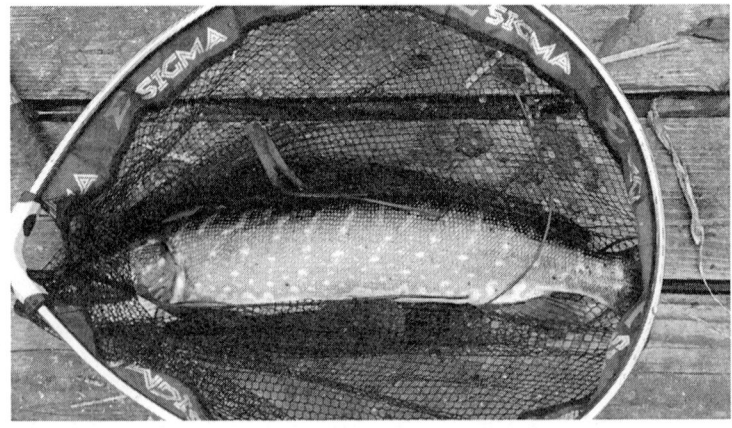

I was not going anywhere near those jaws with my little plastic disgorger but I had a pair of forceps in my pocket to do the job of hook removal. Quickly unhooked, I slid her back into the water and off she swam, apparently untroubled by our meeting. It was only later when I had cleaned off the slime, changed the hook link, re-baited and got the rod back in the water that it dawned on me—I had managed to catch a fish in Roscommon!

More balls of slightly sticky groundbait, more waiting and re-casting, a lot more nothing happening. I tried a bigger hook with numerous ears of corn on it but that didn't work. Perhaps the hook was too big? I dropped to a size 16 with a single ear of corn but that was no better. Next, I tried moving to the other end of the walkway and setting up there in a nice looking swim. That was a similar failure. All this time I was trying to figure out what I was doing wrong. Was I fishing too heavy and the fish were put off by my line? Maybe I should be throwing in more groundbait—or maybe I was over feeding and should cut back. I never did find an answer despite fishing on late into the afternoon.

In the end, I gave up and packed away the gear. It was getting late so my plans to get home in good time were already trashed. With nothing else to show for all my industry if it hadn't been for that suicidal pike, I would have blanked. Yes I know I caught a nice fish and I should have been happy about that but it felt like I was cheating somehow. At no point did I set out to fish for pike and instead had set up to catch roach or bream. Beggars can't be choosers I suppose. That paradox every beginner suffers was oh so true in my case, only experience will lead to more fish but to gain the experience I must go fishing and catch little or nothing.

While the lake was very high, it was not too coloured and I am not going to blame conditions for my lack of success. According to the IFI website Cloonahee holds Bream, Rudd, Perch, Hybrids and even some Tench but none of them distained to take my bait. After mulling it over, I am of the opinion that using sweetcorn was the problem.

It seems that every website I visit, every blog I follow or every dusty book I read on coarse fishing extols the virtues of sweetcorn both as a hook bait and as an addition to groundbait. I'm new to this game so I follow these words of advice in lieu of personal experience but the doubts in my head are real and repeated blanks have built up a body of evidence I can't ignore any more. In future, I will make sure I have a range of baits with me so I can swap as required. For now, I am just happy to have captured a fish in Roscommon.

Later…

Actually more than a whole year later and I am reconsidering that day last summer on lough Cloonahee. It is now Thursday, 26th August 2021, a hot day of blue skies all across the country. I still feel I have cheated a bit as pike very rarely fall for sweetcorn. It was a fluke, pure and simple. So I have decided to return to the scene of my past failure and spend a few hours trying to right that particular wrong. Twelve months on and my coarse fishing has improved greatly so I think it is time for me to try to catch a fish in Roscommon again. Anyway, it looked like it was a good lough and I want to see if I can do better second time around. It was a nice spot for a few hours fishing on a warm summer's day.

As I said before, there are rudd, bream, perch and hybrids in this lough, all of which I am used to catching now. This time I am equipped with maggots and worms plus a much expanded knowledge base. These days I am confident with float and feeder whereas the last visit was a learning experience. Looking back, without worms or maggots I was making life very hard for myself. Other anglers swear by sweetcorn but not me, give me something that wriggles any day.

I rise early in the morning, check the weather and eat a little breakfast. Mist clears quickly and with the heat building already I set off for the county Roscommon. After buying some bait in Carrick-on-Shannon, I wind down narrow lanes taking one wrong turning (so what's new) before doubling back and finding the right road. It's 10.30am before I pull up in the car park at the side of the lough and there is one other car there already. It is a bright, hot day with clear blue skies, not really ideal conditions but I will just have to make the best of it. As a dyed-in-the-wool game fisher the great advantage that coarse fishing has is that the fish will still bite in most conditions. A flat calm on a lough is a death knell when fly fishing for salmon but roach and rudd don't seem to mind too much.

In truth, I am lacking drive and commitment this morning. Coming back to fish Cloonahee feels like returning to the scene of some heinous crime. I know that is ridiculous but the sense of righting a wrong is powerful yet tempered with a feeling of waste. Today I could have been ticking off another county instead of revisiting this one. Common sense tells me that I must be more positive if I am going to catch anything today. I have to shake those negative thoughts as confidence is a prime requirement in my book.

A lifetime of fishing has taught me the value of a positive mental attitude and any time I have lost confidence in myself the fishing has been poor. Just having some maggots for bait is a huge boost of course. Lessons were learned from my last outing to Cloonahee, the most important being the efficacy of the humble maggot. For me, the maggot is king and every other bait pales in its smelly shadow.

Ground bait is another part of my game which has improved (I think). Before it was simply bread laced with some porridge or sweetcorn and the fish treated this goo with the distain it so richly deserved. Now I try different ground baits depending on where I am and what I am fishing for. The base is usually brown crumb, cheap and good for extending any more expensive ingredients. If there are roach around, and there usually is, I add a little hemp. Some proprietary ground bait mixes feature too depending on location.

Along the walkway I stop and have a quick chat with the other angler, a nice chap with a Manchester accent and a leger rod propped up at a jaunty angle. He has landed a couple of perch so far but nothing to write home about. I pick a peg further along, numbered '4' and set up my gear. Half-a-dozen balls of groundbait are added to the swim and I set up my 'normal' rods, one on the feeder and the other on the float. I plumb the swim and it is around 13 feet deep here. Briefly I toy with the idea of using a sliding float but in the end I rig a normal waggler and commence fishing.

My usual faffing about as I arrange my gear ensues, trying to get what I want within easy reach will make the fishing all the more enjoyable. After about 15 minutes, the feeder gives a nod and I lift into a small bream. It is not one of those long, sweeping takes you see sometimes, just a slow pull over to the right. Slime covers everything as I unhook and release the fish. I get why some anglers really don't like bream, they make such a mess of anything they touch but I like them and am pleased to see this small lad. Next the float trembles ever so slightly and a small roach swings in. A cheeky rudd snatches the maggots before another roach, this time a better one, draws the float under again.

I keep feeding the swim with balls of groundbait to try and keep the fish in front of me and I steadily catch fish for the next couple of hours. The wind is only a zephyr but there is just enough to keep me cool. The worms on the feeder rod produces most the bream and only one small lad falls to the float. A nice wee hybrid breaks the monotony. I am having fun!

To keep the bait from being swallowed by tiny rudd I place my bulk shot at the end of the main line. That ensures it sinks rapidly, giving the little fellas no opportunity to snaffle the maggots. Bites on the float are registered either as a faint tremble or a lovely lift bite. The float rises up out of the water like Excalibur and a solid hook up is normally the result. Time slips by under a summer sun, I miss some bites and connect with others. Small silvery fish wriggle as I unhook them, maybe I take a snap then pop them back into their watery home maybe not.

There is a simple wholesomeness to coarse fishing which has drawn me in. Looking at me with my old and basic gear I fear others must take pity on my uncouthness but they miss the point. A session drowning maggots transports me from the reality of today to an innocent world where I am totally focussed on a twitch of the red topped float or a tremble of the thin tip on the leger rod.

Cars appear in the car park and some lads get out and start to unload something. I'm trying to concentrate on my fishing but also listening in to their conversation which I can hear clearly on this calm day. They are here to pre-bait the lake ahead of a competition tomorrow. Starting at the opposite end of the walkway I can see them throwing in groundbait using a big plastic scoop. They are heading my way so I tidy up around me a bit. The big ginger haired fella greets me and we chat about the fishing briefly before he asks if he can pre-bait this swim. Of course I agree and two scoops of pellets fly over my head then scatter 15 yards in front of me. The pellets were in fact sheep nuts. Briefly I try to figure out how much a sack of sheep nuts would cost me before dismissing the idea just as quickly.

About 1pm any last vestige of a wind dies completely and the temperature soars. The fish go off the feed around the same time and it becomes hard work with no bites coming my way. Sticking it out until nearly 3pm, I eventually decide enough is enough and pack up my gear. My phone tells me it is 24 degrees but it feels even hotter. Luckily, the car park is very close by so it is only a few minutes work to take down the rods and walk back to the car before setting off homeward. There are roadworks in Elphin that slow me down but I am soon crossing the county border and am back in Mayo once again.

On reflection, I am happy now that I took the time to revisit Cloonahee. It is a lovely spot to fish and the walkway makes everything so easy. Last year I knew nothing about coarse fishing and apart from the vegetarian pike I landed nothing. This time around I knew what I was doing and was fully prepared. More importantly, I was full of confidence that I would catch something. For me, that is the biggest difference. In the end I landed 6 bream, 10 roach, a hybrid and a couple of accidental rudd. Nineteen fish, the best of them a couple of pounds in weight, would not win me any competitions but it was a hugely enjoyable day out in the sunshine. I am happier now to say Roscommon is completed for the purposes of the '32'.

Cloonahee is a very popular venue but in truth there are so many other loughs in Roscommon I could have tried. Outside of this project I now try to fish one or two new venues in the county whenever I can and it rarely disappoints in terms of the numbers of fish I catch. So much more could be done to open up other lakes for angling but sadly many are off the beaten track, lack any sort of proper access or angling infrastructure such as car parks, stiles, bridges or stands.

Chapter 3
Leitrim

County number 3

Thursday, 10th September 2020

Yesterday I made the decision to tackle another county, this time another near neighbour, Leitrim. In one sense, this should be a very easy place to catch a few fish as Leitrim is full of lakes brimming with all manner of species. My issues are around exactly what kind of fish are swimming around over there. You see Leitrim is a coarse fishers paradise but I am no expert at coarse angling, hence my reticence.

An awful lot of online study had gone into today's trip, venues abound but finding the right one was hard work. It had to hold plenty of fish (obviously) be easy to find, have adequate parking nearby and some structures to fish from. Irish banks tend to be wild and overgrown and as a novice I want to be standing on something stable. Those criteria narrowed down the choice considerably as many of the loughs in the area are pretty wild and poorly served with infrastructure. Add to this the shadow of my near failure on my last trip to Roscommon and you can see why I made the effort to do my research.

I eventually hatched a plan to fish a small lough called Drumgorman Lake, about 3 km to the south of the village of Drumshanbo. According to the IFI website it held Bream, Roach, Perch and Pike. There were some stands to fish from and a carpark right next to the water and as an added bonus the main road from Carrick-on-Shannon to Drumshanbo ran next to the shoreline. It sounded perfect. With all those different species present, I hoped that my lack of skill and knowledge might in some way be mitigated. My seemingly endless research into all matters float and feeder had led me to a plan of attack involving two rods and two different methods which I figured I could employ simultaneously, thus increasing my chances of catching something.

When it came, Thursday morning was dry and the winds were light but forecast to pick up through the course of the day. All the relevant gear was chucked in the back of the motor and I hit the road, bound for lovely Leitrim. For a change, the N5 was pretty quiet and I trundled happily on, heading east and listening to the usual gloom on the radio. Brexit this, Covid that, the latest depressing updates on the total mismanagement of global issues.

At least, the fishing would take my mind off all of that crap for a while. Somewhere between Frenchpark and Carrick the road had been dug up and I had to divert through Boyle, a town I had never been in before. Negotiating the strange one-way system in the town, I emerged on the N4 road and turned towards Carrick-on-Shannon once again. There is a canal only a few yards along the road which looked pretty fishy to me (one for another day). The green and pleasant scenery rushed by as I ploughed on eastwards.

Since the beginning of my early exploits in coarse fishing I have completely lost faith in sweetcorn as bait. Despite being tried frequently, it has produced nothing for me other than a pike (of all things). This time I was determined to get some maggots so I stopped off at the Carrick Angling Centre to pick up a pint. I opted for red ones and invested in some brown crumb for ground bait while I was at it. Chatting with the lads in the shop I explained where I was planning on fishing today. Their view of the lough was it held a reasonable stock of mainly small fish so if all I was after was a good chance of connecting with plenty of small stuff it was a great choice.

That certainly helped my confidence! Next, some brown bread from the local Gala store on the corner of Bridge Street (for me to make myself a sandwich) and I was off on the final, short leg of the journey up the R280 and through Leitrim Village. I very nearly drove past the small carpark at the side of the lake as it is not signposted! Gear was hastily unpacked, rods pushed together and I set up on a fine new-ish looking stand. With nobody else around I elected to fish from the stand, ready to move if someone else wanted to fish there.

I figured loose feeding was a good idea to attract in some fish so a handful of maggots were tossed in while I set up two rods, the 12 foot Shakespeare with a Daiwa Harrier fixed spool and my lovely little ABU Legerlite with the old Cardinal 444A. Both had 6 pound nylon on them. A small 20gm plastic maggot feeder is rigged on the 12 footer then loaded with maggots and put 3 maggots on a size 12 hook. Not overly convinced that the rig looked right, I fiddled about with it to lengthen the hook link then cast it out. I wish I was more confident but as a novice I just have to accept any short comings. A couple of swan shot is all the weight the Legerlite needs and I added a link of pound and a half nylon to a fine wire size 14 crystal bend, tipped with a pair of maggots. This rod was cast to the left. My logic is if there are only small fish in here I can go very light and possibly have a better chance of fooling them.

Maggots, do you hook them by the head or the tail? This kind of vexed me for a while and I was unsure which was the most effective way. It is all these little questions I still need to find answers to. My instinct is to hook them by the tail so they last longer but maybe that's wrong. When the fish are biting well, I doubt it makes much of a difference. Anyway, today they are stuck on to the small hook by the tail. I had wondered why my coarse hooks were made from such fine wire but now I can see they make a big difference when hooking maggots.

To augment the loose fed maggots I mixed up some ground bait and fired a few balls of it into the coloured water, an operation which was rudely interrupted as almost right away I started to get bites. The steady wind blowing from left to right was making bite detection a bit hit and miss but soon enough I connected with a fish on the Legerlite. Winding in, I found what has to be the smallest Perch in the world hanging on to my hook. Ah well, at least it was a start. Of course, being a perch he has swallowed the hook and I have to use the cheap purple plastic disgorger that lives in the chest pocket of my waistcoat to fish it out.

He swims off strongly so it looks like he is none the worse for wear. This is important to me as I have no intention of retaining any coarse fish. Most of my hooks are barbless but some have barbs and I have to check before using them and flatten that sliver of metal as required. Just learning to use the disgorger took me some time. You would have thought that an angler with a lifetime of experience would have been able to use a disgorger but they are not part of a trout and salmon fishers kit so I had to learn how to keep the line tight and then push the tool with just the right amount of force to extract a hook.

More ground bait mixing and throwing and more small bites followed but I wasn't connecting with them. This coarse fishing is a messy business. What between grasping wriggling stinky maggots and kneading equally smelly groundbait my hands are always filthy. A vital part of my kit is an old, disused plastic paint bucket which I half fill with water so I can always clean my hands and an old towel to dry them. Doubts are creeping in already, I am using too much ground bait and over feeding the fish?

Or maybe I am not throwing in enough and the fish are swimming off to find food elsewhere. How do I know? Maybe my hook is the wrong size or the line is too thick. I decide to do something rather than nothing. Changing the swimfeeder size 12 hook for a size 14 seemed to help and after only a couple of casts I struck a solid bite. Half expecting another miniscule perch I am pleasantly surprised to find there was some weight on the end. A lovely Roach of about 8 ounces came to hand, was photographed and quickly released. Happy days! I love roach, to my mind they are a very pretty fish and I smile each time I wind one in. Their small size does not bother me and I can't imagine I will ever become one of those anglers obsessed with catching a two pounder. I think big roach are very rare here in Ireland anyway and a fish of a pound is a good one in this neck of the woods.

More missed bites follow on the float, tappy little affairs which I console myself by grasping at the idea they were due to tiny fish. In an effort to try and turn bites into fish on the bank I change down in hook size again, this time to an 18 and bait up with a single maggot. Bites promptly stop altogether, suggesting I had made the wrong move. On the plus side, I picked up another good roach on the Legerlite, bending the light rod over into an impressive curve for a fish of less than a pound in weight. Ominous clouds had been building in the west and sure enough the rain started and the wind picked up, making conditions less than favourable.

Hunkering down I surveyed my swim and thought the tree roots next to me looked like the perfect spot for a perch to set up home. Re-baiting, I literally lowered my float down at my feet and allowed the baited hook to sink out of sight into the dark roots. Then I waited in the wind and rain. I didn't have long to wait as a lively bite resulted in a firm hook up and a nice perch as soon appeared out of the murk, a fish of about 6 ounces I suppose. As Irish perch go this isn't a bad one.

All the time a somewhat scruffy Robin kept me company, darting down to grab any stray maggots that had crawled out of the bait box. He was obviously well used to this trick. Who could resist the little chap as he picked out a few maggots as a free meal. Little incidents like this add so much to a day by the water. The wind which has been building all day is strong enough now to whip the surface of the lough into little waves and I decide the float is too much trouble to use so I dismantle the brown rod and concentrate solely on the feeder.

Time flew by as the rain first eased off, then returned with a vengeance. Bites dried up so I tried to liven things up with even more ground bait. I had been fishing straight out in front of me but without recent success. Some casts off to my right brought a flurry of bites in quick succession and a few small Roach came to hand but by now I was soaked through and so I decided to call it a day. Sheltering under the trees, I broke down the leger rod and tucked all the bits and pieces away in the back of the car before turning the key in the ignition and heading off homeward.

Everything was sopping wet and will need to be dried out thoroughly before I venture out again. Note to self—must buy a new waterproof ¾ length jacket. The one I am using belonged to my late father and is worn out. I wear it as much in remembrance of him as for any faint protection from the elements. He would be mystified by this coarse fishing malarkey, why go fishing when you chuck everything back? The inside of the windows steamed up as I drove home, not for the first time, nor the last, I am wet through after a spell on the bank. I long ago stopped worrying about damp clothes and see it as just part of the overall experience.

So, what to make of the day and what lessons were learned? Firstly, and probably most importantly, I caught some fish in County Leitrim. I has set out to try and catch Bream, Roach or Perch and had landed 2 out of the 3. Shame I didn't connect with any Bream but I was absolutely delighted to catch the Roach. The first couple were really pretty fish and I now get why some anglers fish so hard for this species. My choice of bait was vindicated and I will make a lot of effort to get maggots when I am going coarse fishing. Not wasting time trying to float fish in the wind was a good move (I think). Dropping the bait into the tree roots looking for Perch was a success too.

Drumgorman is not one of the premier loughs in the county, there are others with much bigger reputations both in terms of the size of fish present and the numbers in them. I had specifically chosen it today because it is one of those 'consistent' loughs, one which normally gives up a few smallish fish rather than huge bags or blanks. In short, it suited a beginner like me. The fact I managed to land some roach and perch certainly vindicated my decision to fish this particular lough.

On the negative side, I failed to catch a Bream (again) and I badly want to land a few of these fish. I read that they should be easy to catch but they are eluding me right now. OK so they are slimy and don't really fight but I still want to catch some! I will persevere and read up some more on the species, then target them specifically on my next outing. I also need to figure out my choice of hooks because I missed a large percentage of the bites I got. Dropping down in size reduced bite numbers but increased hook ups until I went to a size 18, then all action on that rod ceased.

Why? And my hooking ratio was terrible so maybe I need to think about different styles of hook? My ground baiting was a bit haphazard and I need to think about the quantity and frequency of groundbait. I could not hold the shoal of roach in front of me and this means I was doing something wrong. I don't know did I over feed or not put enough in. I need to look into hair rigs as they could help me to convert bites into solid hook ups. I'll do some research first before buying the bits and bobs. This all sounds like moaning but it is the reality of the learning process for me.

Swimfeeders break! I started by tying on a nice little maggot feeder but after a few casts I noticed there was something wrong with it and a little crack had turned into chunks of the plastic body falling off. I changed it for a sturdier one but I will buy some new feeders so I have a good stock. On the subject of tackle, my tackle box badly needs to be better organised. I seemed to be constantly rummaging around for hooks/line and could never just put my hand on what I wanted. I am now looking around for a better tackle box to keep my stuff in some sort of order.

Today saw periods of heavy rain, not at all unusual for Ireland and my mind is straying towards buying an umbrella. The list of potential improvements goes on and on but today was a step in the right direction for me. Will I ever give up my game and sea fishing to concentrate on coarse? Not a chance! Having said that, I am fascinated by this branch of the sport and can't wait to get back out there chasing Bream and Roach again.

It is already obvious that the covid lockdown and travel restrictions has meant very little fishing has been done in 2020. Is this a good thing? I am not too sure. All coarse fish are supposed to be returned so it is not like any less fish are available. My concern is the vast quantities of ground bait normally thrown into fisheries did not materialism this year so have the fish wandered off to pastures new? Or will it simply be a case of a little feed will attract them back within casting range? Only time will tell.

So that is Leitrim ticked off the list, making it the third county out of the 32 where I have caught a fish. It is a very rural, largely unspoilt county with a huge amount of coarse fishing available. If I was a visiting angler, the idea of holidaying in Carrick-on-Shannon would certainly be near the top of the list. It is a nice wee town with lots of accommodation options plus plenty of bars and restaurants for non-angling entertainment. The river Shannon flows through the town with the famous Mudflats section immediately across from the town on the opposite bank and there are dozens of good fishing lakes within easy reach.

For me, it is just over an hour's drive from home so I will be coming back to the area from now on. It doesn't stop there though, Mohill, Carrigallen, Leitrim Village, Drumshanbo, Keshcarrigan and Ballinamore are all excellent villages where visiting anglers will find accommodation and good fishing. To try and list all the coarse angling venues in Leitrim would be next to impossible. Many small lakes are never fished and access is poor to most of them. Who knows what could be swimming around in these forgotten waters?

Chapter 4
Clare

County number 4

Monday, 14th September 2020

    The next county I decided to target in my project the catch fish in every Irish county would be Clare. Once again, I was busy online researching possible venues and plumped for this one, Cloondorney Lough. Situated near to the small town of Tulla in the east of the county it looked to be the best option for me as a raw coarse fishing novice. It sounded like the fishing was easily accessible and the lough held Bream (my target species), Roach, some Hybrids and lots of Rudd. The Rudd apparently ran up to about a pound in weight, a great size for the species in Ireland. Tench, Eels and Perch also inhabited this water but in small numbers. I could just as easily plumped for any of dozens of lakes in the county as Clare is blessed with a number of coarse fishing options.

    County Clare is a popular destination for tourists. Doolin and Lisdoonvarna, with their pubs and festivals, the cliffs of Moher rising majestically from the Atlantic ocean or the lively traditional music scene in the county all attract visitors like moths to a flame. Much of this area is how non-nationals think of Ireland, forty shades of green and all that. Like much of rural Ireland, agriculture and tourism are the staples of the local economy but hi-tec industries are also working across the county these days. Over the years I have visited Clare many times with both work and relaxation taking me to the Banner county, but my angling experiences were previously limited to a bit of sea fishing.

    My plan was to use two rods, setting one up with a feeder to search for Bream and the other with a waggler set high in the water to try for Rudd. In case that didn't work out, I took along plenty of other rods, reels and gear so I could switch around if desired. For bait I had some worms, dead maggots, sweetcorn and bread. So really I was armed to the teeth and ready for anything. The idea of a pleasant day by the side of a lake in county Clare was hugely appealing and I went to bed the night before excited at the prospect of the next day.

Monday and the alarm goes off in the cool darkness of the early morning. The car had been packed the night before so all I had to do was eat my breakfast and sort out some food to bring with me. It would be a long day so I needed sustenance. Six-thirty saw me pulling out of the driveway and off into the darkness. Light was just creeping into the eastern sky as I motored through the villages of south Mayo, crossing into Galway at Ballindine on-route for Tuam.

There the new motorway curves around the town and led me ever southwards. Traffic built up approaching Galway city but it eased again once passed the M6 junction. In two hours, I was passing through Tulla and looking for the brown signpost for the lake on my right hand side. The narrow road was under some sort of repair by the looks of it, consisting as it did of rutted untarred gravel but I found the lough just a little way along on my right and reversed into a neat little space by a small concrete stand. Up until now everything had been going according to plan.

Hopping out of the car I inspected my new surroundings and was a bit taken aback by the colour of the water—it bore a striking resemblance to strong tea. I can only presume this was due to heavy rain but it did not inspire me to see such a filthy lough. As I was contemplating the water two locals arrived and occupied the swim next to me. We had a brief chat and it was clear they knew the lough well and fished it often. What should have been a peaceful spot was ruined by a heavy digger which decided to work right behind my swim all morning. It looked like he was clearing a site for a new house and the clanking of the 360 went on for most of the day. Possibly all this heavy ground works of road repairs and site clearance were part of the reason for the poor water quality I was seeing in front of me.

I was here now so there was nothing else for it but to crack on and do some fishing. In an old plastic bucket brought along specifically for the purpose, I made up some groundbait from mashed up bread, some brown crumb, oats and dead maggots. Following my plan, the feeder rod was set up with the ancient Cardinal 444A filled with 6 pound monofilament running line. A small plastic cage feeder and a hook link of 4 pound b/s nylon with a size 12 hook completed the set up and a lively worm was my bait on this rod. The float rod with the Daiwa Harrier reel and 2 pound running line was set up with a small float and a foot of 1.5-pound hook length to a size 18 carrying a single red maggot fished on the bottom.

Lots of balls of ground bait were hurled into the swim in an effort to attract some fish nearer. Right from the start the float dipped on virtually every cast but hooking the Rudd was proving to be difficult. Eventually I hit one and swung in a typical tiny Rudd. Another couple followed but I was missing 90% of the bites. In between the action on the float, I was continually winding in the swimfeeder and refilling the cage. This session was proving to be trickier than I had hoped.

Time for a cuppa. I had brought along a flask of hot water and a plastic box full of tea bags of indeterminate age. All I know is that they had nestled peacefully in that box of a long, long time. I pulled out the first one that came to hand, dropped it into the cup and filled up with the hot water. Then I made a rough sandwich with some bread and a tomato I had brought with while I let the tea brew. The first sip of the tea was a surprise, it was impossible to tell what I had just brewed. It tasted pepperminty/cranberryish/orangy with a hint of ginger (or maybe lemon).

Obviously there had been an assortment of different tea bags in the container and all the different flavours of tea had intermingled over the time. Ah well, at least it was drinkable. Slurps of the unidentifiable tea washed down the sandwich as I glared at the now unmoving float.

At last, the float dipped again and I struck into another small silvery fish but this time it was a wee skimmer. Growing tired of the small stuff I changed the float rod for my light leger rod and tried worms in the margins as close to the reeds as I dare. Starting with a single worm (nothing), I moved to two worms (nothing) then put on a bigger hook and tried a bunch of worms (yes, you have guessed it, nothing). I didn't think I was doing anything majorly wrong but the fish were totally unresponsive. It was about now I began to have doubts about my conviction that either maggot or worm will work on most days here in Ireland.

I read about the competition anglers who carry a wide range of baits when they are fishing, casters, tares, meat, pastes, cheese etc. In my head, I just needed good fresh maggots or lively worms to cover all eventualities but today I was being proved wrong. The lads fishing the next peg were not catching either so it not just me being useless.

Since bait had failed to produce any fish I broke down the leger rod and set up a pike rod. I fumbled and fiddled in the box to find a wire trace but found one eventually. Half-an-hour of flinging a large copper coloured spoon proved to be unsuccessful but it was a nice change to be casting constantly instead of sitting on the seat waiting while nothing much happened. The rain which had started about midday grew heavier as the afternoon advanced, a warm but never-the-less wetting mist. Water found its way inside my jacket and trickled uncomfortably down my neck.

With little happening, I decided to call it a day at 3pm and packed the soggy gear away in the car. The trusty VW engine burst into life at the first turn of the key and I bounced down the gravel road, retracing my outward journey to Tulla. Unfortunately the junction of the lakeside road with the main road was blocked by a team of lads with heavy machines who were working on the road and I had to reverse back a hundred yards then carry out a 29 point turn to go off in the opposite direct down some more minor roads to get back to Tulla. It rained the whole way home.

So what did I learn from today? I caught some (tiny) Rudd, a species new to me so I was happy about that. The skimmer was very welcome too but it would have been nice to catch something a bit more substantial. The colour of the water looked odd to me and when I mentioned it to the other fishermen they said the lake was never normally that colour. Was it due to the heavy rains we have had of late? Or maybe all those road works had allowed silt to enter the lough. Either way, I am sure the fish were upset by the change and this did not help my cause any today.

It was a long way to travel for a few tiddlers but that is fishing for you! I didn't catch anything on the swimfeeders, all the small stuff were caught on the float. Maybe if I had stuck with the float some bigger Rudd may have showed up, who knows?

Bream continue to elude me. OK, I had a skimmer today but catching the full grown lads is still beyond my ken. I have read that pre-baiting is the secret to catching Bream but that is just not practical for me. To drive for at least an hour or two just to chuck a load of groundbait into a lake then drive home is not a viable option. Instead I need to find smaller waters which hold bream, small enough that I can cover them all in a day. That way I know the fish will be seeing my bait at some point and I can try to hold them in the swim by chucking in groundbait and loose feed.

I am also tempted to try a flavoured ground bait and I'll do some more research on this before I venture out again. Right now it feels like I have so much still to learn about coarse fishing. Every time I think I'm making progress it becomes apparent there are huge gaps in my abilities.

The lough itself was a nice place to fish and it was an example of how so many other lakes could be opened up for coarse angling in Ireland. The concrete stands were very simple affairs which would have cost very little and been easy to make. The two biggest issues for anglers here in Ireland are car parking and access. There are literally thousands of lakes in the Republic which are full of coarse fish but anglers can't get near them. Narrow roads with nowhere to park is the norm. Having to cross fields, often full of stock, is a problem too. Have you tried hopping a few barbed wire or electric fences with all your coarse gear?

It is disheartening when you get to a lake only to be confronted with 20 or 30 yards of reeds before open water. Over the years IFI has carried out some excellent work to try and open up more waters but so much more could be done if there was real government will to do so. This being Ireland, nothing is simple or straight forward. Land ownership is a huge issue here and it is often very complicated with multiple owners of small parcels of land. These would all need to be dealt with and compensation for the loss of small bits of land on lake shores or to create access paths will work out to be very expensive. With ever dwindling game and sea fish stocks, I can see an upswing in coarse anglers over the coming years in Ireland. It would be great if IFI could find the funds to increase safe access to more loughs and rivers for coarse fishers.

My severe limitations as a budding coarse fisher were cruelly exposed for all to see today. I very quickly ran out of ideas and ended up chucking a pike spoon around simply because I did not know what other options I had with float and leger. Bait is a constant nightmare for me with the nearest maggot supplier over an hour's drive away and in the opposite direction from where I was fishing today. I had naively thought dead maggots would work just as well but of course I was a mile wide of the mark with that assumption!

Over the following days I read some more and pondered my relative lack of success. The only Rudd I caught were tiny but that is not to say there were no bigger ones to be had if I changed to fishing on the top of the water. My shotting was haphazard to say the least with little thought beyond getting the float to cock correctly. My groundbait looked pretty unappetising to me and also the fish I suspect. I am sure the consistency was wrong too, I had added too much water and the resulting slop left a lot to be desired. All in all I had fished poorly and I castigated myself for such a poor showing. It was not so much that I failed to land very much but rather that I had not been thinking clearly and putting into practice some of the technicalities of this form of angling which I have been reading so much about. I can do better and will learn the lessons of the damp day by the edge of a dirty lake in east Clare.

So anyway, I have now caught fish in county Clare, not big ones I grant you but fish never-the-less. I knew at the outset of this project that there would be many days when settling for one or two tiddlers will constitute success. That was very much the case today in the Banner County. Management of my expectations is crucial or I will lose faith quickly if there are many more days like this. I strongly suspect that if I lived locally and fished this lake often I would not have bothered to even set up a rod today due to the state of the water. On reflection, I need robust plans for alternative venues when I embark on these long distance trips, much better thought out than I had organised in my head for today. There is a lesson here for any visitors to the country who want to do a bit of fishing. Try to sort out more than one venue in case your main one is not accessible or just not fishing well.

It is the summer of 2022 and I am vexed. The tiny fish I caught when I visited county Clare hardly felt like a resounding victory more like an unfair claim to success. As it happens, I find myself driving through the county on a fine day, not too far from the scene of my difficult days fishing back in 2019. I have a little time to spare so after mulling it over I decide to try once more to catch something from Cloondorney.

I was a very raw novice at the dark arts of coarse fishing the last time I wet a line in this county and I was hoping that I had learned enough to make a better fist of it on this occasion. Turning off the main road I pick my way through Tulla, then along the narrow roads of east Clare in the late summer sunshine. Road signs must be terribly expensive as the local roads here don't seem to have any and a good sense of direction is very handy for those luddites (like me) who don't have satnav. I found the lake handily enough though and was quickly setting up amid lovely surroundings. I had forgotten how pretty this lough is.

A float rod is assembled and about ten feet of water plumbed a couple of rod lengths out. I have no ground bait with me, just a near empty half pint box of mixed casters and maggots. By my reckoning, I have about an hour to fish before I head home. Out sails the small waggler and I sit on my stool, bathed in sunshine. This could be another waste of my time and effort but I am happy just sit here as the summer winds down. I ponder the metaphors that brings to mind.

As expected, some tiny Rudd are showing on the surface. The odd one jumps and confirms they are four inchers like the ones I caught the last time I was here. The bottom seems to be quite uneven in front of me as the float hangs up sometimes when the hook gets stuck on the slimy stones down there. I fiddle about with the float stops to try and find just the right depth and finally decide I am OK for now.

Almost in slow motion the red tip of the float sinks below the surface and I lift into a nice little roach of six ounces or so. A most welcome fish! Watching it as it shoots off I am struck by the clarity of the water. On my last visit here, the water resembled oxtail soup, filthy with suspended matter.

There are very few maggots left in the box now, maybe a dozen or so are still wriggling in the bottom so I have to make them count. Casting slightly to my left brings a quick response and one of the stunted Rudd is soon landed, followed by two more in quick succession. It then goes quiet for a spell until firstly three perch then a tidy roach keep me entertained. Over to my right a dog swims across the lough, chasing a stick its owners have lobbed in and later an elderly lady gets out of a car at the next stand along from me and dives into the water.

She must be in her seventies but she rapidly covers the distance to the reeds which fringe the opposite shore. A short break to catch her breath then she swims back with short, measured strokes. A quick rub down to dry herself then she is off in the car once again. I can only admire her athleticism, I struggle to walk that distance never mind swim it! The fish go quiet and all too soon it is time to go so I quickly pack up and say my goodbyes to Cloondorney once again.

There is a sense of vindication after that short session. I had been beating myself up after coming so close to blanking on my first visit to the lake but I now feel that the conditions were so bad I did well to catch anything that time around. I slip a Neil Young CD into the player and weave my way homewards along the hedge lined byroads of county Clare as the sun dips below the horizon, painting the land gold then purple.

Chapter 5
Cavan

County number 5

Monday, 21st September 2020

It began a couple of weeks ago. You had to listen hard to hear it to start with but it quickly increased in volume and frequency. Now there was robust 'clunk' emanating from the region of the rear suspension whenever I drove over a bump in the road (not an infrequent occurrence here in Ireland). On good roads, it disappeared but as soon as the surface returned to the normal level of inconsistency it came back. I strongly suspected that a bushing in the suspension has given up the ghost and it would need to be changed. I added it to the ever lengthening list of jobs the car needed done. Until I could get around to fixing it I would just turn up the volume on the radio to drown out the disconcerting noise.

I thought before setting off on the next leg of my odyssey that the car might be a problem for me but no, it ran faultlessly while all sorts of other disasters befell me on that Monday in September.

The next target county on my quest to catch fish in every one was Cavan. While I have passed through bits of Cavan on a lot of different occasions, I have not spent any significant time there so it was all a bit of a mystery to me. Cavan is one of the Ulster counties, its northern boundary forming part of the border with Northern Ireland.

When driving to/from Scotland on my annual trips, I pass through a tiny piece of Cavan at Blacklion and I have been in Cavan Town and Ballyconnell on business before now. It is another one of those counties blessed with endless opportunities for the coarse fishing enthusiast so I planned to try for Bream (again) on one of the smaller loughs. Cavan really has an awful lot of loughs to pick from.

While researching possible venues, I hit on a daring plan. I found a lough which straddled the border between Cavan and Longford. With a bit of luck, I could catch a fish on Cavan side of the lough then wander over to the other side of the lake and catch another fish on the Longford side, thus ticking off two counties in one day. The idea really appealed, so I laid plans to attempt just that.

The lough in question is called Guinikin and it lies close to the village of Arvagh. The village itself nestles in Cavan but three counties meet on the edge of the town. Leitrim and Longford are both but a short walk from the middle of the village. Indeed, the town is somewhat famous as it lies at the intersection of three of the four Irish Provinces as Ulster, Leinster and Connaught all converge here. Probably the most direct route for me would be to drive to Longford along the N5 then hang a left up go up the R198.

Instead, I decided to go via Carrick-on-Shannon so I could pick up some maggots at the tackle shop there. That would entail driving through the other popular coarse fishing centres of Mohill and Carrigallen. It probably was much the same in terms of kilometres driven but the roads would be poorer and therefor slower.

The weather had been fine, warm and dry for the previous few days, allowing water levels across the country to drop to something approaching normal for the time of year after a long wet spell. I was hoping that Guinikin was not too high as I wanted to be able to walk around a fair old chunk of the shoreline. In case of bad conditions, I had packed a pair of thigh waders. If nothing else, the banks were likely to be muddy even if they were not under water. Information about the lake was sparse, there was a small carpark nearby which is always a big plus for me. On Google maps, it looked like there was a lane which led to the edge of the lough.

The IFI website stated there were stands to fish from which would be nice if they were there some. In terms of fish, the IFI said there were bream, roach, tench, hybrids, pike and perch present. A nice spread of species to have a go at if the bream failed to appear (as is normal for me). I planned around starting operations with one rod on feeder and the other on waggler. I'd bring a spinning rod with me in case I wanted to try for pike.

The previous day I spent some time sorting out the coarse fishing tackle which had degenerated into chaos after the last few outings. I find that I chop and change methods a lot when coarse fishing and that leads to a host of little bits of used tackle congregating in the bottom of my seat box. Discarded hook lengths, floats still attached to bits of shotted line, empty bait boxes and other detritus all had to be gathered up, cleaned/sorted or safely discarded. Then the necessities like clean towels and spare tins of sweetcorn replenished.

I had read somewhere that bream like sweet flavours in groundbait so I went ferreting around in the cupboards to see if I could find something suitable. Right at the back of a press in the kitchen I came across a suspicious looking wee bottle which proved to be vanilla essence. The best before date suggested to me this was not going to fit for human consumption so I added it to my tackle box.

The tackle shop in Carrick on Shannon opens at 9.30am so an 8.30 departure from Castlebar would put in the parish around the right time. Traffic in the town was heavy but once I was on the main road it eased off and the dry, dull weather made the journey pleasant enough. The knocking from the suspension came and went at intervals but there were no dramas with the car. I rolled into Carrick at twenty-to-ten and after parking strode manfully up to the tackle shop—it was closed!

Bugger, there goes my plans to use maggots today. I was really unhappy about this as I continue to hold no faith in sweetcorn despite lugging a couple of tins along with me. Back in the car I pressed on, passing through Mohill and then to Carrigallen. I had almost driven through the village when it occurred to me there was a small tackle shop attached to a B&B at the end of the main street. Sure enough, there it was just as you are leaving on the left hand side so I pulled over and, clutching an empty bait box, strode up to the wee shop. 'Closed due to Covid' said the sign on the door.

Before I could start cursing properly, someone inside the house knocked on the window and signalled to me. Anne, the owner came out and said she happened to have some bait and after an exchange of coin a pint of bright red maggots were mine. I nearly skipped back to the car, my mood completely changed due to my good fortune. Not far now and I arrived in Arvagh, a bustling village with a one way system.

My chosen lough was on the other edge of the town and easily found. Parking up I got all my gear sorted and ready for action but of a lane to the lake there was no sign. Instead, a deep and foul looking drain led from under the road to the lake and the ground was swampy all around it. Electric cattle fences barred my path and I could already see swathes of dense reed beds around the water. More cursing ensued as I battled my way to the nearest point of the lough but there were still many yards of reeds between me and open water. Setting down all my gear I got out my knife and tried hacking some reeds down but I quickly realised it would have taken me hours to clear a spot to fish from. In the end, I gave up and trudged through the muck and across the fences back to the car. I had wasted a good hour and had still not even set up a rod. I needed a new plan.

All the gear was hastily bundled back into the car and I headed back into the town. Retracing my steps I found a brown sign for Rockfield lough. As I followed the road for a couple of kilometres I could see a small lake and guessed this was Rockfield in a hollow to the right. This lake too was also surrounded by a thick belt of reeds so I beat a retreat, not fancying another battle with more vegetation. Back into the town once again and I found a big lough just before you reach the main street which I later found out was called Garty Lough.

There was space to park and even a pontoon to fish from. After a wasted morning, this would have to do.

Garty is a quite large lough and the southern end of it, where I would be fishing, reaches right into the town. I was lucky to be here on a nice quiet day as I suspect in a wind the open water would become rough in no time, making float fishing very difficult. I can't explain why but I had overlooked doing any research on this particular lough when planning my day in Cavan so I had to make a few presumptions. A lake this size in this part of Ireland meant I could reasonably expect to encounter roach and perch. If they were here, then there will be pike to predate on them.

I suspected it should also be home to bream, and possibly very large bream at that. Given every other option had been too hard to reach I felt this was the place for me so I parked up and got all the gear out of the car again. Past a play park where a mum was pushing a kid on a swing, then over a small bridge to a floating pontoon, what would this lake hold for me?

Midday and finally I set up the gear. My cheap feeder rod with the ABU444 and six pound mono was soon rigged with a small feeder and cast out. Next the float rod and I faffed about setting the depth with a plummet. Both rods were baited with maggots. When plumbing the depth, I found there was about eight feet of water three rod lengths out from the pontoon, a nice manageable depth for me, not too deep not too shallow. Groundbait was made up and balls thrown in, then I settled down with some coffee to see what would transpire. An hour passed and I bent to pick up the feeder rod to check the bait.

There was a muffled 'crack' and the old rod sagged just above the bottom joint. I had managed to strike a big cleat on the pontoon and snapped the rod. Let's just say I was not having the best of days so far!

I packed away the crippled feeder then set up my wonderful old light leger rod and mulled over the day's events from the dubious comfort of my seatbox. All of my plans were in tatters, as was one of my rods. It was 1pm and I had not even had a bite yet. Things were looking bleak. On the plus side, I was settled into a nice swim and I had confidence in my tactics and bait. I would add some more groundbait for a start and this time I added in some of the prehistoric vanilla essence. Mushing it into the mix I could smell the vanilla, very appealing to me if not the fish. Balls of the sweet-smelling goo were chucked into the swim, each laced with some maggots for good measure.

I re-cast then sat back on the seat box to await further events. Very soon the float dipped. I struck—nothing, I had missed the bite completely. The maggots that remained on the hook were well chewed so I re-baited and cast out again to the same spot. Once again, the float dipped and I struck into thin air. This was repeated a few more times. Puzzled as to why I could not set the hook I decided that I needed to make a change. I was fishing a single maggot on a size 18 hook on the float rod so I wound in the leger rod and changed the hook to a bigger size 14 tipped with 3 maggots. First cast with the leger brought a strong bite and a fish on the end. A nice roach of about 8 ounces came to hand and I'm fairly sure I cracked a smile. The float was now being ignored but the leger produced three roach and a perch over the next hour, none big but all welcome. The last swallows of summer hawked flies above me in the gentlest of breezes, life was good.

It went quiet again, presumably because the shoal of roach had moved off, so I took the opportunity to change the hooklength on the float rod, dropping to 12 inches of 3 pound mono and a size 14 barbless hook. I stuck with 3 red maggots hooked by the skinny end for bait. Another two balls of sweet smelling groundbait were flung in and the float sent out to position the baited hook over the spot where the groundbait lay on the bottom.

It is a strange thing but from then on the leger rod was ignored by the fish but the float rod could do no wrong. Bites were universally positive affairs with the waggler giving a tremble before shooting under. In short order, I landed another 3 decent roach and 3 more perch on the float. That made a total of 10 fish for the session, not too bad for a day which had started so unpromisingly. The fish went quiet again about 3.30pm so I packed up and hit the road home.

A post mortem of the day revealed a number of mistakes on my part. I should have checked the bait shop in Carrick on Shannon was open on Mondays. Guinikin Lough was a disaster because I was overly optimistic there would be somewhere relatively easy to fish there. I need to be certain about venues before hiking half way across the country to fish them. Maybe a younger man, equipped with a heavy rake, might have cleared a swim there but it was torture for me just getting across those 7 electric cattle fences.

Not managing to tick off two counties in one day was a shame but that was always going to be a big ask. Breaking the rod was pure carelessness on my part. It was an old rod that I had bought second-hand for a pound or two so it was no great financial loss but it still rankles that I was so fekless. I won't rush to replace it, I have enough rods to see me through the winter and I can think about a new dedicated feeder rod next spring. Bream continue to elude me but I am getting used to that by now. I understand that not pre-baiting is a major drawback but there is nothing I can do about it.

On the plus side, I caught fish in county Cavan! That is a big success for me and I am pretty happy about it. I've discovered a huge affection for roach, they are such a pretty fish and I'm enjoying learning how to catch them. Did adding the vanilla essence to the groundbait make a difference? I honestly don't know but it sure smelled good to me so I will definitely try it again. Getting fish on both float and leger was fun and I am feeling more confident with the coarse gear with each outing. For me, the pluses of the day outweighed the minuses by a goodly margin. Despite the disappointments of the morning, I kept at it and didn't give up.

While fishing, I saw a few heavy splashes out in the lake today which I could not identify as they were too far away. Then a large, silver fish jumped clear of the water not 30 yards from me. Later, another large, silver fish rose at my feet and I saw both very clearly. They were salmon. How salmon got into this lake in the heart of Cavan I do not know. The stream exiting the lake is little more than a drain. I can only imagine this drain links to Lough Gowna which is close by and is part of the massive Erne system.

I must stress that deciding on which lough to fish in Cavan is not easy, there are just so many to pick from! There are literally hundreds of fish holding venues across the county and I will certainly make a point of popping over there more often. Yes, it is quite distant from Mayo but an early start can get me to most parts of the county with plenty of time for a day on the water.

I now need to think about which county to target next. 5 down, 27 still to go. For obvious reasons, I have been fishing those counties closest to me, so from now on the journeys are going to get longer and more arduous. The more distant counties are 4 hours drive or more from home, so at least eight hours will be spent getting there and back.

Fishing time will be at a premium and these long range trips will require much more careful planning than I have put into my jaunts so far. With the winter fast approaching and some counties being in lockdown, it makes sense to keep my powder dry for next year once September is past. A fine spell of weather in October/November might tempt me out to fish for Pike but other than that I will hunker down and make preparations for 2021 once September is over. That knock in the suspension is still there…

Chapter 6
Offaly

County number 6

Thursday, 24th September 2020

Offaly sits in the very heart of Ireland, bounded by no less than 7 other counties. It is another one of those places which I have driven through so many times while commuting to jobs but have never stopped in, let along fished there. In my mind, Offaly was simply a flat and featureless county consisting of nothing but bog which was being systematically stripped by the huge machines of Bord na Mona to feed the hungry power stations so I required a spot of re-education. The most obvious angling opportunities were on the river Shannon which forms the border between Offaly and Galway.

The river is wide and strong here, with shoals of bream roaming around in 30 feet of water. It sounded like too much for a novice coarse angler like me to tackle with any degree of confidence. What I required was somewhere more sedate and intimate. The river Brosna flows across the county but I could not find out too much on exactly where was best to fish so I discounted that river too. How about the canal instead? The Grand Canal could just be the place to try.

The Grand Canal links Dublin in the east to the river Shannon in the west. By the time it was fully open in 1804, it had taken nearly 50 years to build. After a brief period of success, it fell into disrepair for many years. Nowadays, restored to its former glory, it is full of pleasure boats and is home to a good few coarse fish. I read the canal held Pike, Perch, Bream, Eels and some Roach. Pike ran to 5 or 6 pounds in weight but the perch were wee lads with a half-pounder being a good one.

I began to hatch a plan to fish for perch on the canal and found a nice looking stretch at Shannon Harbour, right at the very western end of the canal. It looked like it would normally be extremely busy with pleasure boats but this year, what with Covid and all, there are few people holidaying on the canal and anyway this is the end of the season. One of the big attractions for this spot was the abundance of parking places at the edge of the canal.

Looking at various maps it appeared there would be an interesting area to fish where the 36th lock (the last one on the canal), the river Brosna and the river Shannon all converged. Surely there would be some fish hanging around such a piece of water. If not, between the lock and the hump-backed bridge in the village there were moorings and some wide basins which would also be worth investigating. All in all, it looked as if there was going to be more than enough water to keep me busy for a few hours.

The weather forecast was not great. The day in question was promised to be cool and windy with heavy showers, your typical autumn day in this country. I packed some rain gear in the car and a few spare clothes in case I got very wet. September can be a funny month in Ireland, sometimes we bask in a week of glorious sunshine but equally day after day of heavy rain is just as likely. We are very lucky here and extreme weather events are only something we read about in other parts of the world. Will that change as global warming increases? It seems highly likely that will happen but for now we face wind and rain as usual.

This would be another first for me as I have never fished a canal before. From my very limited knowledge of canal fishing, you need to find the fish first and this can be the difficult bit. The advice was to look for places where the canal either narrows or widens as this seems to attract the perch. Under bridges are also good holding spots apparently. Perch are very accommodating little fish that can be caught on a wide variety of baits and lures so I figured on trying small jigs to start with.

As there were small Pike also present there was a good chance one of them might grab a soft bait too. In addition to jigs, I also packed a small box of spinners. Lacking any of that new-fangled drop-shotting gear I packed a couple of ancient 6 foot baitcasting rods and reels. I planned to give some small jigs a whirl and see if the perch liked them. That would entail moving around a bit to cover as much water as possible and I would need to travel light. As a back-up plan I would bring along my coarse fishing tackle in case the perch were unresponsive and I could try for roach and bream on the maggot or worm.

As usual, I would bring some bread and sweetcorn with me too in case of emergency. Yes, I know, this is far too much gear to be lugging around but with the car parked so close by I thought it better to have too many options than not enough. I harbour a sneaking envy of those modern urban anglers who travel so light, just a pocket full of soft plastics and off they go. Will I ever emulate them? I doubt it, my need to be prepared for every eventuality seems to grow and not diminish with age.

It's the night before and I lay my plans. The route there was straightforward, M18/M6/R357 then cut off for Shannon Harbour. There should be none of the twisty roads of my last couple of forays into Leitrim and Cavan, just good straight road and motorways. I reckon that a tad more than a couple of hours should see me at my destination and as I wanted to be back at home for 5pm that would give me somewhat less than four hours actual fishing. Would that be long enough for me to catch something? I step out into the garden to check the weather before I went to bed, a cold, clear night full of twinkling stars. What would the morrow hold?

Sure enough the forecasters are fully vindicated, the day had broken amid squally showers driven by a wind which didn't seem to know which direction it wanted to blow from. Whatever the direction, it was strong! Eating my porridge I consulted the weather forecast once again, they were now talking about gale force winds and heavy rain with possible spot flooding today. Looks like it is going to be a rough one! Changing weather forecasts are pretty normal here, stuck as we are between continental Europe and the Atlantic ocean.

You can't let a drop of rain put you off doing something in Ireland otherwise you would hardly ever set foot outside the door. Our incredible modern waterproof outer clothes strip away any of the old excuses for remaining indoors during inclement weather, so swathed in Gortex us anglers venture forth.

The trip down to Offaly was uneventful and the roads were pretty quiet. The small bridge over the canal in the village was supposed to be closed so I diverted through Cloghans and came into the village from the south, a fair bit of a detour. Upon reaching the village, it was obvious the bridge was in fact open so my detour had been for nothing. The exactitudes of small details like road closures are not something to depend on hereabouts and it is better to develop an ability to shrug off any lost time as the chance to see a bit more of the country.

I bounced along the rough track on the south side of the towpath, splashing through water filled potholes and reached a parking spot next to the last lock on the canal. Blasts of chilly wind greeted me as I opened the door. Pulling on an extra fleece I quickly surveyed my surroundings and decided to try the jig first in an effort to tempt some perch from the likely looking water above the lock.

Rigging one of the old rods, I selected a 7gram jig and an olive coloured paddletail. Waterproofs and wellies were most definitely the order of the day and the scudding clouds foretold of more rain.

A small van pulled up a two lads got out. The older one, craggy featured and stooped, got busy with something in the back of the Caddy but the younger, red haired fella came over for a chat. He found the notion that I had driven from Mayo to go fishing on a day like today very amusing. They were here to do some maintenance work, 'sure there's always somethin' for doing' as he put it. When I said all we would be doing otherwise was sitting in the pub he said "wasn't that how I spent the last night!"

"Tis sick of the drink I am today." Of fishing he knew nothing, he was a GAA man through and through. When I enquired which code he seemed bemused, "hurlin' of course!" followed by "you fellas up in Mayo wouldn't have a clue about that though."

He wasn't far wrong with that assertion, Mayo is a footballing county to its very bones. The finer points of last season's hurling were by now under discussion but my new pal was called back by his superior as it appeared they actually did have some work to do. I wished him well as he loped off towards the mud stained van, 'there will be no work done this day, sure I'm as sick as a hospital' he replied over his shoulder.

Grabbing the rod I went over to the canal just above the lock and began casting. Problems immediately became obvious to me in the shape of weed, lots and lots of weed. It grew thickly on the bottom and maddeningly floated in great clumps on the surface too. Each cast resulted in a fouled hook, frequently accompanied by a stream of oaths from me. The weed on the bottom came away easily enough so I was not losing any gear but nor was I catching any fish. I gave it twenty minutes or so but this wasn't working at all so I needed a plan B. Back to the car I strode, head bowed, deep in thought.

The weather now degenerated and a troublesome wind sprang up closely followed by a very heavy shower. I got a good soaking but used this time to grab my coarse gear and leg it down to the end of the canal, only about 100 yards from the Shannon itself. There was a steady flow here as the river Brosna came in just up from where I was on the opposite side. Finding a small flat area which has obviously been used by many other fishers before, I made myself as comfortable as possible.

The high bank behind me took the worst of the sting out of the wind but the rain never really let up and all the gear I had with me was saturated. Plumbing the depth I found there was about 12 feet of water in front of me. Given the weed situation above the lock I had ditched the jigs and instead opted to try red maggots on my float tackle with the worm on my light leger rod close in to the reeds at my side.

Casting was difficult in the wind, sometimes the float sailed out fine but other times a gust would catch the float, tossing it around and depositing it anywhere except where I wanted it to land. In addition, I suffered a few tangles when the line wrapped the rod, again mainly due to that damn wind. Alterations to the shot pattern were required as I tried to find a balance between bulk shot at the float to help me cast and spacing them out to get the bait down quickly.

Sometimes the wind whipped up the surface of the water, making it hard to even see the float. Being honest, this was not the most enjoyable day on the bank I have ever experienced but just trying to figure out what to do and then execute it was oddly mentally stimulating. A heavier float might give me more control so I took everything apart and set up again with a large bodied waggler, a task which was far from easy in the wind and rain. This new set up cast much better and I felt much more in control. I trotted the float through the same run for an hour or so without success before the float ever so slowly slid under. I was equally slow in lifting the rod, thinking this was just a bit of weed again but no! A nice wee roach came to hand, sparkling silver flanks and red fins. I had photographed him and popped him back in the water before it struck me, I had done it, caught a fish in Offaly!

I repeated the exercise again with another, slightly bigger roach on the float fished maggot about 20 minutes later but by then the already dire weather had taken a turn for the worse. A veritable monsoon broke and driving rain penetrated every leak in my old waterproofs. A pool of water formed on the seatbox and my maggots were floating in the bait tin. Fishing was extremely difficult as I could hardly see or feel anything in the deluge. Even a half mad Scotsman could not keep this up so I packed away the rods as quickly as I could and started to plod back to the car through the downpour.

Nearing the carpark it became clear the rain was easing off somewhat so I decided to try a few casts from a floating pontoon just below the gates. I was soaked through anyway so a few more minutes in the rain wasn't going to make a hell of a lot of difference. This pontoon is where pleasure boats tie up prior to ascending the lock. In normal days, I am sure this spot was a hive of activity as boats queued there to negotiating the lock. Today there was a solitary empty boat tied forlornly to the pontoon leaving tons of room for me to fish. To me this looked like the ideal spot for perch to hang around so I dropped a worm over the edge of the pontoon while I sorted out the float rod.

I turned to see the tip of the leger rod rattle but when I picked it up and wound in the perch had scoffed my worm and got away scot free. The rain renewed it venomous downpour, horizontal now in a howling wind. I turned my back to it and kept on fishing but it was very tough to see any twitches on the rod tip in the buffeting gusts.

Thankfully, after maybe ten minutes or so the torrents of rain eased off a bit and I was able to see and feel again. Soon the tip of the wee leger rod give another timid rattle and I set the hook in a small perch who had taken a fancy to my cunningly presented worm. I repeated this trick another couple of times with similar sized perch then added another nice roach, also on the worm, before the next belt of weather came rolling in.

By now, there was not an inch of me dry I had to admit defeat. Packing up, I made tracks to the car and some welcome respite from the elements. Water had penetrated my old waterproofs from head to toe and I was cold, soaked and tired. Just standing up in the wind had proved to be exhausting. Dumping all the waterlogged gear by the car I shed the outer layers and hopped into the front seat. A drop of hot coffee and a sandwich revived me a bit and I sat there watching the teeming rain on the windscreen. It was nearing three o'clock and I lacked the will to tackle up again even in the unlikely event the weather improved so I called it a day.

Once more I braved the rain to throw the rods and gear into the back of the car then I turned the key in the ignition and set a course for home, this time driving over the bridge and cutting a big chunk off the journey back north. In the distance, I could make out a white VW van with two lads sitting in it, it didn't look like they managed to get much work done after all. Strangely, the bad weather abated as I neared Ballinasloe and I completed the rest of the journey home in sunshine and light showers.

At home, the sopping wet clothes were bundled up and fired into the washing machine. The left over worms were released back into the compost heap from whence they came while the remaining maggots were frozen for use in ground bait at some point in the future. The rest of the gear could wait until the next day to get cleaned/dried/sorted out. Reviewing the day's events, I had found a really nice place to fish and it is clear that in better conditions and a bit earlier in the year the canal at Shannon Harbour could produce some great fishing. I was reasonably pleased to have managed to winkle out a few fish in truly horrendous conditions.

I know they were small but I was far from disappointed. Once again I had fish to both float and leger tactics. The only real downside is my inability to catch anything other than roach and perch. I need to think about what to do when there is a lot of weed growth. I figured that the float was the answer but would a swimfeeder with a popped-up hook bait been a better option? It did cross my mind to change to that set up but the rain was so heavy the idea of making any more changes was just too much of an effort. All I wanted to do was try to keep as little water as possible from getting through my jacket and trousers.

The next day I dried out all my gear and tidied up my tackle box. Items which were not being used were removed and a few small bits were added. Rods and reels were wiped down and checked over. The old Cardinal 444A was running a bit stiff so I opened it up and lubricated the innards. Groundbait is running low now so a visit to a good tackle shop is required. I need to look at new waterproofs, my old ones are long past their best now and I got very wet in the heavy rain. I'm also going to start bringing my heavy leger rod with me when I go coarse fishing. It can handle heavier/larger swimfeeders and this might help me to add more groundbait into swims and thus attract and hold some bream. In short, more lessons have been learned and bits of the big puzzle are slowly fitting into place.

Counties Dublin and Donegal are locked down again due to spikes in Covid-19 with other counties looking like they will go the same way. At least, I have ticked off another county before it becomes out of bounds. After this burst of activity over that past month, I will be slowing down a bit over the winter and, if the gods are good to me, I will go at it hell for leather from next spring. I had imagined that I would be much further on with this project than I actually am. Just how onerous the whole undertaking is has now dawned on me but I remain resolute (for now at any rate).

Chapter 7
Longford

County number 7

Thursday, 1st October 2020

There is a lot of fishing in county Longford but from what I could see most of it was going to be very challenging for a newby like me. The Shannon forms the western border but I have been shying away from this river simply due to its size. The fish could be anywhere and me fishing one randomly picked spot on the bank and battling those deep, fast flows seemed to be inviting disaster. So instead I found a lake in the north of the county which appeared to be a more likely spot to actually hook something. It is called Lough Sallagh. This body of water straddles the Longford/Leitrim border so I would have to be careful not to stray across the county line as I have caught fish in Leitrim before.

The IFI website said the lake contained bream, perch and roach, in other words the usual suspects. Parking was very, very limited as the road on the side of the lake was single track. It also said the lake was very shallow and very weedy so there could be some issues with that. In the event that Sallagh was unfishable or I could not find a parking spot, I would pluck up my courage and drive down to Lanesborough and try the mighty Shannon. Was the famous hot water section there still fishing now that the ESB flusher is not working? Did the huge Tench of yesteryear still haunt the area? What about the vast shoals of specimen sized Bream—did they still move up the river from lough Ree? Or maybe there would be shoals of silvery roach cruising around in the deep waters. I had no idea but it seemed to be worth a shot if Sallagh was out of ply.

Once again, the most direct route for me coming from Mayo would be to drive to Longford then strike north but I required fresh bait and that would mean a visit to Carrick-on-Shannon. This would add some time to the drive but nothing too disastrous. My plan was to leave Castlebar around 8.30am which should, if the traffic gods were on my side, get me to the side of the lough around 11 o'clock. (months after this day I discovered I could have bought bait at a tackle shop in Longford. Note to self—do more research in future).

I had spent some time since my last trip tidying out the tackle box and cleaning the coarse rods and reels so everything tackle wise was in reasonably good order. I really could do with buying a couple of boxes for all the smaller items of tackle though. Just now there are too many individual tins, each holding one or more bits. Hooks are in an old tobacco tin for example and my selection of swimfeeders live in a disused blue plastic washing powder box.

In particular, I would like to invest in a rig box so that I could have hook lengths made up and ready to go. I reckon that would save me a fair bit of time and hassle. I could also use up the spade end hooks which I seem to have accumulated and are too much trouble to tie when actually fishing. None of this expense was foreseen a few months ago. Back then some floats, split shot and small hooks was all I thought I would need but lo and behold, a bug has bitten me. I really do enjoy this coarse fishing malarkey so a few bob will no doubt be spent.

My hope was that the shallow water would lend itself to float fishing and I would be blessed with fine, calm weather so I could spent the day watching the tip of my float and hopefully see it slide beneath the surface a few times. It is hard to know which form of fishing for coarse species I like best, both float and leger have their attractions. I simply adore using my light leger rod and seeing the quiver tip rattle when there is a bite. Then again, focusing on that little speck of red or orange as it sits there in the surface is hypnotic too. Here in Ireland you can use two rods simultaneously so I can set both a float and leger up each time and see which one works best on any given day.

I checked the weather forecast before going to bed—"a mix of sunny spells and widespread showers. Some of the showers will be heavy with hail and possibly thundery too. Any mist, fog and frost will clear during the morning but the day will be rather cool with highs of just 10 or 11 Celsius in light southeast or variable breezes." Sounded like your typical Irish autumn day to me. I threw an extra fleece into the bag.

Even though I wasn't leaving until 8.30, I rose early on Thursday morning. It's cool now and I put on the gas to warm the house up a little. Cats fed, I set about loading the tackle in the car. For some reason, my thoughts wandered back to the days of my youth and how I would set off every Saturday armed with one fly rod and a small bag containing my only fly box and my sandwiches. Now I go fishing with half-a-dozen rods and enough gear to fill the back of the car yet I don't catch any more fish than I did as a lad. Maybe that will be the next challenge for me once I have completed the 32 counties—fish all year with only one rod. That could be interesting!

I stowed the ABU 234 heavy leger rod in the car this time, just in case I found myself down in Lanesborough. It is capable of casting up to 40gms which would be useful on the Shannon. A lovely rod to fish with, I planned to pair it up with an old silver Daiwa Regal reel filled with 8 pound line. That should be man enough to handle any strong currents and heavy fish down there. Ferreting around in the tackle room I had unearthed some 40gm feeders to bring along too.

The big guns were out. I admit to feeling a lot of trepidation about this trip, Longford felt like a big challenge. Lough Sallagh would be shallow and weedy with poor access and the alternative of the Shannon at Lanesborough looked to be huge and daunting. It felt there would be no easy, middle-of-the-road fishing for me today.

That well-travelled road east along the N5 was not overly busy but thick banks of fog required a lot of concentration. At Frenchpark, I cut off and drove north by east to the now familiar town of Carrick-on-Shannon where I parked up beside the river. Carrick Angling Centre is conveniently located near the bridge. Unfortunately it was closed so I hit the road again, down the N4 then off through Mohill and on to Carrigallen where I got some worms from the B&B there (they had no maggots) before retracing my journey to the junction at the Cloone GAA pitch on that terrible bend.

The minor roads to the lake were not signposted but I managed to guess correctly and peeled off first to the left and then down a boreen to the right. The trees were turning red and gold, making the last stages of the drive very pleasant. For many people, the idea that a long drive can be enjoyable must be hard to fathom but we have little traffic here in the west of Ireland and pretty scenery is all around us. At last, the lake hove into view on the right as the road came almost within touching distance of the water.

There were indeed very few parking spots. I pulled into one near the far end of the lake and got out to take a look. Barely six inches of water were all I could see so I hopped back into the car and found an even smaller space half way along the shore where I could squeeze the VW in without blocking the road. By now, the sun was out and it felt like a summer's day. Donning my thigh boots I waded out to see if there was any deeper water but even 30 yards from the shore I was only in 18 inches of water.

The combination of shallows and bright light did not inspire confidence but I tackled up anyway. The lightest line on my float reel was a threadlike two pound mono so I used that and a gossamer thin one pound link to a size 16 hook. By breaking a worm into little sections, I had suitably small baits. I went slightly heavier on the leger with a small bomb above a size 12 hook and whole worm.

The sun beat down on me as I sat motionless on the seat box. This might be fine for topping up a sun tan but I fished for an hour without a bite. Neither the float nor leger twitched as I sat there forlornly on the grass considering what was wrong. Although a very pretty lough, I felt it was too shallow and quickly lost any faith that I would catch a fish there. Time for some drastic action so breaking down the rods I packed up and hit the road again, bound this time for Lanesborough where the mighty Shannon flows between Longford and Roscommon. Just over half-an-hour later I was driving down the wide main street in Lanesborough.

For those who have never heard of it, let me explain what the flusher at Lanesborough is all about. The surrounding flat bogland was for years stripped by huge machines and the peat which was extracted used to fuel a number of power stations across the midlands. The one at Lanesborough sits right on the banks of the Shannon. Excess hot water was pumped directly into the river and this attracted the fish to the area immediately downstream of the flusher. For many years, this was possibly the premier spot in the whole country for visiting coarse anglers to congregate. Now the power station is closing down meaning no hot water is being pumped back into the river. The question for me was are there still some fish hanging around?

A fine carpark is situated right next to the fishing stands on the Shannon in the town. I opted to start just below the road bridge with a swimfeeder on the heavy rod and touch legering on the light rod. It had clouded over by the time I was set up and fishing and a breeze was beginning to build from the south so conditions were at least a improving for me. The river was very low for this time of year and the anticipated heavy flow was just a sedate one instead, easily manageable for a beginner like me. A thick bed of reeds splits the river here and I was fishing on the Longford side, the Roscommon side is the one used by the boat traffic (not that there was much of that).

I suffer too many tangles when using the feeder and need to do some more research into rigs. For today, I have an eight pound hook length and hope this thicker and stiffer rig will be more compliant. A size 12 hook felt like a reasonable choice to start with, not too big nor too little. I dearly wish I had managed to buy some maggots but worms should still give me a fighting chance. The light rod is rigged with a small bomb on a sliding leger rig terminating in a size 14 hook. I am still experimenting with hook designs. There are so many to choose from, each claiming to be the best. I already have a strong dislike for barbed hooks and will flatten down the barbs on any I have in my box. The downside of this is maggots and worms easily work themselves off the hook when fishing.

I'm overzealous with my first cast and the heavy feeder crashes in to the reeds opposite. I am lucky to get the gear back and I have to rebait as the worm has disappeared. My second cast is much better and I wind in the slack line once the feeder has settled on the bottom. Fishing again at last! A big chunk of the day has gone already and I am only now fishing properly. Fishing the heavy rod feels awkward after the light margin and float rods but I get used to it over the course of this session.

Small hooks and a single worm failed to get any response so I scaled up on the heavy rod and ended up with a size 10 and a bunch of worms. With no bites on the light leger rod, I decided to change over and set up a float on it (being too lazy to go back to the car for a float rod). Casting as close as I dared to the reeds, I let the float slowly work its way downstream, checking its progress occasionally just like I used to when Grayling fishing back in Scotland. I trotted the 17 foot deep water with the float for another hour or more, trying different lines and making my way slowly along the concrete path before at last the orange tipped float is pulled decisively under and I landed a small perch.

It was no monster but at least it saved the blank on what was proving to be a tough day. Soon after that the heavens opened and a heavy squall hit, making it very uncomfortable for a while. In the middle of the downpour, I had another take and I lifted into a nice roach. With one last twist, he shed the hook as I was about to swing him in. A murder of crows wheeled in the cold air above me, mocking my misfortune with loud cawing.

All the while I had been steadily moving downstream to cover as much water as I could. I'd cast in the swimfeeder and leave it where I could see it, then trot the float down and come back to the heavy rod every few minutes. On one occasion, I came back to the swimfeeder just in time to see the smallest of twitches which I struck firmly. Fish on and this one held down deep. The net was soon under him though and I gazed upon my first Hybrid. I was unfeasibly happy with this fish as I was not expecting to bump into a Hybrid here at all. A couple of quick snaps and the fish swam off strongly. That fish put a smile on my face, I can tell you. Deep bodied and feisty, it was a gorgeous creature and one I will long remember. Size is of little relevance to me these days and little ones can be just as amazing as lunkers in my book.

Hoping against hope this was the start of some action I fished on for a while longer but more heavy rain made the job thoroughly unpleasant so I called it a day just after 4pm and made my way back to the car. Just like my last outing to Offaly, everything was sopping wet as I broke down the rods and loaded up all the gear. The inside of the car windows soon misted up with all the wet tackle steaming in the back. Shivering and uncomfortable, it was time to reflect on what in the end had been a difficult day.

Firstly, I had caught fish in county Longford. I have now caught fish from the mighty Shannon and I had landed my first Hybrid. Lough Sallagh was way too shallow in my opinion and I am sure I would have blanked had I stayed there so the move to a different venue was a wise one. Lanesborough is but a shadow of what it used to be now the power station in no longer pumping millions of gallons of hot water into the river. The vast shoals of dustbin lid sized bream and enormous tench have found another billet. Still, it is a nice section to fish and it might be better earlier in the year, say around May or June. I really enjoyed fishing there, it was comfortable and a constant stream of (socially distancing) passers-by and dog walkers provided bits of chit-chat throughout the afternoon.

'Bridies', the tackle shop in Lanesborough has closed down, a big notice in the window curling at the corners proclaiming its demise. The tackle shop over in Mohill shutdown some time ago and it lies dusty and empty now. It must be incredibly hard to keep a small tackle shop open during these hard times what with all the travel restrictions and general lack of customers. Finding bait is becoming increasingly difficult for me and it remains to be seen just how many tackle shops are still open next spring.

Thank God the Carrick Angling Centre is still going strong and the last time I spoke to Frank who owns the tackle shop here in Castlebar he seemed to be doing OK. Long may those shops continue thrive, we need them to keep going. I have tried to convince Frank to stock a few pints of maggots but he is having none of it, saying I would be his only customer for them.

The bait question is so serious I am now thinking about breeding my own maggots next year. It seems to be a simple enough process, if a bit smelly. Apparently the quality of home reared maggots is much superior to shop bought ones which could be another plus. Obviously Helen must <u>never</u> know about this particular project! The question about what colour of maggots is best has also been exercising my mind. Does it make a difference? I suspect it does but when you think about it the fish only get to see maggots when us anglers introduce them in the water. Red has been my preferred colour up until now but a bit of experimentation might be called for.

Realistically I should switch from coarse fishing to the pike from now on. The weather is getting colder and buying bait is proving to be really difficult. I think I will tidy up the coarse gear and put it away for the winter. My next outing may well be to chase the toothy green fellas!

My old car has decided to play up a bit. There was a discernible loss of power for some reason when I was driving home so it has gone off to my mate's for some repairs now and I have asked him to fix the knocking rear suspension while he is at it. Always something…

Later: Prognosis on the car is a failed air mass flowmeter, €350 for a replacement. Looking around for a secondhand one now.

End of October update: Good news—found a much cheaper new air mass flow meter. Bad news, a CV joint has failed and an ABS sensor has packed in along with a rear wheel bearing and a track rod end. That knocking in the rear suspension really has to be fixed too. Oh the joys of running an old banger! All are being repaired now.

7th October: We are locked down again, initially for a period of three weeks but who knows what will happen after that. With no travel outside your own county, the '32 project' is now firmly on hold with only 7 counties successfully fished to date. My performance up to now have not impressed but I am learning as I go along. See you all the other side of lockdown.

Chapter 8
Westmeath

County number 8

Monday, 21st December 2020

After that less than stellar trip to county Longford, we were locked down again as Covid-19 returned to claim more victims. For political reasons, travel restrictions were removed ahead of Christmas and as a result there is a tiny window of opportunity to sneak out for a day's fishing between lockdowns. It is December 2020 and I am taking this chance to attempt to catch a fish in another one of the 32 counties. Of course I won't be meeting anyone either when travelling or fishing, meaning I will pose no threat of spreading the contagion.

It's the night before and I am sipping a whisky in front of the roaring fire. Thoughts flow through my mind about what I am going to do come the morning. It will involve coarse fishing and this alone is enough to peak my interest. My increased enjoyment in all forms of angling has been driven by my new found love of all things roach and perch. That alone would be fine, just fine. The thing is my mind is now buzzing with all kinds of ideas about other forms of angling.

It is like someone has strapped me up to a couple of jump leads and tuned the key in the ignition. I am energised and have found a clarity of thought which I have not seen for many a long year. Learning new techniques and methods, experiencing new waters and catching different fish have stretched me and this in turn has opened me up to new ideas for my game and sea angling. Suddenly I am back to being this wide-eyed and open minded being of my youth, wanting to find out the things I didn't know and to bring my own slant to the fishing. Esoteric? Possibly.

But it is how I feel these days and I don't believe that is a bad thing. So the whisky may be opening up my mind but there is an underlying and ultimately fundamental change going on in me. I am really enjoying my fishing now, much more than I did even last year. And now I am going to county Westmeath in the morning.

The obvious venue to fish in this midlands county is Lough Sheelin. Sheelin is home to a stock of large brown trout and is a mecca for dedicated fly anglers. The thing is, for my purposes tackling a difficult water like Sheelin was a chancy option with a high probability of failure. Sure, if I boated a good trout it would be great but I have blanked on Sheelin too often to take it lightly. The other great trout loughs of Ennell and Owel are very demanding waters too, so instead of waiting for the trout loughs to open again next spring I decided to fish the Royal Canal now in the depths of winter and try to tempt some coarse species. Closer to Dublin there are apparently some very productive stretches of the canal but in Westmeath info was a bit patchy regarding hotspots.

There is good access just off the M4 motorway near Mullingar which was tempting but in the end I settled on a stretch at Ballynacargy. At this point, I have to confess I had pencilled this trip in for late spring next year and not the week before Christmas. Only the temporary easing of lockdown has tempted me out.

The Royal Canal apparently holds bream, roach, hybrids, perch, tench and pike. I suspect but am not sure that there could be some rudd in there too. I read that local anglers were deeply concerned about plummeting stocks of fish due to poaching but it sounded like there were still some fish there to be caught. I packed a float rod, a leger rod and a spinning rod in the car, hoping that would cover any possible eventualities. The rough plan in my head was to travel light and keep moving with just the float rod, hoping to run into some bream or roach. If that did not work, then I'd switch to the feeder and if that failed to produce the goods I'd try the spinning rod for pike and perch.

As usual, I had a back-up plan in case Ballynacargy was a failure. Along the road to the east lies the town of Mullingar and the canal passes through there too. It has fished very well in the past so I planned to head over there if Ballynacargy was blank. To be honest, I was expecting a tough trip this time. I am still very much a beginner at canal fishing and I would be guessing where the fish might be at either location. Added to that the time of year and I was certainly going to be stretched this time around.

Yesterday I poked around in my relatively new compost heap to see if there were any worms to be had. I was none too hopeful as it still looked woody on top but as I got near to the bottom of the pile I found some lovely worms. I gathered about 30 of them and left the rest in peace (for now). All the worms were the same size, around 3–4 inches long meaning I would get two baits out of each by simply cutting them in half. Enough to last me for the duration of this session I figured. There is always a tin of the dreaded sweetcorn in the bag in case of emergencies.

Since my last trip I have been busy online, treating myself to some bargains on eBay. My new rucksack/stool would get its first airing. This exactly what I bought it for, roving along a towpath with the minimum of gear. Rig and tackle boxes, bought dirt cheap, now house all my smaller items of tackle and are a huge improvement on the odd assortment of tins they replaced. My trepidation at fishing canals, while still very real, has abated somewhat on the back of success in Offaly last autumn.

There is nothing like catching a few small fish to settle the nerves and the snippets of knowledge I am gradually picking up have given me a sort of platform to work from. Just having the basics to set up and know broadly what to do is comforting. I am no expert, nor will I become one anytime soon, but I am learning as I go and thoroughly enjoying every minute of it. I have planned as much as I can so I head off to bed.

Light. It is light. I waken slowly and am disorientated. Why didn't my alarm go off? Probably because I forgot to set it! OK, so I am starting later than planned but that is alright, there is no great panic. While it is a fair distance to Westmeath, it is not the longest of my trips. I'm hoping against hope the roads will be quiet for a Monday. It's very wet and the temperature is hovering around freezing as I set off into the grey gloom. The old Golf runs well, the extensive repairs mean she will last me a bit longer. Wipers swish as I motor across the dank grey landscape.

The usual road east along the N5/N4 brought me to the long straight between Rathowen and Ballinaleck. Here I turned off on to the L1902 and followed this road, across the river Inny, down to the village of Ballynacargy which is right on the Grand Canal. This part of the country is rarely visited by tourists. It is prime agricultural land but it lacks the grandeur and romance of the west, the history of Ulster or the city life in Dublin. Here there are cattle chewing the cud, lazy rivers and canals winding amid low lying green fields. Large tracks of the land around here were devastated by Bord na Mona as they ripped the peat bogs apart to fuel power stations in the last century.

This practice has largely stopped and there is a degree of remedial work being carried out on some of the damaged bogland. It will take generations for that effort to come to fruition but at least a start is being made. Hamlets and small villages dot the middle of Ireland, places where the pace of life has barely altered for a hundred years. Those within commuting distance of the city can tell a very different tale though as thousands of people flocked to live within striking distance of the well paid jobs in Dublin. Today I was beyond that belt of blighted towns, out in the silage scented air of Westmeath on the banks of the Royal Canal.

Truth be told there is not much too the neat little village of Ballynacargy. It consists of two streets, a fine church, one shop, a petrol station and a few pubs. I ducked down a lane beside the church and parked near a small stone bridge over a channel which fed the canal. Mallards were noisily poking around in the shallow water, untroubled by the rain. Beyond, the wide basin looked pretty desolate in the watery vista. I am afraid I know little about canal construction but I am guessing basins like this one were built so boats can turn around.

To think that these canals were dug by men with just a pick and shovel amazes me. Thirty minutes digging for worms exhausts me so how men could keep it up hour after hour, day after day seems to be superhuman. Working the barges which used the canals was dangerous, low paid work too and many men died transporting goods across the country.

The mist was drenching from the moment I stepped out of the car. This was going to be far removed from my day dreams of balmy summer days on the towpath. There is a lock at one end of the basin so I decide to start proceedings immediately below it. First I put the light leger rod together and cast half a worm out. Setting up the float rod next, I plumbed the depth. I mucked up this process by putting on shot which were too heavy and it took me a while to cotton on to my mistake. It shouldn't have—the canals in Ireland are very shallow so I chastised myself for not seeing my mistake quickly.

Split shot sizes and weights utterly confuse me but I need to learn about them to avoid wasting time again. There is a steady flow here and the float trots nice and slowly down into the basin before I wind in and recast. A small rivulet feeds into the basin at my feet, the muddy water gradually discolouring the canal. Will this put the fish off? I nip back to the car for something or other and as I return I see a mink on my bank. He is too quick for me and he escapes before I can reach for my camera (a gun would have been better). Mink are a curse, murdering other wildlife. Taking a look around me I see the pike anglers have been a bit careless with their casting resulting in a couple of fancy baits hanging ingloriously from the wires which cross the canal.

Despite the ravages of Covid, I feel very safe as there is nobody around here. The small village behind me is quietly going about its business but nobody comes near me here on the edge the canal. The thick, grey mist envelopes me as I crouch by the side of the water, silently going about my business. Casts, baiting up, watching the float with hawklike intensity—I am utterly absorbed and in in a little world of my own.

The little leger rod is such a joy to fish with. I bought it secondhand for a fiver, ten feet of brown fibreglass with the softest tip you can imagine. If I ever hook anything big on it, I'll be in bother but for silvers it is a wonderful tool. Water drips off the tip ring as I watch intently for offers. Hushed traffic noises from the main street behind me, two men talking outside the church, the ducks squabbling in the channel. Cloaked in wet greyness, I feel apart from the rest of the world, just me and the rods.

I have been fishing for about half-an-hour when the leger rod gives a slight rattle. Letting it develop, I finally lift into a small fish which quickly comes to hand. A nice 6 ounce roach to start with and he is released after a snap. It doesn't matter what else happens today, I have my fish from county Westmeath and I am delighted. Roach are such pretty little chaps and I love them dearly. I wish I had some maggots with me but instead the worm will have to do. Weeks after this trip I find out there is an excellent tackle shop in Longford where I could have bought a half pint of maggots but I was blissfully ignorant of that fact on this day. We live and learn I suppose.

It goes quiet again so I start casting in different directions. I flick the float 'upstream' towards the locks and almost immediately it disappears. I miss that one but the very next cast produces another firm take and this time I set the hook. This is a much better fish and it fights really well all the way to the net. Out of the water I am unsure of exactly what I have just caught. Initially I figure it is a good roach but the colour is golden, like a rudd. I check the mouth (up for rudd, down for roach) but this just adds to the confusion, both mandibles are the same length. None the wiser, I popped the fish back and it swam off strongly. I reckon it weighed around a pound.

I like to fish with the lightest float possible, given the conditions on the day. Even now, many months after taking up coarse fishing I am still experimenting with shotting patterns. If I need to cast more than a couple of rod lengths, I add bulk shot at the float so it will cast better. For fishing close in, I like my shot to be 'shirt button' style. While it would be very nice to know if I am right or wrong, I strongly suspect there is no such thing when it comes to shot patterns. Some days one set up works then on others you need something completely different.

Now the perch show up and I land a couple of small lads. Perch in Irish canals don't seem to grow large, unlike some in English canals. I don't care, it is always lovely to see these aggressive little fish in their brilliant colours. They are such obliging wee fish, always willing to grab the bait on even the quietest of days. The biggest problem with small perch is they swallow the hook. When I started out coarse fishing, I found retrieving the hook was difficult but I am getting much better at using the disgorger now and a quick flick soon frees the little barbless hook and the lovely striped fish is popped back into the brown water at my feet.

It all goes quiet for a long time and I try searching along the bank but without success. A hundred yards below me there is a bridge over the canal where it narrows which looks like a great spot to me but I fail to register a single bite there. Returning to where I started I pick up another three roach over the next hour, hardly scintillating fishing but hey, I am out in the fresh air so I don't mind. All of them fell for a piece of worm on the float and none of them would have weighed more than a few ounces.

I get the distinct impression the roach shoal is constantly on the move and I am doing a poor job of persuading them to stop in one spot for a while. All the time the mist gets heavier and heavier, soaking everything. In the end, I decided that the return for getting so wet is not worth it and I pack up. Four roach, one roach/rudd hybrid and two perch was the grand total for the session. I have had a lot worse days!

Not for the first time I toss the sopping wet gear in to the car and head off on the long, winding road back to the west. Back at home I returned the unused worms to the compost heap where they can do what worms do for the next few months. The wet tackle is given a rudimentary drying but I will sort it out properly in the morning. For now, I want nothing more than a bite to eat and to unwind after the drive home. Those quiet hours spent in a sleepy Westmeath village were lovely. I know that sounds crazy but the wet does not really bother me much and the few small fish I landed brought me an awful lot of enjoyment. Shrouded in the quiet mist, everything dripping wet by the old canal was a relaxing experience for me. Not everyone's cup of tea I suspect but we are all different and find stimulation in so many different forms.

We can expect a severe lockdown to come into force almost immediately after Christmas Day and not the 6th of January as previously stated. My take on it is that this next lockdown will go on for many weeks so there will be no fishing for me in the near future. Added to the lockdown, I have taken another interim management role which will last for the first 3 months of 2021, meaning I will be kept busy making some money instead of angling.

Taking stock of where I am on the 32 journey I see that I have caught 49 fish in 8 counties to date, exactly a quarter of the total. I am well pleased with this, given the horrible year we have all had. I am astounded how many of the trips have been coarse fishing ones. I guess that just goes to show how ignorant I have been about fishing here in Ireland. At this point in time, it is next to impossible to make any firm plans. Who knows what 2021 will bring and what restrictions we will be living under? I always knew I would have to be flexible and adjust my plans as conditions dictated but little did I think being locked up at home would be my main barrier. I feel thankful for the trip to Westmeath today, it was a joy to be fishing again.

Later…After Christmas 2020 the country went into lockdown once again. Travel restrictions were strictly enforced again so angling was completely out of the question. The work contract was extended by an additional month which kept me very busy right up until the end of April but the fishing rods remained unused for the first four months of the year. By May, I was itching to get back on the road and tackle some more counties.

Chapter 9
Mayo

County number 9

Wednesday, 19th May 2021

My home county. I know it like the back of my hand and have fished on most of the available waters, mainly for trout and salmon. OK, so I don't really need to put myself in the position of trying to catch a fish here but I wanted to. It just felt right that I dedicated one day to catch a fish in Mayo for the sake of the project, a sort of 'if a thing is worth doing it is worth doing right' mentality. There is also another, more cunning side to this need for a Mayo fish, I want to try and catch an atlantic salmon and Mayo offers me by far the best opportunity to do just that. It is the middle of May and we can travel again after the lock down was lifted.

For those of you who do not know about this county, let me give you a brief outline. Situated on the far western edge of Ireland the county is blessed with spectacular countryside, abundant natural resources and populated with welcoming and friendly locals. These days it is a popular tourist destination but in the past it suffered greatly and many left here to find better lives abroad. The famine of the mid-nineteenth century took the lives of thousands in Mayo, the poor land being largely given over to potatoes at the time. When the crops failed due to blight, the population starved or fled.

Those dark days of hunger and death are history and today there are modern manufacturing plants, more diverse agriculture and a vibrant tourism sector support jobs across the county. In short, it is a great place to live.

Some of the great Irish fisheries are in Mayo. Delphi, Burrishool, loughs Conn, Carra and Mask spring to mind. The rivers Moy, Erriff, Robe, Owenduff and Owenmore all flow across the land. We have lakes filled with voracious pike and Clew bay still has stocks of sea fish for those who want to avail of action in the salty water. To say I was spoiled for choice when deciding where to fish is a total understatement. There is one lough which is very special to me though, so I plumped for Carrowmore lake in the northern part of the county.

The ancient barony of Erris covers the wild lands around Bangor and there, sitting like a jewel amid the bog is Carrowmore. As far as I am concerned this place is unique, I know that in my wide angling experience I have never fished anywhere like it. From early in the year, salmon swim up the short connecting river from the sea and lie in the familiar spots in the lough. As the water warms they come in greater numbers until by April there are hundreds of them with more of their kin arriving each day when conditions are favourable.

By June, the first runs of sea trout arrive, mainly small fish of a pound or so but with some much larger ones too. This lough is unusual in that it is very shallow and with a bottom covered in peat silt which has washed off the surrounding bog. That means the water is easily churned up on windy days, turning the water brown and making it unfishable. It was there I would make my stand.

I blanked on my last visit to Carrowmore despite there being fish in the lake so I was hoping for better luck this time around. Angling has been a bit hit and miss so far this year with some anglers catching regularly while others are struggling to meet fish. A storm is forecast for the end of this week which will churn the bottom of the lake so this trip was aimed to put in a few hours before the lake became unfishable. I have mentioned the lake being churned a few times so had better explain what that means. Strong wind causes waves on the surface of loughs which in general is a good thing for us salmon fishers as it makes the fish easier to deceive and seems to make them more active.

The issue on Carrowmore is the combination of shallow depth and peat silt bottom. That means any significant wave action stirs the silt up and turns the water a filthy brown colour. Under these circumstances the lake becomes unfishable and many days are lost each season due to the water being churned. It takes days for the water clarity to return to normal.

This was going to be a big day for me. The usual preparations were made and I arranged to meet my mate Ben in Bangor as we still have to travel separately due to Covid restrictions. Fishing on your own on the loughs can be hard work sometimes so we decided to share a boat for the day. I drove up under bright sunshine and with hardly any wind to shake the roadside birches and whins. In the end, we meet up in the neatly tarred car park at the harbour and nattered about the fishing as we tackled up. A few other cars were there too which is normally a good sign and the usual banter ensued with our fellow fishers.

I tied up a 3 fly leader made from ten pound mono then scanned the contents of my fly box. A Goats Toe Muddler for the bob position, Claret Bumble (of course) for the tricky middle slot and a Golden Olive hairwing creation of mine as the tail fly or 'stretcher' as it used to be called. That would do to start with, old reliables and different colours in their make up for the salmon to pick from.

Boat loaded and engine primed, we set off up the lough, dodging the rocky shallows just outside the harbour. Years ago I was in a boat with another angler who swore blind there was a short cut through the shallows and made straight for the harbour at full tilt. The resounding bang when the propeller hit a stone came as a shock and we limped home on the oars. An expensive error of judgement! Today, light clouds began to roll in from the west and it looked like there was enough of a wind to give a ripple as we motored up the lake in rapidly improving conditions.

With that faint wind coming from the west, we could set up to drift the mouth of the river, probably the most favoured lies on the whole lough. Long drifts are possible and the knowledge you are almost certainly covering fish makes for exciting fishing. We were both fishing with slow sinking lines but many anglers use floaters on this lough. Our casts snaked out in front of the boat, tossing the three flies on each line twenty yards ahead of us. All through the long winter we wait for days like this afloat on Carrowmore and now here we were gently drifting along the shoreline under a springtime sky of palest blue. The wind began to veer more to the north as the morning wore on.

By judicious use of the oar, Ben guided us along the mouth of the Glencullin river over prime lies but there were no takers apart from a few small brownies. We repeated the exercise one more time with similar results then moved over to the Barney Shore, another well known salmon lie, as the wind was favourable for that drift. I had a small sea trout and a brownie and Ben added another pair of small trout but the salmon were still eluding us. We could see other boats around us and none of them were meeting fish either. Salmon fishing is rarely a sport of hectic action so patience is more than a virtue, it is a necessity for us fly fishers.

With the fishing quiet, we adjourned for lunch, sandwiches and tea wolfed down as we sat on the shore with sky larks serenading us from on high. Why do sandwiches and tea taste so good when eaten on the edge of the water? Sitting on a turf bank we chatted about this and that, generally putting the world to rights. There was warmth in the sunshine that had broken through a thin veil of clouds which had been coming and going all morning. I took the opportunity to change all the flies on the cast, going for a Green Peter on the bob, a Wilkinson in the middle and a Beltra Badger on the tail. I figured the bright flies suited the day now the sun was shining.

Lunch over, we pushed the heavy white boat out and clambered back in. Then we settled down for more drifts off the mouth of the river where the salmon lie with their bellies on the soft bottom with 5 feet of water or less covering their backs. Any clouds had burned off by now and we were treated to blue skies and a fierce sun which reflected off the surface of the lough making it hard to watch the flies. Another drift over the Glencullin lies was fruitless so we fished two drifts over the shallow further out which is marked with an orange buoy. This can be a real hotspot but not today as we failed to stir so much as a trout. This is typical of salmon fishing, long hours flogging the water with no signs of fish. It takes a strong will and a hefty dose of self-belief to keep going some days.

Ben suggested the Barney Shore again and I did not object as the wind direction would drift us nicely along close to that stony shoreline. Here the high bank ends abruptly and there is shallow holding water for about 100 yards out into the lake. This is classic Irish lough fishing for salmon, shallow water ruffled by the wind, the creaking of the oar and it pulls us out a little or to dodge a near sunken rock in our path. Cast and retrieve a shortish line with three flies. Show it to them then whip the flies away. Cast again.

More pulls on the oar out the back of the boat to keep her on line or to follow the contours of the bottom. We set up on the drift close to the shore, trying to judge the depth so we are not too shallow. Stonechats were singing that familiar weird song of theirs and I was watching some Sand Martins swooping over the fields out of the corner of my eye. Then it happened...

Ten yards from the boat the water broke and the tail of a big fish lashed the surface as it turned down. Simultaneously, the line tightened and I lifted into solid resistance. 'Salmon' said Ben but I was not so sure. 'Feels small, maybe a sea trout' I countered, reeling in the slack and watching what the fish was doing.

She swam towards the boat at first, staying deep and shaking her head. I stamped on the wooden boards, our usual tactic to keep the fish away from the boat and potentially swimming right under it, sheering the thin leader on the rusty metal keel band. She moved off to my left and very obligingly kept going all the way around to the back of the boat. This is where you want a fish to be so that you have room to play it out. By now, Ben had reeled in his line, stowed his rod and had grabbed an oar which he used to move the boat away from the shore. These actions as so well-rehearsed that neither of us need to ask the other, we simply get on with the jobs while the lucky angler is concentrating on playing the fish.

The ratchet sang as the salmon went off on a short run but it did not go far, instead turning and coming back towards the boat under heavy pressure from me. I don't like to see fish being allowed to run too far and possibly drowning the line so I play salmon quite hard. My rod was hooped over and the line disappeared into the water almost vertically as the fish swam near the bottom. Another short run ended with the fish rolling just under the surface and we both got our first good look at it.

"Fresh fish," said Ben, not wasting words unnecessarily. "Bigger than I thought," I chipped in. Yet another short run, this time to my right then back down to the bottom she went again. My wrist was aching by now!

I heard the net being extended as I applied more pressure to bring the fish up to the top. There she thrashed, always a nerve-wreaking moment but the hook held. I could see she had taken the bob fly. Circling now, the fish was beginning to tire but she still managed to dive once more then head off to my right again. I checked Ben was ready and led the fish towards the net. She shied away at first but I maneuvered her back and with her head up she slid into the waiting meshes. The relief was palpable and grinning like a pair of lunatics, we shook hands and quickly dispatched the salmon. The whole battle had probably lasted less than ten minutes. Ten minutes of doubts, fears and anxiety. I have fished most of my life and landed hundreds of salmon but the thrill of the fight never leaves you.

I put the fish into a bass to keep it fresh after fitting both tags through the gills. Now we had to get the boat back in order to resume fishing. The net was first dipped in the water to clean off some of the slime then stowed away, my tackle checked after the rigors of the fight and the oar put back into the right position. We set up to fish the balance of the drift and started casting again as we discussed every minute detail of the take and the battle. In salmon fishing, it is often the case a second fish can be lured soon after the first one so it pays to fish hard when one is in the boat. Today though the lough was not going to play that particular game and we fished out the long drift without any further action.

We did the same drift again, then back out to the buoy and over Glencullin once more too. Not a fish stirred so we decided to stop for another cuppa. We both felt the conditions, while very bright, meant there was the chance of another fish so we next headed off for Paradise Bay about half way down the lough. A couple of drifts failed to produce anything and so I decided to call it a day. I was tired and my wrist was aching after what had been a long day. Under an azure sky dotted with cotton wool clouds we drove back to the harbour, both deep in thought. Today it had been my turn but is could just as easily been Bens. Why that fish had taken my fly and not his we will never know but that is part of the attraction of salmon fishing.

Gerry, one of the local Fisheries Officers, was at the harbour when we pulled in and he checked my catch to see everything was in order. We chatted for a while about fish and fishing and Ben decided he would go back out to fish on a while longer. I got out of the fishing clothes and packed everything into my car. The wind was dropping now and the sun was starting to sink in the west. The long road home seems much shorter when there is a salmon in the back of the car!

So there you have it, Mayo has been crossed off my list of the 32 counties. I had fished hard all day, kept persevering in marginal conditions and never gave up hope. This does not always work but I believe persistence is critical to being a successful salmon angler. I slept soundly that night, trust me!

Carrowmore is well known in angling circles and many anglers travel from far and wide to fish there. If you are considering a trip to try the lake, I would urge you to make the effort to come. I am of the opinion this is the best salmon lough in Ireland at the moment. Of course you can blank, but the months of April, May and June usually see a good head of fish in the lake and I firmly believe that just having fish in front of you is a big part of the battle when trying to catch a salmon.

Tying a Green Peter.

There can be very few fly fishers who have never heard of the Green Peter. Tied originally as a copy of the medium sized green bodied caddis which hatch on summer evenings on Irish loughs it has become synonymous with lough fishing and subject to just about every variation you can think of. The fly I used today is close to the original so let's take a look at it in detail.

Hook sizes vary enormously depending on when and where you are fishing. A size 10 covers a lot of options here so I will use that here. Use the hooks you have faith in, I personally go for a Kamasan B175, the heavier gauge wire adding both weight and strength.

Tying silk on the fly which caught the salmon today was black 8/0 but again, use what you like. Sometimes a fly tied with a fluorescent yellow tying silk seems to work better.

When starting your tying silk at the eye end of the hook, be sure to leave sufficient space for the wings and head hackle which will be added later on. This is one of the most common mistakes I see in fly tying so be sure to give yourself sufficient room. Tie in a prepared red game cock hackle by the butt then run the tying silk down to where the bend starts, creating a layer of silk on the bare metal. Now tie in a length of fine oval gold tinsel. A word of caution here, there are some very poor quality tinsels on the market these days. Spend wisely and only buy the best quality. Nothing worse than making a lovely fly only for it to fall apart in use. Bind the end of the oval tinsel down by running the tying silk over it back up to where the hackle is tied in. Cut off any waste end and then run the tying silk back down to the bend again.

Now dub the tying silk with green fur. Once again, the colour is open to interpretation. You won't go far wrong with seals fur dyed the colour of garden peas. Form the body by winding the dubbed silk and then give it a roughening with a piece of Velcro or something similar. Grab the body hackle with a pair of pliers and wind it down the body in 4 or 5 open turns. Tie in with the oval gold and reverse wind that up through the hackle before tying it down and removing the waste. For a beginner, this all sounds very daunting but trust me, a bit of practice will see you flying through this process and making lovely palmered flies.

Wings on this fly were made from hen pheasant secondary slips tied low over the back of the fly, just like the original. I could write a book on the variations of Green Peter tyings and the wings can be made out of a host of different materials depending on what you plan on using the fly for. Now tie in and wind at least 4 turns of a red game cock hackle in front of the wings. Secure the hackle, remove the waste end and form a head with the tying silk before whip finishing and varnishing in the usual manner.

Chapter 10
Galway

County number 10

Wednesday 26th May 2021

If I am honest, I should have really ticked Galway off right at the very beginning of the '32' project as I have caught numerous fish in this county over the years. Sea fishing out of Clifden, mackerel bashing off the rocks in Galway Bay, casting flies for brown trout on the Clare river—the list goes on and on. A fisher could spend his or her life in this county and still not fish all the available waters. Some of the angling greats fished in Galway and wrote extensively of their experiences so there is no shortage of literature to digest if you are researching the area. I used to come to Galway frequently when I lived in Scotland and loved the city (especially the nightlife), the surrounding countryside and the fishing. But for the sake of this project I wanted to catch a fish in the county this year so I made plans to try for some trout on mighty lough Corrib.

I did consider many other venues across this large and diverse county. Down in the south there is great coarse fishing on the Shannon at Portumna which I have yet to sample. Although the famous sea trout fishing in Connemara is but a shadow what it used to be, they are still running the great loughs over there. Then there is the Galway Weir Fishery in the heart of the city but the treacherous bottom puts me off there these days what with my poor balance and dodgy knees. Lough Innagh was very tempting too, beautiful and occasionally bountiful. In the end, though I plumped for the big lake, Corrib.

Anglers across the globe are familiar with the Corrib, it holds a special draw on fishermen's imagination. Since the dawn of sport fishing the vast, wild waters of this lough have provided spectacular angling for those lucky enough to cast a line here. For many years, I kept a boat on the upper part of the lough at Salthouse

Bay and got to know it reasonably well, catching (and losing) some terrific trout in the process. The days spent exploring the bays and islands, the offshore reefs and craggy shorelines were a joy and I learned a lot about my own abilities as well as the ways of the fish. Days of high expectation which came to naught were balanced by exciting sport amid glorious surroundings. Corrib is a special lough which captures your heart.

For those unfamiliar with Corrib, let me give you a rough outline of the fishery. With a surface area of over 170 km^2, it is the second largest freshwater lough on the island of Ireland (after lough Neagh up in the North). It lies to the north of Galway city and a small part of the northern end lies in county Mayo. Roughly divided into two parts, the northern basin tends to be deeper and rockier with the south basin (known locally by the uncouth name 'the sump') being shallow and open.

The lough is narrow and full of reefs where the two basins join. Islands, large and small dot the lough and I have heard numbers for these island vary between 365 and over a thousand. I guess it all depends on your exact definition of when a reef becomes an island. While brown trout are the principle quarry species, the lough is also home to pike, ferox, salmon, perch, bream and roach. Visiting anglers are well catered for by the local boatmen who can be hired from villages around the lough. This is no place for a beginner, you need to know exactly where you can motor and fish, keep a close watch on the weather, know how to handle a boat in all conditions and be prepared for every eventuality. Sadly, lives are lost all too often when this lough is not shown the respect it deserves.

In terms of the fishing, the Corrib caters for every taste. Some people troll for large trout and salmon while many others prefer to dap natural mayflies, daddies or grasshoppers. I much prefer to fly fish despite the knowledge a dapper will out-fish me most days both in terms of the numbers and the size of trout caught. It is late May now and that of course means one thing and one thing only—the mayfly. My plan was simple, fish either wets or dries depending on the hatch, move until I found the fish and to enjoy my days out on the lough. I say 'days' as I was fortunate to be sharing a boat with that fine angler, Dr John Connolly of Pontoon for four days on the Corrib.

Sometimes I fish with a 6 or even a 5 weight outfit but here on the Corrib you can run into some seriously large fish so I brought along my 7 weight outfit. Wet fly usually catches average sized trout with the dappers picking up bigger fish but even still trout in the 5 to 10 pound range are caught by fly fishers each season so it pays to fish on the heavy side. That extends to you leader material and I would personally hesitate to drop below 6 pound breaking strain when making up my wet fly casts. I know anglers who shudder at the thought of anything in single figures.

I was lucky enough to be staying overnight at the lovely Mask Valley Lodge, situated on the shoulder of the hills overlooking Mamtrasna. The car was parked outside, surprisingly free from excess fishing tackle for a change, making way for some food and clothing instead. The day had dawned fine and still, powder blue skies o'er the greening hills of Mayo. Sheep bah'ed and thrushes sang is if intent on bursting their chests. Steam curled from my coffee cup as I sat on the balcony and counted my blessings.

To be honest I could have easily lazed there all day, just sitting admiring the countryside and drinking coffee by the mugful but I instead had to be off, the game was afoot. I had slung the rod and the rest of my gear into the back of the car the night before so there was not much more to be done. I would be ghillieing John for these 4 days but I hoped to pick up a rod for a while too, depending on how the days panned out. The winding road past rough fields of sheep took us through Cornamona and on to the peninsular, the car full of music (Rory Gallagher if you must know).

Pulling up on a narrow grass verge I stepped out into a riot of colours and smells from a nearby garden. Inside the house someone was listening to the news in Irish on a radio and the dulcet tones of the reader floated from the open front door on the faintest of breezes.

No wind. I looked out across the bay before doing anything else, as all us anglers do. The might Corrib slumbered under a mirror calm surface, perfectly peaceful. The trees on the peninsular stood straight and tall, no signs of the slightest movement in their branches. I was not overly concerned though as the wind usually picks up as the day goes on. Here at the small private harbour where our hire boat was moored I met up with John. We had not seen each other for a few weeks so there was a bit of catching up to do. You must remember, this is Ireland and it is best not to rush anything. Family, the state of the world, a dash of politics and fishing (of course) all had to be chewed over before anything else.

Doorus is a peninsular which juts out into the upper part of the western side of lough Corrib. It has long been associated with excellent trout fishing, in particular when the mayfly are hatching. Islands, reefs and shallows dot the waters around the peninsular and the whole area is a fishers heaven. Friends had been fishing there the day before and while they had lean pickings they saw the dappers pick up many good trout up to in excess of 5 pounds in weight, but there had been a bit of wind yesterday and that was a crucial difference.

The time honoured rituals of loading the mountain of gear into the boat ensued. We met up with Jim and Brian who were also fishing today and after catching up on all their news we made loose arrangements to meet up at lunchtime. Just to add a bit of spice to the day an aggressive swan got a bit too close for comfort as we pulled away from the shore and headed out for our first drift. Apparently he does this to all the boats and has been known to break a poorly stowed rod before now. Over in the distance I thought I could see a small wave so I drove to the rocky reef in the middle of the large bay where, sure enough a corduroy ripple gave us the smallest of chances to fish.

The paltry westerly wind was to say the least fitful and only 30 minutes in to the day that faint breeze died completely, leaving us becalmed. Motoring around we hunted for a patch of rippled water, however small. This went on for a while until a zephyr from the north gradually built up sufficiently to ruffle the surface ever so slightly. It wasn't much but it was just enough to allow us to fish again. John stuck with his preferred team of wets while I opted for a pair of dries. It is fair to say that we were equally unsuccessful for the next two hours. Mayfly were hatching in reasonable numbers by now but very few trout had shown an interest in feeding on these surface flies. It felt like the right time to stop for a spot of lunch!

When I first started fishing on the Irish loughs the ritual lunchtime break for a brew on the shore was lost on me. Why on earth did the locals stop fishing for an hour when they could be casting. It made no sense to me as a young angler, I was there to fish, not waste time drinking tea and talking. Those dreaded words from my boat partners 'we'll just pull in for cuppa' were torture to my ears and the whole messing about filling and boiling the damned Kelly kettle broke my heart. Ah, the impatience of the young!

At the very epicentre of this ritual is of course the kettle itself. Invariably battered and blackened, its totemic status in Irish game angling is unrivalled. Somewhere along the way I bought one and mine too displays battle scars garnered on rocky shores and pebbled islands from Corrib to Conn. Nowadays I would not be without it. I bring it in an old hessian bag with some firelighters in a plastic box. This bag is the third item to be stowed in the boot of the car before setting off, only the engine and fuel tank are ahead of it.

So what changed? How did I go from hating lunchtime to looking forward to the traditional break? My guess is I mellowed with the passage of time as most of us do. The driven and focussed man I used to be has slowly learned to hurry less and appreciate more. Sitting on a rock, talking to friends or strangers as the smoke and steam curl up into the sweet spring air now seems like a gift from heaven. Angling for me has morphed into the sum of many parts instead of just bent rods and leaping spotted fish.

Of course there are days when wet and miserable weather make that reviving beverage more than just pleasant, it verges on the lifesaving. Hunting for dry twigs to burn poses a challenge nearly as great as catching a fish on a rainy day so some of us cheat a bit by secreting a few dry pieces of kindling from the woodpile at home in our bags.

If I had to conjure up a single image that conveyed Irish angling, I suspect it would not be of a great fish, a screaming reel or even the vista of the sun setting over a lough, no, it would be a Kelly kettle with a wisp of white smoke rising and the lads laughing and talking in the background.

Pulling into an island we decamped and started to walk over to a table in the trees where two fellow anglers were sitting. A string of profanities greeted me and I recognised Liam and Paul, lads from town. I had not clapped eyes on Liam for years so we had some catching up to do. Firing up my kettle, I was horrified to find I had left my mug at home and had to beg a loan of one from the lads. We spent a while recalling our various fishing experiences and there was the familiar raid on my fly box by the boys.

Meetings such as these are such an integral part of Irish lough fishing, something to be deeply cherished in this mad world we live in. I am not good socially, finding it hard to talk and aware of my limitations but put me on an island with some fellow anglers and I come alive. We drank strong tea from cracked mugs, sat on stones dumped there by the ice age and told tales of fish landed and lost.

"Do you remember that time on Carra…"

"Sure, the fish yer man Sean lost on Mask last week was a pig of a fish, he hooked it off Devenish and it ran him half way to the Schintillas."

'Did you hear that so-and-so has a new boat?'

There was an awful lot of stories to both told and heard but in the end it was time to go back out on the lake. Parting on the gently sloping shore, the lads all headed off in different directions, the sound of engines fading in the distance. It had been great to see them all, especially on an island in the middle of the Corrib.

During the lunch break a faint wind had picked up from the north west, not much now but maybe just enough to get the fish moving. Hastily packing up, John and I cleaned up after ourselves then returned to the boat and I pushed us off into deeper water. My outboard burbled into life and we headed for the inner islands, weaving through the reefs without so much as a scratch on the keel for a change. I set us up on one lovely drift after another, ghosting over reefs and pale submerged stones or hugging the edges of tree covered islands. We flicked flies into all the likely spots, me pulling on the oars to hold position or to direct the 19 footer around points or jagged rocks.

Close to a rocky island shore John lifted into a fish but it turned out to be a lightly hooked 6 incher which had grabbed a Green Peter. Back it went and we resumed the drift. Just enough of a wind was blowing now to create a small wave and a trickle of mayflies were still hatching, so some faint vestige of hope remained. The maze of small rocky islands and shallows means the boatman has to be constantly paying attention to the drift and working the oars to position the boat correctly.

Fishing with one hand on the oar and flicking out casts with my other hand, I tried to cover as much water as possible. It takes years of experience to handle a drifting boat properly on the big Irish loughs. Local knowledge is everything here and a mistake can easily lead to a grounding, or worse.

Despite all the boat handling, I was still concentrating on the fishing. With my eyes fixed intently on my pair of dries I had a perfect view as a trout head-and-tailed, inhaling the Yellow Wulff on the end of my leader. A delayed strike found purchase and I was in at last. Deep dove the fish then he ran out to my right before surfacing and thrashing the water with his tail. After a good fight which featured one more blistering run, I netted a fine trout of about a pound-and-three-quarters. The lads wanted some fish to cook so this one went into the bag. Relief was writ large on my face, the day had been slipping away without me moving a fish until then.

Dried and treated, once more the flies were sent back out. The wind died down a bit, reducing the surface of the water to being only slightly ruffled. The mayfly hatch, which had never been strong, subsided into the occasional dun. John and I fished on for another hour or more but that was all the sport we had for the day. Given the time of year this was a poor return but conditions had been tough and all the other boats we met had similar catches of just one or two trout.

    We motored back to the tiny harbour, faces reddened by the sunshine. I am old but John has a few more year on even me so I bade him take a rest while I unloaded the boat and secured her firmly to her moorings. The other boat came in shorty after us so I gave them a hand to empty their boat and tie that one up too. They had no fish but like us had seen feeding trout earlier in the day.

    Sharing some curse words for the excess of sunshine and the lack of wind we divested ourselves of waders and piled our gear into the respective cars. Heavy engines, still hot from use, were lifted off the transoms and up to the cars. Years ago we just left the engines on the boats as nobody would dream of stealing them but those days are long gone. Another day on the lough was over.

    So I had achieved my goal and landed a fish in Co. Galway. Under the circumstances I suppose I should be happy I caught one but I honestly feel I should have done better. Mayfly were hatching and a few trout were moving to them. I didn't try to fish the mayfly nymph and that was possibly a mistake. Calm water often means the best hope of success is going to be with the a well sunk nymph. I had just convinced myself the dries would pull up a few fish but in the end that trick only worked the once. Ah well, there is always the next time.

The flies.

Wulff patterns are in legion and like most western anglers I have boxes stuffed with different variations. Today the yellow one finally fooled a trout. It is tied with wings and tail made from squirrel tail dyed yellow, a lemon yellow seals fur body and a hackle consisting of many turns of a grizzle cock hackle dyed yellow. If you want, you can add a rib of oval silver tinsel or globright no. 4 floss silk. Hook sizes are 10 or 12 normal shank and I use yellow or fire orange tying silk in 8/0. Very simple but a great pattern at the height of the hatch.

Just varying the colour of the squirrel hair tails and wings gives you a range of options and my box is full of all sorts of variations on this theme. Some days a green or olive Wulff is better but if in doubt the yellow is a good starting point on Corrib, or on Mask for that matter.

John's Green Peter was the standard red arsed version tied on a size ten hook but with a few legs added to give it a bit more movement.

Chapter 11
Armagh

County number 11

Wednesday, 2nd June 2021

Not the most noted of Irish counties for angling I suppose but I still found a venue to try. After the recent game fishing outings in Mayo and Galway this would be another coarse fishing trip for me and one that would be slightly different to my usual canal shenanigans.

Armagh is one of the northern counties, sandwiched in between Tyrone, Down and Antrim as well as Monaghan and Louth in the Republic. The vast expanse of Lough Neagh forms the northern boundary. I have only ever zoomed across this county on the motorway, often times in the dark, so know little or nothing about it. When I worked in Belfast, this was a weekly occurrence and trips over to Scotland to visit family and friends took me along the same route. Armagh was just another few miles of green lands beyond the tarmac to me. I did start to read up on Armagh prior to this trip but gave up after a few pages, it was just a litany of murder, religious war and plantation.

I found it all too depressing when I was supposed to be planning a fishing trip so I abandoned the blood-soaked pages and instead read up on the finer points of stillwater float fishing, an altogether more relaxing pastime.

I had opted to try the lake at Loughgall. Set in a country park, it looked to be a nice spot surrounded by trees and with good access via a pathway all the way around it. Stocked with roach and carp, there were some tench, pike and perch also present according to the blurb on the 'net. From a study of Google Maps, I could see an abundance of stands to fish from too and it all sounded like the ingredients for a relaxing day were in place. The only cloud on the horizon was a report I had read that the fishing was now terrible after a zebra mussel infestation had caused the water to clear. This kind of mixed messages are a constant problem for me when planning trips and it adds to the uncertainty and worry.

Fishing is never an exact science and blanks are part and parcel of the game but when you are travelling long distances to fish you want to give yourself the best of chances. The saving grace for me was the presence of perch, these little warriors are usually obliging and I was banking on tempting at least one of them. I had no intention of bothering the carp. In the north, you are only allowed to use one rod (unless you buy another rod licence and permit) so there was no way I would be hunkering down with the heavy gear and boilies or any of that malarkey. No, I planned on keeping it simple and trying for the smaller stuff either on the float or maybe with a leger.

I figured I needed a 'plan B' so I looked at the river Bann which flows through the county. The upper Bann around Portadown has a good reputation for bream and roach so I decided it would be my back up water in the event of a blank at Loughgall. Some stretches of the river have been developed for angling and other pursuits so I looked it up on the internet and there were some glowing reports of good bags of bream and roach. As far as 'plan B's' go this one was most definitely on shaky ground. I am useless at catching bream, have no experience of coarse fishing on rivers and the river looked to be devoid of any features to focus on. I was anticipating another difficult day…

Getting there seemed to be easy, just follow the usual road to the north via Sligo and Enniskillen. A fair chunk of my life has been spent travelling that road and I have seen it slowly improve over the years. The fine piece of duel carriageway between Dungannon and Ballygawley replaced a boring and badly worn road a few years ago and the twisting, winding, narrow stretch that links Enniskillen to Sligo is gradually being upgraded to remove the worst of the lethal bends. Lord only knows how often I have chugged along this ribbon of tarmacadam, but at least I was going fishing this time. To make the most of the day I was bringing my outboard engine up to be serviced at Sands Marine on the shores of Lough Neagh not far from where I would be fishing. This involved a slight detour but it was worth doing while I was in the area.

One of the very few good things about growing old is the cheap angling permits in Northern Ireland. If you are a young pup aged 18–60 this costs you a whopping £77 for a season permit in 2021 but oldies like me aged over 60 only pay £17.50 for the season. You need a rod licence on top of this but that only sets us 'mature' anglers back a fiver. I had bought mine on line and now I double checked that the printed copies were in my jacket pocket.

I know I could just flash the email on my mobile but us elders cling to the old ways and a slip of printed paper feels more real somehow. How much longer will paper be with us? I know the industry better than most having worked in it for twenty years and the dire predictions of the paperless office came to naught. The changes in our approach to the environment are a different story and manufacturing paper consumes massive quantities of raw materials and power. I doubt if this can continue for much longer.

I timed my journey to coincide with the tackle shops in Enniskillen opening so I could procure some bait. Digging in the compost heap produced a tin of worms to bring with me but I really wanted my preferred maggots. My deep and abiding love of maggots is founded on the fact they work. OK, it gets a bit self-fulfilling when I use maggots all the time but they are an astonishingly consistent bait. A new venue with some mixed reviews, limited time to fish and rustiness due to lack of any coarse angling for six months made it feel like I needed every possible aid on my side. The old familiar jumble of tackle was in the back of the car of course so I would be able to switch methods if I felt the need.

Gentle, melodic tones awoke me at 5am. I consider the invention of the ring tones on mobile phones to be one of life's greatest dichotomies, an assault on the ears in most cases but the calming tones of my alarm make the transition from sleep to groggy wakefulness quite pleasant. Coffee, strong and dark, drunk as I make up some sandwiches for the day, one last check I have most things packed then I am off on the road once again. The open road, not much traffic for the first leg as far as Sligo, just the rhythm of the tyres on tar. Roadworks slowed me down a bit but I pulled on the handbrake outside the tackle shop in Enniskillen just as they were opening up.

One pint of their finest red maggots were soon wriggling in my bait box and I hit the road again amid rush hour traffic. I had flirted with the idea of investing in some pinkies and I am sorry I didn't. I have yet to try them out but fancy they might be very good. At least, it would have been something new to try out. Enniskillin between 8 and 9 in the morning is usually chock-a-block with traffic but for some reason it was not too bad today. Just after 10am I dropped off the engine with Nigel and after a brief chat hit the road again. Along the motorway, I doubled back through Portadown / Craigavon and on to Loughgall.

Flags fluttered from lamp posts everywhere and sectarian graffiti was daubed on numerous walls. Once out of the towns the last leg of the journey was on a twisty, winding road through apple orchards which give the county its nick name.

Turning into an impressive stone entrance then down a winding road with the golf course to one side, I found the large car park and got out into the pleasant sunshine. In the reception, my licence was checked, so now all I had to do was decide what to take with me to the water's edge. The lake was supposedly very deep so I was planning on using a swim feeder and based my choice of rod around that.

It felt odd not taking my light leger rod or the float rod this time. With a 'clunk', the car doors locked and I was off down the path to the lake, bathed in warm summer sunshine. It was busy already, golfers turning up to tee off, young mums pushing buggies or trying to herd boisterous toddlers and others just out for a walk on a nice day. Walking around the lake, I plumped for a stand which looked out on a small weedy bay. The substantial timber stand with '78' stapled to it would be my spot for a few hours.

Setting up a small maggot swimfeeder, I lobbed it out into the greenish water and settled down to see what would happen. Six pound nylon on my reel should have been strong enough should a hapless carp come along. I fed the swim often to try and attract some fish and also dropped a few maggots close in. I missed using two rods (you are only allowed to use one in Northern Ireland) and really felt handicapped without the options two rods gives me. The first hour passed pleasantly enough, the warm day making it thoroughly enjoyable just to be out in the fresh air, but there were no fishy responses to the feeder. I reeled in and switched to a sliding float but this was completely ignored too. Today was indeed proving to be a challenge for me.

My feeder fishing is still pretty erratic and results vary widely. A typical session will see me rig the feeder rod with either a cage feeder or a maggot feeder, usually a 20gm size. These days my normal rig is a twizzled boom to a hook length which can vary from 6 to 20 inches. Hook size is usually a 10 or 12 but I do go as small as a 16 if I am after smaller fish. When fishing for tench, I often use a hair rig. Bait is either maggot or worm. On the waters where I fish long casting is not necessary (at least I think so) and I rarely go much beyond 30 metres out. Often it is just a gentle lob as close as I dare to nearby weeds or rushes.

And that will often be that for the whole session. I vary bait sometimes, swapping between maggot and worm but most days that is the extent of my changes. I used to be more adventurous but saw no big improvement in catches so these days I have drifted into the lethargy of just leaving it out there and hoping for the best. Not that such a lazy approach has not borne fruit, some of my best fish have come to the feeder which has been neglected for 20 or 30 minutes! Basically, what I am saying is I need to up my game with the feeder!

The water was very deep even close in, making the float a difficult option to fish successfully. I changed back to the feeder and this time I fished it at very short range, all the while loose feeding maggots with my catapult. Still nothing so I ate a sandwich and thought about what was going on. Three other anglers were in sight and I had not seen any of them bend a rod into a fish meaning I was not alone in the ignominy of blanking. A pair of swans swam nonchalantly past me with their 6 cygnets in tow.

They floated by just inches from the stand, such beautiful, graceful creatures. As I watched them I became aware of some small fish in the weeds on the bottom of the lake at my feet. It was impossible to tell what they were or indeed exactly how big they might be but they were silvers of some description. Here was a possible target for me.

The feeder rig was swiftly removed and I set up a small float with bulk shot on either side of it to cock the float but no other shotting. My idea was to see if the small lads would take a maggot on the drop so I tied on a size 20 hook on two pound hook length and baited it with a single red maggot. Small handfuls of maggots were then trickled into the swim just under the tip of the rod. When dropped in (it was so close I didn't need to cast), I could watch the wriggling red maggot slowly drop down through the water column, slowly spiralling down until it disappeared in the weeds. I kept this up for maybe 20 minutes until the float gave a tremble and when I struck out came a small perch. Success had come in the spiny shape of a 6 incher but they all count and I had landed a fish in county Armagh. A few minutes later an even smaller perch came to hand by the same method.

I shall refrain from regaling you dear readers with rest of the afternoons catch, whipping out small fish is difficult to relate as a page-turner! Suffice to say I ended up with 4 perch, 2 roach, one skimmer and one unidentified 'something' which looked like a tiny silver bream (but different to a skimmer). None of these fish were more than eight inches long. Eight tiddlers after driving all the way from Mayo does not sound like a great return for all my efforts but in truth I was pretty happy. During the afternoon I did not see anyone else catching a fish. I suspect those lads were targeting carp so long hours of nothing happening would be the norm for them. Would I have caught something if I had stuck with the feeder?

It is a good question and maybe the fish would have switched on at some point and given me some sport with roach or bream but with the day slipping away so quickly I needed to be more proactive, even if that meant angling for small fish.

To be honest it was actually quite stimulating trying to catch the small stuff. They would bite very quickly with the float giving a rapid dip only to pop back up almost immediately. My reactions are not what they use to be and lots of bites went unanswered. I focused hard on the float most of the time but there was a clear area of water to my right where I could watch the hooked maggot descend in to the depths and a I saw it taken a couple of times on the drop. They moved so fast that I didn't see the fish, just the maggot disappearing from sight.

I knew when I started this odyssey that there would be days like this, days when the big fish were not biting or I was just not fishing properly. Or conditions were against me or Lady Luck was sitting drinking gin in a bar instead of watching over me. Days when I would struggle and need to find ways of catching something (anything) to save the blank. Today I had to resort to fishing for small stuff but at least I had figured out a way of tempting them and trickling the loose maggots into the swim worked a treat at holding the little lads at my feet.

By 4pm, I had had enough and packed away the gear. The air felt heavy, as if thunder was not far off as I loaded up the car and heading back to the motorway. Picking up the now serviced engine (thanks Nigel), I turned for home, the road now clogged with commuter traffic. By Dungannon, the heavens opened and I crossed back into the Republic at Belcoo/Blacklion in a downpour.

It was a long day but an enjoyable one. Armagh had always bothered me and I suspected if I was going to blank anywhere it would be here. Instead, I landed eight small fish, lost about the same number and missed dozens of bites in that busy final hour. If you had offered me that at the start of the day, I would have gladly taken it!

Fishing in very deep water presents some issues for me. Lobbing out a feeder is the obvious tactic but what do you do on days when the fish refuse to take? Sliding float was my back up method today but that didn't work either so I am left wondering where I was going wrong. Perhaps I need to invest in some method feeders, the idea that the ground bait and hook bait are together sounds like it should be very good.

The carp anglers seem to use method feeders a lot but would they work just as well for bream and tench? My lack of coarse experience is obvious on days like today and I'm sure an experienced angler would have found a way to catch some bigger fish. As a learner though it felt good to be able to winkle out some small stuff when all else had failed.

Northern Ireland will always perplex and fascinate me in equal measure. How so much can be crammed into six small counties is incredible. History, horror, beauty and hope all merge into one glorious, terrifying and wonderful space. I've spent a lot of time there over the years and seen the good as well as the bad so I don't see it through rose tinted glasses. From a purely angling perspective, it has an awful lot to offer and I can only scratch the surface for the moment. My hope is that when I retire I will be able to devote more time to fishing across the border.

Chapter 12
Fermanagh

County number 12

Wednesday, 9th June 2021

Once in a lifetime

Fermanagh is synonymous with coarse fishing, period. The Erne system and a wealth of other lakes set like jewels on a cloth of green are a coarse fisher's paradise. Anglers come from all over to fish the pole or swimfeeder, heaving out impressive bags of roach and bream. Competitions around Enniskillen often feature weights in excess of 100 pounds. Fantastic piking is to be had in the county too. Obviously when tackling Fermanagh I would be coarse fishing, right? Au contraire! I had another plan in mind altogether.

Fermanagh, one of the northern counties, is landlocked. It shares a lengthy border with the Republic as well as co. Tyrone. Right at the extreme western edge of the county there lies a small lough called Keenaghan, so far to the west in fact that a small part of the lough is actually in Donegal. In this lough live a healthy population of stocked brown trout and it was these little beauties I wanted to catch. In choosing Keenaghan, I was making a strategic decision. You could make a very valid argument that Lough Erne is a more productive fishery and certainly holds larger trout.

My issue with Lough Erne is I have absolutely no knowledge of the system and simply locating fish could be a nightmare for me on such a large and complex water. The same really applies to the coarse fishing. There are well known stretches all over the county but having never fished there trying to track down a shoal of bream or entice some roach from broad, deep waters felt like too big a challenge for me. I wanted somewhere more 'intimate', somewhere that I could stand a reasonable chance of locating a few feeding fish. Plus I am so much more comfortable with a fly rod in my hand, despite my slowly improving coarse fishing skills. I feel confident on small loughs full of trout, it seems like half the battle has already been fought simply because I know the fish are there to begin with.

This lough is shaped like a letter 'Y' lying on its side. It is small by Irish standards but is still best fished from a boat. Rules allow only electric engines and since I don't have one I decided to fish from the bank. The idea of trailering my boat all the way there then rowing for the day before manhandling the boat back on to the trailer on my own did not appeal, so I would tough it out from the periphery instead. I had no real idea of how good access was around the lough but I read that there were a few stone fishing stands placed where necessary. I liked the sound of them! So waders would be required in case I needed to get past reeds or to reach deeper water.

The other day my four year old neoprene chest waders gave up the ghost in spectacular fashion when they ripped at the seams while I was in deep. A new, cheap pair were acquired and these would do fine for this trip. Given my near total absence of a sense of balance these days my trusty wading staff was definitely going to be required.

A contact on social media told me he fished this lough and recommended it to me. He also said it got good hatches including some mayfly. I looked up the NIdirect website to get an idea of the stocking policy and they apparently put 5,000 brown trout into Keenaghan during 2020, the first 1,000 going in in January. More went in during March, May and June. Stocking was suspended during April due to Covid-19 restrictions. I was hoping they followed broadly the same pattern this season and when I looked it up on the NI direct website I saw 3000 trout had gone in this year so far. That is a pretty heavy stocking for a smallish lake. Surely there would be a few of them still in there?

Dropping Helen off at work first, I hit the road amid rush hour traffic. Usually I plan trips to avoid the worst of the cars and trucks on our roads but today I had to put up with an excess of my fellow road users. I had grown used to the feelings of trepidation on these '32' trips but this time I was really looking forward to fishing a new lough. Many anglers here in Ireland despise stocked fisheries but I see them as an integral part of the angling scene. They make a pleasant change from the big loughs, a chance to try out new ideas and methods.

The Fisheries guys in the north stock a lot of small lakes like Keenaghan and this has to be applauded. They may not be the most spectacular or technically challenging but they attract new anglers to the sport while at the same time providing something different for old hacks like me.

I had brought along my 5 weight Orvis with a floating line, hoping any action would be in the upper layers of the water. Recent warm weather should have encouraged the trout to look up for hatching insects at this time of the year. In case I was completely wrong, a backup of the 7 weight with a range of reels holding various sinking lines nestled in the back of the car.

As I would be wading and moving around I filled a couple of fly boxes with some likely patterns and stuffed them in a waistcoat. This lot, and more, were stowed in the back of the car as I motored along, the glorious countryside slipping by, a dull and windy day but warm. Ireland can be cold and grey in winter, but here in June it sparkles with new life.

This trip involved a direct route for me. Up the N17 to Sligo then along the N15 to that newish bypass at Ballyshannon (birthplace of one of my musical heroes, Rory Gallagher) before peeling off on to the tail end of the N3 as far as Beleek where I crossed into the UK. A mile or two beyond the town a left turn brought me down a narrow, tree lined track to a car park at the water's edge. In total, it is about 135km from my home in Mayo. Given the length of some of my '32' fishing journeys this felt like I was in my own back yard.

One other reason for selecting Fermanagh this time was I was going to be heading over to Scotland the next week and didn't fancy another long drive. There is a car park right beside the edge of the water where I pulled up and shut off the engine. Stretching as I extricated myself from the front seat, I began to I tackle up and appraised my surroundings. The lough appeared to a bit smaller than I had imagined but it looked 'fishy' enough. How do I explain the term 'fishy'? I can't! A lough either looks like it holds lots of fish or it doesn't and the exactitudes of the definition are impossible to write down. Anyway, on this fine summer's morning Keenaghan looked decidedly fishy to me.

The wind would be blowing in my face from the car park bank so the lovely light Orvis stayed in its tube as I set up the 7 weight with an intermediate line and three flies. No point in making life difficult for myself. A car pulled up, soon followed by another, both sporting UK number plates of course. The drivers obviously knew each other but beyond a friendly 'how are ye?' in my direction it was hard to see why they were there.

No fishing tackle appeared to be present. Waders and jacket donned, I toddled off to the first of the stone jetties and started to cast into the wind. I was a bit rusty to start with and tangled the line a couple of times within the first few throws. After that, though the casts fairly flew out. My slowly sinking line settled below the surface and I fished a jerky retrieve to impart some 'life' to the flies. I had tied a Black Goldhead on the tail with a Green Peter in the middle and a smallish Claret Bumble on the top.

I had not been fishing for very long when a white truck came bumping along the narrow road to the car park. My attention drifted to watch the driver negotiate the tight track. What was a lorry like this doing here? While I was gawking at the lorry a fish plucked at my flies but didn't take properly. It had hit the flies deep, the black goldhead on the tail doing its job of dragging the other flies on the leader down to where I hoped the fish would be. I turned to get a better look at the white truck again as it slowly lumbered towards me and it was only when it was but a few yards away that it dawned on me—it was a fisheries truck and it was here to stock the lough!

I fished on as the two lads in the cars greeted the truck driver. Now it made sense, these guys worked for the fisheries too and would be assisting the driver to transfer the fish into the water. Huddled together they planned the details of the stocking. With regimental order, the truck was positioned on the concrete ramp, a large diameter plastic pipe fitted to the tanks and with a 'woosh' suddenly hundreds of trout were being sucked into the lough not 30 yards from where I was stood.

For about ten minutes, the poor trout were whisked out of the plastic tanks and deposited in the lake. I enjoyed some lively banter with the lads about how I should be paying them and then they shut the valves and packed away the pipe, before the truck was off again, bumping down the track. The whole operation had not lasted more than ten minutes. By now, the water in front of me was heaving with the new arrivals. I had been more interested in the mechanics of the process while the fish were being sucked down the pipe but now it was time to concentrate on actually fishing. I have often heard that fish are hard to catch when newly stocked and they take time to settle but I always had my doubts about that. Now I was about to find out for myself.

Of course I tangled my leader while trying to cast a bit too far in the wind and lost time sorting out the resulting knots. Back in action once again I tried to get some idea of what the fish were doing but they were jumping, rising and splashing all around me in no particular order. Resolving to keep my head I began to cast about twenty yards out, fanning my casts from right to left.

Allowing the flies to settle, once I was happy they were a few inches under the surface I began to retrieve quite quickly. A dozen casts went out, then a dozen more. Should I change flies? Finally my line tightened and I struck into a trout but it came off almost immediately. Before I had time to retrieve the slack and re-cast, another fish had grabbed the tail fly and was safely landed after a brief struggle.

Quickly released, I cast out and this time two trout were hooked! Both fell off but a few chucks later I had another brownie. And so it went on, cast, fish, release, cast, fish, release, etc. Double hook ups were common, trebles happened three or four times. Casting to fish which showed almost always resulted in a hook up but fishing blind pulled them too. I photographed some but my mobile was getting all slimy so I stopped after a dozen or so.

I don't understand why there was a gap before the fish took my flies but once they started they kept going. Sometimes the line would tighten as I was letting the flies sink, walloping into the goldhead on the drop. Many times I hooked one fish only for others to grab the other flies during the fight. It was hard to figure out what was going on as a fish often fell off only for another to grab the same fly before I could get the line in. How could I describe this madness? I think carnage is the best I can come up with.

The fish fought reasonably well but the double and treble hook ups meant it was mostly a case of being hauled around until they tired each other out then me dragging the total weight unceremoniously ashore. Unhooking was undertaken hastily to try and get them back in the water as swiftly as possible. Luckily, most of the trout were lip hooked with only a couple hooked further back.

Fish were all around me so I kept casting and catching. Takes varied from gentle tugs to electrifying jolts, almost all of them unseen as the fish were deep. Fights were usually short affairs with little in the way of jumps from the hooked fish. Double and treble hook ups degenerated into a heaving match between me and about four pounds of trout, each trying to head in a different direction at the same time.

I thought about stopping when I had landed 20, but that number came and went and I was still catching. The fish were typical stockies, about 14 ounces in weight and generally in good condition apart from some chewed tail fins and stunted pectorals. I swapped flies just to see if that would make any difference but to be honest I could have thrown in bare hooks and probably caught just as many! A black goldhead was probably the most effect fly but a peach muddler caught a few as well.

By now, I was well lubricated in fish slime. My right arm was getting a bit sore and yet still the fish savaged my flies as soon as they hit the water. An hour after the fish had been stocked there were less of them showing but still the same frequency of takes to my flies. Finally, after an hour and a half of this madness I called it a day. I had landed 36 trout, lost twice or maybe three times that number and must have risen close to another hundred or so. All fish were safely returned to fight another day. Reeling in felt to be both a relief and a sadness that this amazing experience was coming to an end.

I plodded back to the car to think about what had just happened. The trout were still taking freely but I had had enough for one day. As I broke down the rod I could see trout still showing out in the lake and even as I drove off I saw a few jumping where I had been fishing only a short time before. It was a strange sensation to be going when there were trout to be caught but enough was enough.

Never before in my long angling life has this happened to me and I doubt it will ever happen again. Was it fun? Yes, for a while it was exciting but that very quickly wore off. There was no skill attached to catching the fish, no metal gymnastics we anglers normally associate with our fishing. It was too easy. Sure, like you, I have spent so many days flogging the water for no return and would have given my first born child for an hour of non-stop action.

When it actually happened, the joy was short-lived and the mechanical actions of heaving in fish after fish soon pall. I am glad I stopped when I did, to keep on hauling out trout after trout would have been a pointless exercise. As it was, I had three dozen good trout in 90 minutes, a feat I will surely never repeat again. It made for a memorable day right enough! Once in a lifetime you might say.

For the sake of the '32' project, I can categorically cross Fermanagh off the list. The day turned out to be very different to what I had expected and I guess I did not really learn much about Lough Keeneghan. It is a nice place with good facilities, including a disabled access platform. I'd like to fish it again on a more 'normal' day. What would be really nice is a day on a boat there in May or June with a good hatch of fly. Proper fishing if you like.

The drive home was uneventful and I was glad I had returned all the fish, the thought of gutting and filleting really did not appeal to me that evening! I got some more work done in the garden on my return and the tackle in the back of the car can wait there until the morning. I will never have another day like that and it was an incredible experience which I know many of you will be envious of. I was extremely lucky to be in the right place at the right time for once. It will keep me going through the many blanks which no doubt await me.

The successful patterns for me were a black goldhead (the dressing is in another chapter), a normal RA Green Peter, Claret Bumble, Invicta and Peach Muddler. I greatly doubt it mattered a jot what flies were tied on the end of my line, those newly stocked trout would have taken anything small enough to get into their mouth.

Chapter 13
Meath

County number 13

Monday, 28th June 2021

    The Royal County

    My research into finding somewhere to catch a fish in Meath threw up lots of options but none of them really 'sang' to me. No gasps of excitement when reading about possibilities, no heart-fluttering watery discoveries. Meath is a large county situated in the east of Ireland stretching all the way from Westmeath in the heart of the midlands to close to Dublin city.

    The Irish Sea marks the extreme eastern edge of the county around the town of Drogheda. Mainly flat agricultural land, it also hosts many commuter towns. The marketing guys sell Meath to tourists as the heart of 'Ireland's ancient east' which is fair enough I suppose. Kells and Newgrange are both in Meath for example. The rivers Boyne and Dee were spectacular salmon fisheries in days gone by but they have both faded to a shadow of their former selves and it would not be the silvery salmon I would be after this time around.

    Coarse fishing is cropping up a lot in my ramblings across the country, more often than had expected to be honest. This is the direct result of naivety on my part and also a reflection on the poor game fishing we see these days here in some parts of Ireland. Years ago the loughs and rivers of Ireland were full of trout and salmon but that simply isn't the case anymore. Abstraction, pollution, dredging, overfishing, invasive species and the rest of modern day 'progress' have reduced our game fish populations greatly across vast swathes of old Ireland.

    In their place, we now see huge shoals of roach, dace in some southern rivers and even chub in the river Inny. Anyway, it soon became apparent that my foray to Meath would in all probability entail a spot of float or leger fishing. And what harm? I have grown to love dabbling in the black arts of maggot drowning. Currently I lack any degree of sophistication or expertise in the genre but the learning process is proving enjoyable and fulfilling.

So I looked at my options for coarse angling in the county. The Mentrim loughs up near to Ardee sounded very good but it is a long auld trip from here to Ardee and I was hoping to find a spot nearer to home. Then I looked at the nearly straight path of the royal canal as it cut across the county and found a place called Boyne Dock just inside the Meath border not too far from the town of Kinnegad. I settled on there and planned accordingly. I hold my hands up here and confess there was a large element of laziness on my part in choosing Boyne Dock, Kinnegad is just off the motorway and is easy to get too without a long, complex journey down winding country roads. Would this lack of effort on my part come back to haunt me?

I am attracted to spots on the canals where the shape of the waterway changes, either narrowing or widening, or where locks interrupt the long miles of straight, featureless towpath. I surmise that places like this must be attractive to the fish so I hunt out basins, bends, locks and harbours. That is how I came to select Boyne Dock. Here, a small basin had been excavated, a widening where I hoped the fish might congregate.

On the map, it does not look like much but any slight change in shape inspires my confidence. On the down side, I had read nothing about the dock and it seems to have either slipped under the radar of anglers or, heaven forbid, is utterly useless. I was about to find out.

I was planning for roach but hoping for bream and praying for tench. The usual coarse gear came with me including the never used pike rod. It is always along for the ride but somehow never sees action. Maybe today that would change, if there are no signs of roach or bream the spinning gear will be given an airing.

A light rod for drop shotting also made the cut so the option of targeting perch was also available to me. Yes, I know, this is far too much gear to bring with me but I have a dread of missing out on an opportunity when doing this 32 project. The thought of driving home fishless just because I didn't bring this or that bit of tackle keeps me awake at night. So the pike rod and some spoons were tucked into the car along with all the other tackle which I might or might not require.

The usual process of loading up the car and setting off on the road to the east has been well rehearsed at this stage. Not for the first time I was off down the Dublin road. Stopping off in Longford, I picked up some bait from Denniston's shop. To be honest the timing of this trip was based around the opening time of the bait shop. At 9.30 am, Denniston's fling their doors open to the world and I could avail of their finest grubs. My complete and unshakable faith in maggots shows no signs of abating so I bought some red ones and white ones. I thought I had brought along a few worms for good measure too.

These were dug from the compost heap the previous evening, a mixture of small reds and brandlings. None of them were any great size but they would be good enough to tempt a perch I reckoned as I popped them into a small white container. It was only when I stopped in Longford that I realised the hard won worms were not in the car—I had left them at home! I bought a few more at the shop. Denniston's is a fabulous place, it sells musical instruments and fishing tackle so it is pretty much Nirvana for me.

Back behind the wheel and the miles slipped by as I mulled over the prospects for the day. If the dock did not fish, I would be forced to try walking along the towpath, searching for a shoal of roach or a stray perch. There are worse ways of spending a day I guess. My decision not to make the longer trip to Ardee prayed upon my mind though, doubts swirling about in my head as I cruised along at a steady, if unexciting, 55mph.

An uneventful journey saw me turn off at Kinnegad and only a few miles further on I swung into a large, tree lined car park near to the dock. A number of cars were already parked there but as it turned out none of them belonged to fishermen. I had the dock to myself.

The canal here is raised above the surrounding countryside. Indeed, when approaching the dock the R160 road passes right under the canal as well as the railway. Kildare was but two fields away to the south. So it was here, amid the verdant fields on the very edge of the royal county that I would try my luck. It is quite ironic that I have taken to canal fishing at this stage of my life. Many years ago I lived in Kirkintilloch, just north of Glasgow.

Formally an industrial centre for heavy engineering, the town had slid into depression and decay over the years but one major part of infrastructure remained, the Forth Clyde canal. Every day I walked Nessie, my faithful collie, for miles along the towpath and it never once crossed my mind to try fishing there. At the time, I simply had no interest in coarse fishing so passed up some great opportunities. I now understand the canal there is full of roach, perch and pike. Ah well…

It had rained while I was driving from the west but the forecast was for a dry afternoon. By the time I had reached my destination, there was some blue sky showing amid the fluffy white clouds. Unloading all the tackle, I set up two rods, one for the float and the other with a leger. My thinking was to target roach with float fished maggot and aim for perch by legering a worm on the bottom. The old 13 foot ABU float rod, Daiwa Harrier reel and 4 pound line and a small float was soon set up and I used the 10 foot margin rod with a wee red Firebird reel that I found in the bottom of a cupboard filled with 6 pound main line for the running leger. Size 14 hooks on both rods felt about right at least for a start.

The basin was small but it gave the appearance it could be home to a few fish. Weeds looked like they might be a problem though and my decision to delay this trip until late June looked like a mistake. Before commencing fishing, I raked out a swim and baited it. Small balls of brown crumb with a little hemp mixed in and flavoured with vanilla provided the ground bait, my aim being to attract fish into my chosen swim and then try to keep them in front of me with a trickle of loose feed. Opting for a size 14 with a couple of maggots on it I fished over depth on the float rod.

A worm, also on a size 14, was my chosen end gear for the leger. One of the big issues when fishing Irish canals is the clarity of the shallow water. This leads the fish to be very easily spooked both by unwary movements on the bank or by overly thick line. For that reason, I was using 2.6 pound breaking strain hook lengths. I realise this was taking a chance because if I hooked a decent sized fish it could easily break me off in the weeds. The internet had informed me that there were good tench and even carp in this canal but I was pretty sure the best I could hope for was a 6 ounce roach or a minuscule perch.

The towpath was a hive of activity with a constant stream of dog walkers, hikers and cyclists making the best of the nice weather. This is Ireland so every passer-by stopped to exchange some chat with me. What was I fishing for or how many had I caught, that sort of thing. The Irish love to talk! Casting in the light leger first, I then set up the float rod. The canal is shallow, only two-and-a-half feet deep in the middle so a very light, small waggler was all that was required.

Settling into a rhythm, I fished steadily for an hour or more, occasional balls of ground bait interspersed with some loose fed maggots decorating the swim. Some small rudd could be seen messing about near the surface a few yards away but otherwise all was quiet. The water was gin clear and weeds grew right to the surface out with the small area I had raked. This was proving to be a tough gig. While I really wanted to be catching some fish just sitting there on my wee stool in the sunshine was a lovely way to spend a few hours. As usual, I started to tinker with the end tackle, going for progressively small hooks on the float and lengthening the tail on the leger.

At last, the float gave a slight tremor then dived but I missed the bite. By now, I had dropped to a size 20 hook with a single maggot, bulk shot at the float so the bait would drop through the water just like the loose ones that I was feeding in. I fished on, glued to the float and wishing it would register a bite. I ate a sandwich, drank some coffee and scowled at the stationary float. I had to try something different. Taking the float off I changed it for an even lighter one and re-shotted the line.

I also swapped the tiny size 20, a huge looking size 16 taking its place. Two red maggots adorned the new hook and off into the cool water they sailed. Almost immediately there was a tap at the float but it came to nothing. I loose fed a handful of maggots and re-cast. This time there was a positive take and a small perch came to hand. A few casts later a slightly larger perch repeated the exercise. OK, so I was not breaking any records here but at least I had not blanked. Canal perch were always going to be part of my catch for this project. They are such obliging little fellas and here on the edge of Meath they had saved my day. A quick photograph and then they were slipped back into the crystal clear water, none the worse for our brief meeting.

It went quiet again for a while but a cast to the very edge of the raked area produced a solid bite and I lifted as the float slid off to my left. This was a better fish which required netting. A lovely hybrid fought well and was quickly snapped and then released. To say I was happy with this fish is an understatement, it had made all the planning and driving worthwhile. Hybrids are particularly lovely fish and I am uncommonly fond of catching them. There is definitely a bit more fight about them than either roach or bream which just adds to my appreciation of the wee mongrels. It went quiet again after that fish so I settled back in the sunshine and simply soaked up the joy of being outdoors on a fine day.

The small rudd had been occasionally knocking at the maggots all afternoon and one was unfortunate enough to get himself hooked and landed. They are such pretty little fish! True rudd are becoming ever more scarce in this country with loss of habitat and cross breeding with roach the main causes. Years ago every small farm had a pond to supply water for the animals and human needs but they are being filled in to provide more acreage to grow grass. That loss of biodiversity hits hard and the poor rudd who thrived in small farm ponds have fewer and fewer possible homes each year.

All this time the leger rod sat there, completely unmolested. Single worm, worm chopped in two, bits of worm threaded on up the line—none of these worked. Was this because the fish didn't want worm or is there a flaw in me legering technique? Probably both is the likely answer. In the short time I have been coarse fishing my ability to catch something on the float has steadily improved but leger and swim feeder lag a long way behind. I am not even very sure why I opted for a bomb today instead of a feeder. It just felt like the right rig given the shallow water but whatever my logic it was badly flawed and the old margin rod enjoyed a day of rest.

That wee rudd turned out to be the final fish of the day. It all went dead after that and try as I might I could not get any more offers. I blamed the high temperature but it just as easily have been due to my poor angling. I'm also of the opinion that coarse fish of most species switch off from about 3pm onwards most days. Of course there will be exceptions to this but I have now seen the same thing happen too often for it just to be coincidence. In the end, I decided to pack up and head off home.

Packing up was the work of only a couple of minutes and I was then back down the track to the waiting car. A group of cyclists were there, a sea of lycra in dazzling colours. Like us fishers they have their own uniforms. Somehow I could never see the attraction of cycling and especially the figure hugging, multicoloured clothes which seem to be so important. Drab olives and browns of my fishing clothes are a much better reflection of my own personality and how I want to just blend in and not stick out.

As I filled the back of the VW with tackle the bikes moved off in a long single file heading for the towpath. There is plenty of space for us all on the towpaths of the canals of Ireland.

So what to make of all that? In the bright conditions in very clear water I suspect I actually did OK landing one good fish. Early morning or late evening would definitely have given me a better chance but beggars can't be choosers. My normally reliable method of a legered worm in the margins failed to register a single offer even though there were some perch knocking about. Raking the swim took me ages and I think I need a bigger rake. Weed growth is luxuriant in the canals at this time of year and effective raking is a must if you want to contact fish.

So Meath is crossed off the list. After the shenanigans up in Fermanagh during my last outing, this was a return to reality with a bump. I am beginning to suspect I need to be more flexible with my times on these longer trips so I can fish early or late rather than during the middle of the day. It's all a learning curve!

Canals pose so many problems for me, it feels like I will never really get to grips with them. Of course, the middle of the day in high summer is not going to be the best time to try and fish them and I need to limit my expectations accordingly. Boyne Dock is easily accessible and is a nice spot to while away a few hours. Just because I had a slow day does not mean it is always like that and I am tempted to try it again in the future. Having said that, those lakes up at Ardee sound very good!

Chapter 14
Laois

County number 14

Monday, 19th July 2021

Good god, what was I going to do about Laois? As far back as the end of last year I had been looking for a suitable venue there. No major loughs, no coastline, little in the way of rivers either. No canals for me to gently float some maggot down. No hill loughs or rushing streams. Maybe there was a small tench lake or a stream with a few roach? Or perhaps a farm pond with a host of small rudd in it? I kept pumping 'Laois, fishing' and similar search terms into Google but I was not finding much in the way of quality angling. So Laois was very firmly put 'on the long finger'. I planned other angling escapades but forgot about the O'Moore county for now.

Fast forward to July 2021. This had been going on for too long and I had to make some real efforts to find a spot to fish down there. In the intervening period, I had made occasional desultory efforts to research Laois but they had come to nought. Now I sat down and spent some time refining the search and studying maps. Coffee was drunk, the cats did their best to distract me but I stuck to my task for once. Trolling the internet for places to fish has become a regular, and not unpleasant part of life for me since starting this project.

For an oldie like me, the ability to access so much information with a few taps of the keys is still a wonder. I grew up in an era when you went to the local library to carry out any research or reached for one of the encyclopaedias which virtually every home had at the time. Now, I simply refine the search criteria and out pops as much detail as you can possible want. Possibly the fact that all this information is so easy to access means it is undervalued by many people. Anyway, I spent a lot of time working my way through the different angling options in Laois. I had been sure it would be some coarse fishing that I'd find and so it proved.

Before we get into the fishing, let's take a look at Laois. Firstly, for those of you not from Ireland the name must present some problems. Spelt 'Laois' it is pronounced 'Leash' There are some complications to that but we will skip over the finer points of Gaelic pronunciation and just settle for 'Leash'. Formally known as 'poor and proud', it is now a prosperous county. Lying to the west and south of Dublin it shares a border with most of the other midland counties.

Home to a lot of beef and dairy farms, there are a scattering of towns and villages and the main road from Dublin to Cork and Limerick bisects the county. I have travelled across it many times but until today I've never stopped the car, switched off the engine and pulled on the handbrake. The river Barrow flows across the county and provides good fishing but I have a half-baked plan to fish that river in county Carlow so I'd save the Barrow until then.

It's a typical summer's morning, warm air filled with the scent of blossoms in the garden as I slurp coffee to waken me up. The sparrows and starlings are making an unholy racket in the trees, not helped by the cats who are on the prowl. I am looking forward to the day ahead, the change of scene and prospect of fishing somewhere new is always appealing to me. The recent hot, bright weather is continuing and for this reason I will be targeting Rudd today with the outside chance of a tench.

Laois is easy to get to from Mayo, there is a good road that goes all the way there. The easiest way there for me was to go to Athlone then to Abbyeliex via Tullamore and Portlaoise. I left it late to set off, planning a leisurely drive there, a peaceful days fishing and maybe stay on until the evening if the fishing was slow through the day to try and tempt a tench as darkness fell. All in all this would mean a very long day for me.

I had a few maggots left over from my last outing and I took some frozen dead casters out of the freezer to add to my ground bait but I required some better quality bait. Research had earlier revealed there was a tackle shop in the village of Mountrath so I headed there first. I picked up a loaf of bread in a Centra but walking up and down the main street I could see no tackle shop. Then I spotted a small metal sandwich board type sign on the pavement extoling the virtues of Shakespeare tackle.

No signs above the door gave any further clues but inside the tiny premises I found all I needed for the day and even better, some great advice from Fran who owns the shop. Maggots, in both red and white, would be my mainstay today and I got a bag of black groundbait too. So where was I heading?

I had decided to try a small lake called Gill's Pond on the edge of the quaint village of Ballinakill. According to my research it held rudd, roach, bream and a few tench plus some bonus carp. Surely even I could catch something there? Ballinakill is a pretty village, a bit off the beaten track and it slumbered quietly under the blazing sun as I arrived there. Turning off on to a minor road I found the pond with ease. The first thing that strikes you about it is the amount of weeds which cover a large percentage of the surface. It looked more like a field than a lake!

I called one of the club members when I arrived, his number kindly written on the door of a small hut at the entrance. Connor appeared as if by magic, stripped to the waist and sweating profusely as a result of clearing some vegetation on the far bank. A down to earth and helpful lad, he gave me some good information about the lake and what to try. Coin changed hands (for which Connor apologised profusely), my net was dipped in disinfectant to prevent the spread of any disease then I set off for the far end of the lake.

Connor told me to take the car around there to save me walking under the hot sun and so I was able to have the car only a couple of yards behind me as I fished. Setting up on peg 1, I commenced operations at around 2pm under a cloudless blue sky and 27 degree temperature. The journey over I could now concentrate of my fishing.

OK, so conditions were rubbish but I was hoping the fish might come on the take as the sun dropped below the horizon. I had carefully read the rules which are posted on the door of the hut. Unfortunately, you are only allowed to use one rod so my idea of setting up the leger rod for bottom species while I float fished for rudd went out the window immediately. Reduced to only the one rod I opted for my old twelve foot Shakespeare which is a bit of an all-rounder. I was no sooner standing at the peg when a family of swans appeared and spent the next 20 minutes in the swim.

Eventually they headed off again but this visitation was repeated numerous times over the course of the session, each time requiring me to stop fishing and even once they had gone the swim was left dirty from all the weeds the birds had pulled up. These birds obviously equated fishermen with free food. My idea of using bread flake on the surface to try and tempt the rudd was now not going to work, all I would attracted were the bloody swans! I tried to think this problem out but my lack of coarse experience led me to opt for fishing on the bottom to try and winkle out a roach or skimmer. On reflection, this was probably not the best option.

I started off with a helicopter rig fished as close as I could to the lily pads on my right but other than a couple of half-hearted taps the maggots were ignored. I kept this up for a while under the unrelenting sun but the time was slipping away and I was fishless so I needed to make another change. What to try next though? It was blistering hot and so I decided to try the float for rudd which famously do not seem to mind warm weather. The swans were always close by and I reckoned that trying bread would simply attract the birds back into the swim so instead I rigged up a light float to fish on the drop and baited the size 18 hook with a single maggot.

The very first cast saw the float dip and I wound in a small rudd, vindicating my change of tactics. A few casts later a roach accepted the maggot. I missed lots of bites but I was catching pretty steadily now. There was nothing of any great size but the float disappeared frequently enough to make up for the lack of anything of stature. The same pattern was repeated throughout that afternoon, I would get maybe 20 minutes of fishing and land a few small fish before the dreaded swans came back into the swim and I had to put the rod down for a while. I loose fed maggots and kept a steady stream of balls of groundbait going into the very edge of the lily pads in the hope of getting some tench to start feeding. Was I overfeeding?

Possibly I was but I find it dreadfully hard to know how much or how little groundbait to chuck into a swim. That my line was too heavy also concerned me but I was very loathe to go down any lighter what with there being tench in the lake. I have made that mistake far too often and been broken by big tench in the past for me to fall for that one again.

A carp swam by, totally ignoring me and my baited hook. It looked to be about five or six pounds in weight, enough to put a good bend in the rod. Connor had said there were a few in here alright but I was finding the going hard enough without making life even tougher for myself by fishing for ultra-picky carp.

The sun beat down relentlessly on me. My old cowboy hat came in useful in keeping the worst of the rays off my head and neck but I think I need to consider buying an umbrella. In some ways, this is the final angling taboo for me, an admission I have reached an age where comfort is most important to me. Up until now I have justified not requiring an angling brolly by telling myself it would just be another item to lug around, one that would rarely be used and in probability end up being blown away some windy day. Here though, on a blistering day in Laois the notion of a brolly to shelter under was very appealing to this par-boiled fisherman.

One skimmer (small) put in an appearance and then it was back to the rudd again (smaller). Everything I was catching was small! By 6pm I decided to go back to the feeder to try for something bigger, so setting up a new rig I threaded a piece of artificial corn on to a hair rig to pop up the bait from the bottom slightly. My idea here was that a bigger hook and bait might attract a tench while at the same time dissuade the small stuff from biting.

Tappy little bites bothered me for a while (rudd) but I did manage a good bream on this set up plus some other small stuff. In the end, I decided the noise of the swimfeeder hitting the water was too invasive so I went back to the float, this time a waggler shotted over depth and a size 10 hook baited with a bunch of maggots. Another skimmer, some roach and a solitary perch fell for this tactic. A lift bite saw me strike into a small tench at last but this lad managed to throw the hook after only a short while. What is it about me and tench just now? I can't seem to land one for love nor money.

The swans were slightly less invasive after about 6 pm, whether they had tired of annoying me or realised I was not going to feed them bread is debatable. I had stupidly left my sandwiches out in the sun and hunger drove me to eat two of the driest, curliest sambos ever for my tea, washed down with warm water as I had left that out in the sun too! This type of silliness is typical of me when I am fishing, I just lose focus on everything else when there are rods and reels to be attended too. That whole multitasking thing that everyone goes on about simply does not work for me, ask me to do more than one simple job at a time and it will end in disaster. Around half-past-eight the sun finally began to lose some of its power and the air felt pleasantly warm as the session wore on towards its climax.

Fishing ends at 9pm on Gills lake so here I was, packing up just as the place seemed to be coming alive. Lots of small bubbles in the margins suggested the tench were finally coming on the feed while the ever active rudd were going mad on the surface now. I was frantically casting out the float, getting small nibbles or line bites then cranking the handle to rebait as fast as I possibly could. Some more small Rudd came to hand but the tench evaded my best efforts. Nine o'clock came and went with me still chucking out that float and maggots.

Finally I had to accept defeat as time had run out for me and I had to leave. Tiredness was creeping up on me by then anyway and I had the best part of a three hour drive home ahead of me. So I broke down the rod, thankful the car was parked immediately behind me and there was no need to lug the heavy tackle too far. The final tally was 15 rudd (mostly small but there was one good one), 4 roach, two skimmers, one decent bream and one small perch. 23 fish on a day when nobody in their right senses would be out with a fishing rod was an acceptable return I think. Fishing in Ireland under a blue sky with temperatures of nearly 30 degrees was never going to be easy. The heat had allowed all the maggots in my box to pupate so I fed them to the fish.

Darkness fell as I drove along the near deserted roads home to Mayo, an indigo blue velvet canopy above me as the miles slipped past. Bob Seger on the CD player sang of young love in the mid-west, broken hearts and of growing old. At 12.20 am, I pulled into the driveway at the house, tired and stiff. A quick brew then off the bed, contemplating the day's events.

Looking back on the day I think I could have done better if I had been more flexible. I stuck rigidly to maggots, usually one or two at the most on a small hook. My idea all along was to try and tempt a good Rudd with the hope that a maggot could lure anything else as well. Casters (which float) were definitely worth a try but I failed to consider them. Perhaps a change to a large hook on the feeder with something like a worm kebab might have been worth a try for the Tench which are most definitely in there. When I had been talking with Connor at the start of the day, he had mentioned the tench seemed to waken up at the end of the day and I had fixated on that, pushing any other options to the periphery of my thoughts.

Gill's pond is well run and a very pretty place to fish set in a lovely part of Ireland. It obviously holds a big head of coarse fish in it and it is a pity it is so far away from me as I would definitely fish there again if it was closer. Given the terrible conditions of extreme heat and brilliant sunshine I was more than happy with my catch for the day and my choice of a pond stuffed with rudd had been fully vindicated. The swans had been a royal pain in the posterior all day but it was their home so I just had to suck it up. I know I didn't always make the right choices of set up today but I am still learning so mistakes are just part of that process.

I remain pretty sure if the swans had not been there and I fished bread flake near the surface I would have caught a lot more rudd and maybe even some good ones. When all is said and done though, that is one more county successfully fished in my quest to do all 32. If I get the chance to fish Gill's Pond again in the future, I will grab it.

Chapter 15
Dublin

County number 15

Part 1, Sunday, 20th June 2021

Dublin. The Irish sea to the east, the mountains of Wicklow to the south and the rich farmlands of the pale to west and north. The depressingly inevitable scatter of commuter belt towns encircling it. Capital of the Republic and home to more than a quarter of the entire population, here was an angling challenge for me! I know parts of the city quite well having worked there for a brief period but most of it is out with my ken. The sprawling housing estates and business parks are a mystery to me and will in all probability remain so. Dubliners ('Dubs' to the rest of the population) are a mixed lot, some of the nicest people I have ever met hail from the fair city but it has a nasty side too but then again I expect you can say the same for every large conurbation. Tourists flock to Dublin and are well catered for by all manner of paddywhackery but the attractions and blandishments of the city centre were not for me. I had fish on my mind.

It was not too easy finding a spot to try and catch a fish in Dublin. The county boundaries basically just encompass the city itself with very little rural ground. Could I bend my own rules and indulge in some sea fishing? I thought long and hard about fishing from the piers at the harbour of Dun Laorghaire, the transient home of the ferries to England. I had read they get lots of mackerel there during the summer months. The thing is, mackerel are either there in numbers or they are not, so there was a high risk of driving all the way to south county Dublin only to find there were no fish present.

Anyway, I felt uncomfortable changing my self-imposed rules at this late stage. I needed somewhere a little less risky. That was when I started to think about the canals. Both the Royal and the Grand canals flow through the city and they both have reasonable stocks of coarse fish. Just knowing perch, bream and roach were definitely present gave me a bit of confidence. The internet is full of video footage of guys catching pike in the very heart of the city with traffic a few feet away and commuters watching as they haul out an essox. I am too private for that level of publicity so I settled on a stretch of the royal canal far from the madding crowd and right on the county border.

Better stretches of the royal canal are to be found further west but the whole point was to catch a fish in Dublin county so I nailed my colours to the mast and made my plans around a section of the Royal Canal to the east of Leixlip. The stretch between Collins and Cope bridges had apparently seen some decent fishing over the last few years so I figured it was worth a try. Normally I bring everything possible with me when coarse fishing but this time it would be different. I needed to be able to roam the canal to find feeding fish and that meant travelling light.

I'd bring the old 13 foot float rod and a reel full of 4 pound line then the rest of my tackle and bait would have to fit in the pockets of my waistcoat or the small rucksack on my back. The plan was to float fish but with some feeders and weights in the bag I could swap to bottom fishing if necessary. In the car, I would have a spinning rod in case I failed to catch any bream or roach. I figured that small spinners might tempt a jack pike if all else failed. I must confess all this sounded decidedly sketchy and fairly major doubts cruised the backwaters of my mind. Lacking any better plan though I decided to go with this one.

The Royal Canal stretches from the centre of Dublin to the Camlin River at Cloondara, just before it meets the Shannon near Tarmonbarry in county Longford. There is also a connecting stretch which runs all the way to Longford town but this has not been repaired (yet). Begun in the dying years of the 18th century, it took many decades to complete and like so many other canals was soon overtaken by the new-fangled railways. It fell into disuse and was only resurrected again in 2010. Now it is used for recreation instead of commerce and there are plans for the tow path to form part of the ambitious cycleway which links Moscow to Galway. I was not planning anything remotely as taxing!

Although I had read that the canal basically fished all year round, I wanted to go there early in the season before the weeds became too overgrown. Once the water starts to warm up in late April and May the canals here in Ireland rapidly fill with all manner of vegetation. Good for the fish as this provides habitat for their food but a right royal pain in the derriere for us anglers. Lockdown and then family commitments knocked those plans on the head and instead it would be the tail end of June before I made the trip east. My weed rake was most definitely going to be required regardless of the time of year so it was checked and carefully packed in the small rucksack/stool I was taking along.

Work has taken me to the fair city many, many times so the journey there would hold few surprises. Setting off very early on a Sunday morning was deliberate for a couple of reasons. During the week traffic at peak times can be horrendous and I wanted to avoid the worst of the jams so planned to be there before then. Parking near where I wanted to fish was going to be very limited so I wanted to find a safe spot before anyone else. A supplementary reason was the afore mentioned tench in the canal and early mornings are traditionally the prime time for those fish.

I felt uncommonly excited about the upcoming trip to Dublin. This new found enthusiasm for a day on the water has been pent up due to the covid. Looking back, for a number of years I have been very jaded and at times even not enjoyed my fishing. I suspect I had fallen victim to a self-inflicted malaise. We all fish for different reasons, some want to win competitions, others to test their skill. For some, it is the social interaction with fellow anglers and others it is catching the biggest fish. I most enjoy the mental conundrums faced when starting out a day, solving the problems which end in a bite/rise/take. Where are the fish, what are they eating, how can I attract them?

These and a thousand other challenges are what I love about fishing and it was a dereliction of my mental approach to the questions which sucked the enjoyment out of my angling. Fishing had all become very similar and to a degree even predictable for me. The small amount of fishing I was able to do during 2020 changed all of that mainly due to the coarse fishing that I began to learn about.

Turning up at a new venue, using gear I was unfamiliar with and trying to catch species I'd not captured previously proved to be invigorating and mentally challenging. This also had an unexpected side benefit in that I appreciated my game fishing so much more, possibly because my fishing consciousness had been reawakened. Now the idea of a day on the canal trying to catch a roach or skimmer has me genuinely excited.

So off down the long road I went. Leaving the motorway just as it enters the city I found my way to a spot near the canal and parked up. I had been ruthless when packing the rucksack the night before and only the bare essentials had made the final cut. For bait, I had some worms and maggots and there was some sweetcorn hiding in the bottom of the rucksack too. My plan was simple, if necessary I would clear a swim with the rake and then fish single maggot below a small waggler. Loose feed a few maggots to try and attract and then hold some fish. If that didn't work, then move along and try another swim. Repeat this until I found some fish.

Across a yard used by a rowing club lay the canal. Other than a gentle bend there were no obvious features on this part to attract fish, they could be anywhere. Stringing up the old float rod with the Japanese reel and light line, I took in my surroundings. The railway track on the other side of the canal follows it closely for many miles. The rumble of traffic on the motorways could still be heard too. While not exactly urban fishing, it was still much more noisy than I am used to. No harm, the whole point of the '32' project was to sample as many different angling experiences as possible while catching fish in each county. Canal fishing in an urban environment was every bit as valid as fly fishing for trout in the wilds of Connemara.

I found a likely looking swim and gave it a rake to clear some of the weeds and stir up the bottom a bit. Plumbing the depth I found barely 3 feet of water in the middle and less near the edge. A small crystal waggler was my first choice. Setting the float so the hook would be on the bottom I tied on a two pound hook length with a size 20 spade end hook attached. Bait would be a single red maggot and I tossed in a few others as loose feed. I was fishing at last! The reason for fishing so light was the clarity of the water, it really was gin clear. I figured my usual 3 or 4 maggots on a size 12 was going to be too much in these conditions.

Sunday morning joggers and dog walkers were out in numbers and among them that most heinous of the great unwashed—the passer-by who thinks they know all about fishing. What starts off as a casual 'caught anything yet?' quickly degenerates into a full blown instructional lecture, based on this person's encyclopaedic angling knowledge gleaned from that one time they went fishing on holiday.

I fished hard, raking out swims, baiting them up, fixing the float in an icy glare for hours. I tried different spots, went down to one pound hook length, used chopped worm then tried worm and maggot. Floats were changed for ever lighter ones, shotting patterns adjusted to change the rate of fall and I loose fed maggots into swims all day. All of this failed to produce even a nibble. The hot sun beat down on me as the insects buzzed around in the heat. Nothing at all stirred though until a tiny perch fell for a single red maggot. Only slightly longer than my thumb, this fish was barely out of the cradle. I am sure it is the smallest perch I have every caught in my long angling career. That was it, that was the total for a whole day fishing the Royal Canal in Dublin. At 5pm, I packed up and headed for the car and the long road back to Mayo. I was gutted.

I drove home crest fallen, not even I could count the tiny perch as being an acceptable fish. I would have to try again at a later date. I knew when I started this odyssey I was bound to blank sometimes but failing so spectacularly in Dublin was hard to swallow. The long road west seemed to take an age to negotiate and all the while I was asking myself what I could have done differently.

I saw no signs of a good fish all day, bar a few minnows in the margins the place looked dead. No tiny bubbles rising to indicate fish grubbing about on the bottom or dark shapes drifting slowly through the weeds. I had fished fine all day and I really didn't think I was scaring fish off. I need to learn lessons on days like this but I don't know where to start with this one. The fact I saw no other anglers is perhaps an indication that the fishing was poor.

It was very much a case of back to the drawing board for me. I spent a significant amount of time searching for another venue. I didn't fancy returning to the Royal canal after the abject failure in June so I had to find somewhere else, but where?

Part two, Sunday, 25th July 2021

The wounds of my last foray to the capital have healed so it is time to return to the capital. In the end, I decided to try the other canal in the city, the Grand Canal. It too has stocks of pike, perch and roach, is of a similar depth and construction as the Royal but links Dublin harbour with the river Shannon in county Offaly via a more southerly route. My idea was to fish it with jigs, looking for perch and jacks around the lock gates where there should be less weeds. I'd bring some maggots with me too so I had options if the jigs failed to produce. This would be 'urban' fishing, a backpack with some small bits and a rod, not much else. The section of the canal I was targeting passes through a landscape of industrial and commercial sites with some housing mixed in. Busy roads and even a motorway crossed the waterway and the towpath is heavily used by everyone from friendly dog walkers to drug addicts. It would be far removed from my usual gentle days of solitude in a small boat on a western lough!

I don't own any specific jigging or drop shotting rods or reels so I would just make do with an old spinning rod and a small fixed spool filled with light fluorocarbon line. I was not anticipating hooking anything large so I did not bother with a net. The whole idea was that I could quickly move between different spots until I found a few fish. The majority of the canal would be shallow and weedy but I hoped to find deeper, clearer water at the locks, three of which were strung out along my chosen stretch.

I eschewed another early start, to beat the rush hour traffic on a weekday I would need to be on the road at 3am so instead I opted for a more leisurely mid-morning start and departed Castlebar at 9 o'clock on a slightly misty summers day. The M50 was not too busy when I got there and I turned off at the Red Cow then found a parking spot near to the canal.

I admit to being nervous about leaving the car parked in such a dodgy area but I figured nobody would want to steal such an old wreck and made sure not to leave anything of any value inside. Across a bridge then down to the towpath which had been developed into a wide cycleway. Three locks I was targeting were grouped pretty close together it and my hope was they would be less weedy than the open stretches of canal. Would this be another disaster or could I wangle out a few decent fish today?

My chosen rod for the day was a light 7 foot ABU spinning rod of great vintage. I had bought it in Aberdeen in the 1970s, but to be honest it had hardly been used since then. The brown fibreglass is still in great condition. Rated for 2–10 grams it should be OK for what I demanded of it. I matched it with my elderly Daiwa Harrier fixed spool reel, a cheap and cheerful set up which should see me through the day. In my small rucksack, I had stowed some soft baits, a few small spinners and plugs, a plastic box of hooks/weights/swivels/floats and a couple of small bait boxes containing the live bait. No net, weed rake or other essentials.

I set off for the closest lock, feeling full of trepidation. With one failure already under my belt, I was under pressure to do much better this time. Beyond watching some very entertaining videos on dropshotting I know nothing about this method, adding considerably to the challenge. The guys on YouTube made all look so easy, just jiggle the wee lure up and down and perch or pike magically appear on the hook. I treated the videos with a healthy dose of Scottish scepticism.

I started off with a basic drop shot set up of a 3.5 gram weight and one of those swivel/hook thingys which I stuck a small plastic grub on (you can tell already that I am out of my depth here). The maggots in my bucket were the backup but I needed to feel I was 'doing something' this time rather than waiting for a float to dip. I manfully strode up to the nearest lock, a steely glint in my eye. 'Make my day suckers' I muttered in my best Clint Eastwood voice as I dropped the grub into the dirty water by the lock gate. I jiggled it up and just like I had seen in the videos. Nothing. I must have the wrong colour—I changed to a yellowish one and tried again. Nope, no good.

I moved the weight a bit closer to the lure so it would fish closer to the bottom. Nothing. I tried casting and then bumping the weight along the bottom. That didn't work either. I tried both sides of the lock gates but with a similar lack of success.

"Yer's not goin' ta catch any bleedin' fish there mister." The broad Dublin accent from a child's mouth was a shock to me and here were a pair of ankle-biters behind me. One wore a bright red top that looked far too big for her while the other, younger lass was dressed in britches that were out at the knees. Neither of their faces had been in close proximity of soap and water for a long time. "Ders fishes up der," said the one in red, pointing to nowhere in particular. "We seen a fella fishin' der before."

I thanked them for their advice and walked off up the path. An hour had gone and I was still to see a fish let alone hook one. The next lock was further away than I thought but I sauntered up there under the low, grey clouds, trying to figure out what to try next. I settled on sticking with the drop shot for now.

This next set of locks were much more promising. A deep, clear pool below the gates was fishable but try as hard as I might I could see no fish swimming in it. The rush of water from over the top of the lock gates created a fast flow immediately below and it screamed 'perch' to me. After checking the terminal tackle was in order, I lowered it into the canal. With the much improved clarity of the water, I could watch the jig as it descended into the depths and didn't a pair of good sized perch rush out of nowhere and try to grab the plastic grub.

Both missed it and I wound in to try to repeat the exercise. Back down went the jig and this time a solitary perch came to investigate but he too declined to bite. To cut a long story short I drop-shotted this spot for the next 20 minutes and most drops I had a follow but not one fish actually swallowed the lure. Time for a re-think. Sitting on the lock gate I considered my options and figured a natural bait was worth a try.

I only had the short spinning rod with me but it would have to do. I rigged a small crystal waggler float, plumbed up and added a 2.5 pound tail with a size 16 hook. Soon a pair of red maggots where sent wriggling into the water. After only the second or third drop (it was not even a cast), the float bobbed and I struck into a nice roach which promptly fell off the hook as I was swinging it in. Damn! I couldn't count that one. A few minutes later the float disappeared and I lifted into a modestly proportioned perch which made it safely to my sweaty paw. Perch are such gorgeous fish and this one in particular looked bloody marvellous to me, my first Dublin fish.

I fished on and landed one more perch and a smallish roach. The fast current and back eddy was making bite detection tricky and control of the baited hook almost impossible. Sometimes I was snagging on weeds but it was very hard tell when. Then, on the umpteenth drop my float slowly sank and I lifted to free the hook from the weeds only to see a huge perch surface with my hook in his mouth. The great fish gave a slow roll and was gone. He hadn't been far of a couple of pounds in weight that lad!

I could see what was happening here, the currents were strong and very variable so I was losing contact with the hook as it was washed in different directions deep below (there was about 10–12 feet of water). I took off the crystal float and in its place went for a hefty pellet waggler, rated for 3 grams. I then put my bulk shot just above the hook and changed up to a size 12 holding a bunch of maggots. Some loose feed was chucked in, then I dropped the new set up down. It took a while but eventually the float dipped and I lifted into a nice perch. It wasn't the big lad I had lost but it was still an OK fish.

I caught another roach, no great size but very pretty. For some reason, I decided to take another look at the pool below the run I was fishing. Laying the rod down I watched intently for a while, my eyes slowly adjusting to the water. Sure enough, I could make out a dark shape on the bottom, then another and many more. There were perch in there and what was probably roach too. I slung the big blue float out and the maggots settled on the bottom. Minutes passed but then the float trembled and I struck into a nice perch.

Some kids, under the supervision of 3 adults stopped at the lock above me. I paid then no heed as I was considering another change of tackle to fish lighter in the gin-clear pool. There was the usual noise you associate with a gang of kids then a resounding splash as one of them jumped in to the water above the lock.

The others soon followed and they were having great fun. I was concentrating very hard on my float when out of the blue a wet-suited child hurled herself directly into the swim, not 2 yards from my float!

Letting out a howl of delight as she surfaced, a broad grin on her face, she next extolled the virtues of the water and encouraged her pals to join her. By now every self-respecting fish was in the next parish so I wound in. One of the accompanying adults came over to me and said the kids would not be there long and they would be out of the water in a hour or so. I thought about it for a while but decided to head back to the car. On the way, I dropped the float into the dark water under a bridge and in three casts pulled out a small roach and two small perch.

Back at the car I took down the rod and slung all the gear in the back. Some random lad tried to cadge a cigarette from me and wouldn't take no for an answer. I slammed the car door shut and locked them before speeding off, leaving him shouting something unprintable towards me. You gotta love Dublin!

So, what to make of all that? I had landed 6 perch and 3 roach before the cannonballing kids brought the session to a shuddering halt, so I was reasonably happy with that result. Only that I had found the fish below the lock I fear I would have returned to Mayo with another blank. It was very irritating that the kids showed up just as I had found a shoal of fish but that is life and we just need to move on when stuff like that happens. The little spinning rod was a poor tool for fishing the float but the alternative of dragging more than one rod with me today was just not an option for me.

Drop-shotting still needs further investigation. It certainly got a response from the perch but they would not actually take the plastic. I will do some more research and maybe even invest in some of those dinky little 'creature' baits.

Dublin has been very firmly crossed off my 'to do' list. Two trips across the full width of Ireland it had taken but I had done what I had set out to achieve. It looked to me as if the stretch I was fishing used to be good. There were concrete pegs all along the towpath but they were all badly overgrown and had not been used for years. I'll be honest, I won't be in a rush to fish there again but it was an experience and I learned a bit more about fishing.

Chapter 16
Monaghan

County number 16

Tuesday, 3rd August 2021

Where do you even begin with county Monaghan? Seriously, was there ever a county so well endowed with coarse fishing venues? A hell of a lot of head scratching went into deciding where to fish to tick this Ulster county off my list but in the end I made a decision, well sort of…

Monaghan is in the Republic, another one of the border counties which butts up against the UK. Cavan, Meath and Louth encircle it from west to east and it pokes up into the UK like a big, jagged tooth. Characterised by the rolling drumlin landscape, this is a fertile farming area of small fields and hedgerows. There are no large centres of population here, Monaghan Town and Carrickmacross being the two main towns. Oh, and there are lakes, lots of them. Most of these are filled with fish which makes Monaghan a very attractive county for the likes of me.

I scoured the internet for information about the angling opportunities in Monaghan and was not disappointed by the range of venues available to us anglers. I know I am critical of the IFI (often justified) but they seem to be on top of things in this county and there is a wealth of information for anyone who wants to fish here. In addition, and slightly unusually for Ireland, there has been a lot of development work carried out to improve access for anglers. Car parks, footpaths and fishing stands are common on the lakes in this part of the country. This is hugely appreciated and the IFI should be congratulated for this excellent work. If similar works could be carried out in parts of Roscommon, Clare and Leitrim a huge amount of fishing could be made available to both locals and visiting anglers.

I looked at Ballybay and around Clones, both very tempting centres with a lot of lakes to try. In the end, though I opted for Carrickmacross. I liked the look of some of the surrounding lakes and felt I would have a good chance of landing some fish there. Truth be told I have actually caught fish in Monaghan before. Many years ago I worked in a papermill in Aberdeen and the product was sent to various plants in Britain and Ireland for further processing. One of those plants was in Kingscourt, co. Cavan.

I got to know some of the lads in that plant and visited them in 1979 for a bit of fishing. I stayed with Pat at his house in Carrickmacross and we fished for trout in some of the local lakes as well as on Sheelin. There were some great nights drinking porter till the wee hours after successful days with the rods. Happy days indeed. For the purposes of this '32' project, I would disregard those triumphs of long ago and pit my wits against the little fishes of Monaghan once again.

My plan was a simple one. On the outskirts of Carrickmacross, there are three lakes in particular which are grouped within a few miles of each other so if I was struggling on one water it would be easy to switch venue. Here is what the IFI have to say about all three lakes:

1. Monalty Lake is located approximately 3.25km S.E. of Carrickmacross on the R178 Dundalk road on the right hand side of the road. Turn right after approximately 3.25kms and this roadway runs right beside the lake. There are a number of swims on this eastern shoreline and parking and access is also located in this area. Some local fishermen fish from small punts moored to platforms in the lake and boat fishing can produce the best results as the mobility allows the angler to locate the feeding shoals. This lake covers an area of 16 hectares with depths to 6m. This lake holds good stocks of fish including roach, rudd, bream, hybrids, tench, pike and eels. Bream, hybrids and tench to specimen size are to be found in this water and annually it records many specimen bream over 9 and 10 lbs in weight and the Specimen Fish Committee certifies these fish. Maggots, sweetcorn and bread are all effective baits. Anglers fishing in the early months of March and April and the later months of August, September and October produce best results.
2. Lisanisk is located on the R178 Dundalk road on the outskirts of Carrickmacross and is well developed. A spacious off road car park is

provided and there are a number of angling stands on the road side of the lake. This 5-hectare lake has a maximum depth of 2.5m and produces great tench fishing. A number of large carp have also been taken in recent times. As well as tench and carp this lake holds good stocks of bream, roach, hybrids perch and some pike. This lake has a very weedy bottom as is best fished by float or pole.

3. Capragh Lake is located on the Crossmaglen road 4.5km N.E. of Carrickmacross. This lake has a good off road car park beside the lakeshore and there are many fishing stands around the lake. This lake which covers an area of approximately 12 hectares has depths ranging from 3m to 12m. This lake contains bream to specimen size and good stocks of roach, rudd, tench, perch and pike. Pike anglers will also find it possible to launch a boat on this lake.

I think you will agree these are good, concise appraisals of all three lakes. I planned to start on Lisanisk and if that was no good make a move to Monalty with Capragh as a final back up should I still be fishless by mid-afternoon. I like having back up plans on these trips, it gives me a way out if one venue is not fishing well. I guess there is an argument that I dilute my attention to one venue by holding one or more in reserve. That is certainly a possibility but I find the peace of mind knowing there is a 'plan B' more of a benefit than a hindrance. The drawback with all of this was with three water to fish it was turning in to a very, very long day.

Another plus point for me in Carrickmacross was the tackle shop there. Anglers Choice have a huge range of gear and bait so I planned to hit the shop first when I arrived in the town. Aside from the all-important maggots the guys there would also have up to date information about where the fish were being caught.

It is the night before and it is Bank holiday Monday and so Helen and I go for a bite to eat for the first time in a year or so. We have to dine outside the restaurant but it's a warm evening and we enjoy a lovely meal and some wine. Probably too much wine truth be told as we return home and sit outside in the garden talking till the wee hours. Eventually we retire for what is left of the night and at 5am my alarm sounds. Time to get up and go fishing but boy am I tired!

As a youngster a scant 3 hours in my bed was more than sufficient but at my advanced age I need much longer to be able to function properly the next day.

Bleary eyed, I shuffle around the house gathering up my gear. It takes me ages to load up the car and make something to eat. The idea of postponing this trip today briefly flits across my mind but I push those negative thoughts away and finish making my sandwiches.

With all this talk of big fish, I pack my heavy leger rod and a reel with eight pound line on it. I have no plans to directly target the carp that were in Lisanisk but the heavy line would give me a fighting chance of landing one if it picked up my bait accidentally. I have tangled with carp before and they are doughty fighters but the old ABU rod would be a match for all but the biggest of the species. Lisanisk held tench apparently and they would be my target species if I fished on that lake but carp could very well snaffle a bait intended for Tinca Tinca.

A look in the bait fridge reveals half a pint of red maggots which were still in good condition and also a few worms so I brought them along for the ride. I could add them to the groundbait if nothing else. One last check that I have everything with me then I switch on the engine and hit the road.

Monaghan is another one of those awkward journeys for me with a trek through the middle of Ireland. Three hours behind the wheel should see me there I figured but slow traffic, especially tractors, can stretch that out when on some of the lesser roads I would be travelling. I wanted to arrive in Carrickmacross at 9am but I am late in leaving. Oh boy am I tired!

Longford, Ballyjamesduff and Kingscourt were negotiated as I ploughed on ever eastwards. I am getting used to the roads in this neck of the woods now. With the old car and no sat nav. I rely on map reading and memory to find my way around the highways and byways of Ireland. There are occasional lapses but I possess and good sense of direction and generally manage to find my way around pretty easily.

Road signs are much better than they were when I first came to Ireland but there are still many smaller roads which are unmarked. While the road was quiet for the first few miles, the plague of summertime tractors soon slowed me down. Sometimes at only a little above walking pace I gradually closed in on my destination.

Somewhere to the west of Virginia I round a bend to see an elderly man standing in the middle of the road, waving me down. I slam on the brakes and come to a halt a few feet in front of this guy. A farmer, resplendent in a worn flat cap and wellies, he wants a lift and before I can offer any meaningful protest he has hopped into the passenger's seat beside me. The stench of fresh cow dung fills the air as my new friend tries to tell me where he wants to go but it is just a list of local farms from what I can gather so I set off in the only direction I can. "Past O'Donnell's now and up the road to Casey's, ye know where that is?"

I have not a clue but keep on driving and after a few miles my pungent pal waves a hand towards a large slatted barn just off the road. Out he gets and without so much as a 'thank you' he is gone. The remainder of my journey is completed with all the windows wound down!

I arrived in Carrickmacross after the rush hour to find the streets were not too busy as I tried to find my way to the tackle shop. Angler's choice is just to the north of the town centre, pretty easy to find. Once inside I buy some fresh maggots and a bag of groundbait. It would be easy to part with some serious cash here, it is a cornucopia of coarse angling tackle and I have to steel myself not to buy some goodies. Back in the car I need to make a decision on where to start and I plump for Lisanisk. It is the closest lake and from what I have read it might be the easiest.

Being low on energy this morning and not looking for any major challenges, Lisanisk will do to begin with. Back through the town centre and it is only a short journey to the small car park which serves the lake. Once I have got all the gear I need out of the back of the car I slowly make my way to the bank and find some fishing stands. With no local knowledge, I simply pick one at random and proceed to tackle up. Here in lies one of the biggest challenges of this project, I have no prior knowledge to base big decisions like what stand to fish from.

I tend to look for some structure such as weedbeds or maybe an island close by but it is always a gamble. Lisanisk has lots and lots of weeds so I just plonk my gear down on the second stand I come to.

The heavy leger rod, which I had been placing so much faith in remained in the car and instead I bring the 13 foot float rod and the 12 foot swimfeeder. Six pound line on the feeder rod reel is probably a bit light if I run into a carp but I view that eventuality as remote. On goes a short helicopter rig and a maggot feeder and I bait up with a bunch of maggots on a size 10 hook. Groundbait consisting of brown crumb (of course), Sensas lake, a small tin of corn and a little hemp is mixed and balls tossed in, feeding a swim two rod lengths out directly in front of me and a bit further out to my right. Then, at last, I cast out, hard up against the lily pads where the balls of ground bait are slowly disintegrating on the bottom.

I turn my attention to setting up the float rod but this takes me ages as the swimfeeder gets bites right from the off. I miss the first couple before setting the hook in the third one. A small skimmer comes to hand, is snapped and quickly popped back into the green water. Well that didn't take long! Skimmers are an enigma, such willing little fish but they can be so annoyingly difficult to hook some times. Well that is my experience of them so far anyway.

More skimmers are lost and landed before I finally get the float rod into action. A size 12 baited with 4 maggots doesn't even get time to settle on the bottom before the float dips and a tiny rudd is hooked. That make a mockery of my idea that the bigger hook might dissuade the smaller Rudd from biting. The water seems to be filled with rudd feeding close to the surface and virtually every cast sees the float dip as one of the little rascals has either robbed the maggots or they are wound in.

It is all action as both rods are constantly getting bites. In the end, I give up with the float, the hook is sinking too slowly, giving the rudd the opportunity to nip the baited hook on every cast. Cutting off the rig and making up a new one is just too much work when there is so much action on the feeder. I break down my beloved float rod, its work for today over and I now concentrate on the swimfeeder instead. This lake must support a huge head of fish because virtually every cast receives the attention of the rudd or skimmers.

Warm, humid air feels hard to even breathe in today as I cast out, tighten up to the weight and watch for the pulls on the rod tip. These come quickly and the skill today is simply in setting the hook. At a rough guess, I connect with only every third or fourth fish which says a lot about my general condition today. The hook link begins to look a bit tatty to me so I take the time to change it and renew the hook itself at the same time. Dragonflies buzz around me, those big brown ones. Martins swoop low of the still green water and above there are swifts screeching. The sounds of an Irish summer.

After a couple of hours, I consider a move but a combination of lethargy on my part (induced by last night's frivolities) and a belief that something bigger must come into the swim sooner or later due to the heavy feeding I am giving it means I sit tight in the same spot for the whole session. Of course nothing bigger does show up and instead I swing a steady flow of pewter coloured skimmers and tiny golden rudd to my hand. I tried chopped worm for a change from the maggots but the rudd found them easy to strip from the hook even as it was sinking quickly past them. Checking the clock on my slime covered phone I see it is 2.30pm. I've had enough and decide to call it a day. By then, I have landed 31 skimmers and 17 rudd.

The biggest of the skimmers would not even reach a pound in weight and every piece of gear is covered in snot. My rods and reels, the lines and end tackle are all caked in slime from the skimmers. My clothes and skin are liberally dosed with the stuff too so there will be a big clean up when I get home. Just taking down the rods and the short trudge back to the car seem to sap the final vestiges of energy from me and the long road home feels like impending torture. The heavy tackle box is heaved into the car along with all my other smelly gear. Once I am moving though the journey back home passes quickly enough and I turn into the driveway just before 6pm.

A post-mortem of the day would reveal the previous night's revelries meant I was barely fit for an arduous journey and a lot of fishing. I should have moved after the first hour and tried to find better quality fish but I was just too tired. I know I am going to regret not fishing the other lakes as I had originally planned. Sadly I guess I am just too old to go burning the candle at both ends any more.

That's a pity as enjoying a few glasses of red wine and fishing are both pastimes I thoroughly enjoy. What would have happened if I had been in full health and well rested? I think I would have fished the other lakes as planned. Both my 'back up' lakes have an excellent reputation and to be so close to them without wetting a line was an awful waste. Who knows if I would have caught anything but I would have enjoyed trying.

There is a hell of a lot of coarse fishing around Carrickmacross and I will make plans to visit there again. Any coarse anglers contemplating a trip to fish in Ireland could do a lot worse than basing themselves in the town. It's a busy place with all the facilities you could want on a fishing holiday and there are plenty of lakes to pick from within a few miles.

Interesting to see that the feeder out-fish the waggler today too. It is normally the other way around for me but this time out the float rod was just plagued with tiny rudd. The helicopter rig I was using did not seem to be vastly different from the ones I have fished with before so it is hard to figure out why it was so lethal today and yet so useless at other venues.

Today was something of a milestone. I have now landed fish in 16 of the 32 Irish counties, exactly half way to my goal. While disappointed in my performance today, I am pretty chuffed with progress to date. It has been stop-start and hard to get any sort of rhythm going but to be half way there make me feel good. Monaghan was a long journey and I can see that I have left all of the longest trips until the second half of the project. Many more miles will need to be covered if I am too complete what I have started.

Chapter 17
Antrim

County number 17

Wednesday, 18th August 2021

Antrim occupies that far north eastern corner of the island of Ireland, an ancient kingdom with strong traditional links to my home country of Scotland. Indeed, I think I am right in saying there are but 12 scant miles of salt water at the closest point between the two countries. I recall being on holiday on the Scottish island of Islay many years ago, looking out from Port Ellen on a beautiful summer's day and being amazed how clearly I could see Antrim on the horizon. A countryside of rugged coasts, hill farms and small towns, it has become famous as a result of it being some of the locations used in GoT. It was not dragons I would be searching for but a few much smaller and hopefully more obliging scaly creatures.

The northern part of Belfast city is in Antrim. The city sprawls across the lowlands on either side of the river Lagan with co. Down to the south and co. Antrim to the north. The river widens into a large bay and towns line both sides. Behind Carrickfergus on the Antrim side there are water supply reservoirs, some of which have been stocked with trout. Perhaps one of these could be a suitable venue? That was certainly my initial plan but I started reading up on trout fishing in Antrim and was surprised by just how much of it there is. Antrim's rivers and loughs cater for a large and enthusiastic group of anglers who live in and around the county. I mulled the various options over but really found it hard to make a firm decision. In the end, I hedged my bets in a quite unique way.

Up in the hills of northern Antrim there sits a lough called Dungonnell. It has been formed by a dam and holds some wild brown trout. This would be one of my target venues for the morning, up in the solitude of the glens with just the sheep and calling curlews for company. Hill lough trout are usually small creatures but fishing in lonely spots has a certain attraction for me. Having said that, I read that trout up to 5 pounds have been caught in this lough.

For me, this was going to be one of the longest journeys in my 32 project. Being perfectly honest, I have been putting this one on 'the long finger' for most of this year, always finding an excuse not to tackle it. This was solely based on the distance I would have to drive there and back. It would entail a very long day with considerably more time spent driving than actually fishing. That in turn meant less time to find fish and figure out how to catch one or two. Tiredness was obviously going to be a factor on the day as well.

Initially planned for Tuesday, I felt ill that morning so postponed the trip 24 hours. The idea of a very long day behind the wheel when not feeling your best did not appeal so I drank plenty of fluids, got some rest and gathered my strength for the 'morrow. Wednesday arrived, cloaked in grey and cool for the time of year. Feeling much improved, the bits and bobs required for the day were assembled and loaded in the half light. An early start was required as the trip to Dungonnell would take well over 4 hours behind the wheel.

Through the never ending roadworks in Sligo just after 7 am, Enniskillen at 8 and then on to Dungannon. From there, it was on to the long and winding road via flag bedecked Cookstown and Magherafelt to Toome. As I crossed the river Bann and an idea struck me, how about a few minutes fishing the Toome canal? This would only be a slight diversion and it was a piece of water I had heard of but never fished. I knew it was a famous pike fishery but I recalled reading somewhere it had roach, perch and bream in there too. I took an exit at the next roundabout and found a cark park right beside the canal. Quickly setting up a light spinning rod, I strolled along the path to a set of locks and was fishing a small jig within minutes.

The water was very scummy further down but pretty clear at the locks. Some kids on paddleboards, resplendent in bright orange floatation vests, were having fun further up but they soon dropped down to close where I was fishing. Sure enough, the paddleboards were just the start and jumping in to the water plus general mayhem quickly ensued. Changing to a float set up made not a whit of difference and not so much as a single bite came my way. I decamped to a stretch of the canal above the locks for some peace and got plenty of it. I didn't register a single bite up here either. Loose feeding maggots failed to improve the situation and so I finally admitted defeat.

Retracing my steps I soon passed the kids who were still screeching with joy as they hurled themselves into the water. At least some people were enjoying the canal this morning. Returning to the car I was alarmed to find I had wasted two whole hours for no return. Tactically, my decision to try Toome had been a disaster. What would the rest of the day hold?

There is a 'B' road which leads from Toome to Ballymena via some twists and turns. From there, the A43 led me to the hamlet of Cargan then on to lesser roads until finally the dam hove into view as I crested a hill. A small tarred car park at the dam with space for a dozen cars provided a safe spot to leave the motor. With each mile I had travelled north, the weather had deteriorated and a thick mist cloaked the hills as I pulled up.

Hungry, I indulged in a sandwich washed down with some coffee as the world turned grey and damp outside. Just as I finished my impromptu lunch the mist cleared slightly, it was time to crack on! Waterproof jacket, waistcoat and boots were swiftly donned, then I set up the old rod with a reel containing a peach coloured line. The damp clung to me as I tied on a small daddy on the top, a size 14 Claret Bumble in the middle and a green-tailed Kate on the end.

I like to fish close in on hill loughs. These waters often deepen quite quickly so the trout can usually be found near to the edges. A slow and quiet approach is necessary though so as not to spook them. Short casts, show it to them then whip it away is my normal style. Starting near the dam, I worked my way along the western shoreline with the wind coming over my right shoulder. It was immediately obvious the peach line I had taken to be a floater was in fact a sinker.

No matter, I would fish just as happily with the wet line. The bank was rough so a neat 'one step per cast' fishing was not really feasible and instead I hopped like a waterproofed goat from one rock or tussock to another, casting as wind and stance allowed. This is a lovely way to fish for trout, you have to concentrate on so many different factors to get it right. Gradually I made my way along the edge of the lough, shrouded in the mist which had started to thicken once again.

Soon after I started there was a sharp tug and a swirl but that trout did not stick. I cursed, took another step and cast again. Not long after that another fish tweaked one of the flies but he was also too quick for me. The mist really thickened now and my visible world was painted in streaming grey. Flicking the flies out beyond an underwater rock brought an immediate response but no firm hook hold. I worked my way along the bank for perhaps two hundred yards, rising a dozen or more trout and not one of them did I manage to hook. By now, it was raining properly and so retracing my steps I returned to the car, wet and fishless. Time to get the thinking cap on!

I had noticed that every rise to my flies had happened within the first couple of pulls of my retrieve, and after that the fish had shown no interest. Sheltering under the tailgate of the Volkswagen I set about changing my set up. That sinking line had to go, I was convinced the trout wanted a fly high in the water. A search in the reel case soon produced a yellow floater the right size and in a few minutes I had a new leader tied on too. Next the flies came under scrutiny. All rises I had been able to see appeared to be at the middle or tail positions.

Maybe the claret bumble was a bit too small? I put a size 12 version in the middle of the new leader. That green-tailed Kate made way for a conventional Bibio on the tail. Perhaps the green tail had been too gaudy for the conservative trout in this lough? What about the bob fly though? Scanning the contents of the box my eyes fell on a row of my much loved deer hair caddis. Grey ones, green bodied ones, black ones with a wee silver tip—all were good patterns but somehow not quite what I wanted today. Then I spotted it, a fiery brown DH caddis on a size 14 hook—perfect!

Experienced anglers reading this will know that feeling you get sometimes, a knowing this fly is going to work today. Carefully I tied the little caddis fly on to the top dropper. Tackle alterations complete I sat under the tailgate until the rain had eased a little again before I venturing back to the water's edge. Everything in the visible world around me was dank and dripping.

Casting the old yellow floating line was a joy, it fairly sailed out across wind and wave. So much of my gear has been bought second-hand over the years, including fly reels with lines on them. Some of the lines were rubbish that had to be binned but others were in good shape so I cleaned those up and added them to my armoury, the only downside being I had to guess what they were. Floater, intermediate, forward or double taper—there are so many types and designs of fly lines now it is not easy to figure out exactly what is what. For now, it was certain the peach line I had started with was a medium sinker and the yellow one on the reel now was a lovely, silky floater.

So here I was working my way along the same stretch of rocky shoreline. Wet and fishless but with new flies on. I started at the same place as before but now the water felt lifeless and of trout there was no sign. I plugged away, timing my casts to coincide with lulls in the gusty wind. The floating line cast much better and added a few yards to each throw. A splash and sharp tug broke the rhythm of the casts, this one was hooked. It fought with dash and verve for a small trout but he came to hand without any drama and I had my prize, an Antrim brownie.

Of course the Fiery Brown DH caddis nestled in the corner of his mouth. Dark, as most hill lough fish are, the spots on his side merged into a sold dark brown along his back, a lovely fish. The fly easily twisted out, he was soon back in his watery abode none the worse for his mistake. The fish was no sooner released when the heavens opened and I made a bolt for the car. Waiting for a while for a clearance which never came, I watched the ceaseless rain through steamed up windows.

Another sandwich was munched and time slipped away with the teeming rain showing no signs of abating. In the end, I decided to change venue again so I packed up, happy with my solitary success. Disrobing under the tailgate, rod and reel were hastily dismantled and thrown willy-nilly into the back of the car. A resounding clunk as it was slammed shut then I was off back down the narrow road. It had been a brief session and one which I felt had been spoiled by the weather but at least I had caught one.

Now for a trek along the byroads of Northern Ireland and a complete change of angling experiences again. I was headed for the short Movanagher canal near the village of Kilrea to do a bit of float fishing. Here the River Bann is blocked by a weir and to allow boats to navigate the barrier a canal had been dug along the right bank and fitted with a set of lock gates. The coarse fish greatly appreciated this section of quiet flowing water and promptly took up residence. Roach, pike, perch and bream allegedly inhabit the canal now and it is a popular venue for matches.

I thought that some maggots might tempt one or two of them so I set off down narrow roads bereft of signposts. I had a vague idea of where I was going but to be honest there was a lot of guesswork involved as I crawled along quiet country roads hemmed in by hedges and lacking any indication which way to go. One junction completely flummoxed me and for a few miles I had no idea where I was going but I found an alternative road which brought me to a village I recognised. It took me an hour but I finally made it to my destination. Thankfully the rain which had driven me away from Dungonnel eased as I headed west.

After parking up, I surveyed the canal and decided on one of the old concrete pegs as my swim for the remainder of the afternoon. Not that there is much to pick between them all but this one, number 4 as it turns out, would do for me. This being Northern Ireland I was only allowed to use one rod when coarse fishing so I had brought along the 12 foot rod and a small amount of coarse gear. Plumbing up I found the water was about ten feet deep in the middle. Different venues have different rules about the use of groundbait here in the north but you are allowed to use it on this wee canal.

I mixed some up and tossed in three balls to try and attract in some fish then cast out my crystal waggler float with a pair of red maggots on a size 14 hook. The maggots which were left over from my last coarse fishing outing the previous week and had come from the bait fridge at home were turning to casters so I added those pupa to the ground bait. Then I waited. In fact, I waited for the better part of an hour before anything happened.

Trickling in a steady stream of loose fed maggots is a favourite tactic of mine and today was no different. 6 or 8 maggots chucked in every second cast generally feels about right to me and I am pretty sure this helped to pull a few perch into the swim. My surroundings were lovely and the old concrete fishing pegs provided comfortable lodgings. After the rough terrain and soggy conditions of Dungonnell, it felt like pure luxury to have a seat and a firm, level footing. I was even beginning to dry out a bit. The contrasts between the two angling genres can be stark sometimes but both fly and float exert a huge appeal on me. What is it they say? "A change is as good as a rest." I'll drink to that.

Finally, the crystal gave a wobble then dived and I was in. A smallish perch was quickly reeled in, unhooked and released. More followed in a steady procession. The first one was small but the were some 8 ounce ones too. Bites varied between subtle little dips of the float to instant disappearances or sideways pulls. There is nothing subtle about the dear old perch and each of the ones I hooked had swallowed the maggots. A barbless hook is a 'must' if there are perch around, as is a good disgorger. As a kid I was forever being stabbed by the spines on small perch in my eagerness to unhook them but experience in handling them has thankfully consigned those stabs of pain to my memory banks.

A tally of seven was reached before the sky darkened in the east and the rain came back again. It was half-past-four in the afternoon. Of roach and bream there was no sign and pulling out small perch had lost something of its appeal. With the prospect of a second soaking looming, I decided it was time to head home again so I packed up and began the long journey west. Traffic was much lighter but there were still a few late summer tractors on the roads and it was nearly nine pm before I turned into the driveway at home in Mayo.

When I got home, I mulled over the logistics of the day. I had been driving for a total of ten hours and had fished three venues for a total of five-and-a-half hours. I had driven a total of 675 kilometres, by far the longest journey of the 32 project to date. All for seven small perch and a solitary half pound brownie. BUT (and this is important), I had landed fish in county Antrim. Trying the canal at Toome had proved to be a mistake but that's fishing for you and there no guarantees so I accept that blank and move on.

Similarly, the trek across country to try and catch fish at Kilrea was a lot of effort for not much return in terms of fish caught but I saw a bit of the countryside and enjoyed fishing that venue. I recall reading somewhere that these canals fish better in high water conditions when the coarse species seek shelter from heavy flows in the main river. On another day, I feel sure both canals would fish well. If Dungonnell lough was close to me, I would have it haunted! It is a beautiful upland fishery and if the trout are all around the size of the one I landed it would be a great place for someone like me. Instead, it is literally at the other end of the country and as such I will probably never fish it again.

Chapter 18
Carlow

County number 18

Sunday, 12th December 2021

It had to come one day and it came last week. Mick, my mate the mechanic, shook his head and we both peered under the bonnet of the old Golf at the much maligned machinery therein. The list of faults was just too extensive this time for me to consider any further repairs so the decision was taken there and then, the old girl would be scrapped. It was strangely emotional seeing her loaded on to the flat bed and going off into the darkness a few days later. All those miles, all those memories just whisked away like that. I bought a cheap and well battered Renault in her place so the 32 project was still on.

Storm Barra had rattled the windows and felled trees across the south and west earlier in the week and the cold, windy weather lingered on long after the eye of the storm had passed. Being cooped up indoors for days on end was taking its toll so I decided to fish this Sunday and even more exciting, I would tackle another of the 32 counties. An uncomfortable day beckoned but what else can you expect in December? Being honest, winter fishing is something I find less and less enjoyable as each year slips past.

I used to love it, the cold and wet didn't knock a stir out of me at all when I was a young man but these days I hate the chilly weather. Just being cold is enough to ruin being outdoors for me so a selection of thermals, fleeces, waterproofs and hats are necessities when I do venture out. Met Eireann were promising rain with strong winds all day which is always a pretty safe bet here in Ireland.

Carlow does not immediately spring to mind when thinking about Irish angling. Gentle farmland and busy towns, just about commutable distance from Dublin; that is how it always struck me. Situated in the south east of Ireland,

Carlow is one of the smaller counties, sandwiched between Laois, Kilkenny, Kildare, Wexford and Wicklow. Carlow Town is a thriving community with lots of shops, pubs and restaurants to be enjoyed. It is hard to believe but this will be my first '32' jaunt since August, where does the time go?

By now, you will have all gathered that I am no fan of the OPW (office of public works) but the information on their website on river heights is excellent and I was able to see the river Barrow was running at half a metre on the gauge and slowly dropping near where I planned to fish. Water temperature had dropped quickly at the end of last month but had steadied recently at just over 5 degrees. If that was good or bad for roach and dace fishing, I had no idea.

The river Barrow is one of the country's great waterways despite many man-made diversions. It flows very roughly north to south and empties into the salt at Waterford along with her sisters the Suir and the Nore. Much of the river has been canalised and numerous weirs make it hard for salmon to penetrate far upstream. OK a few salar still force their way into the system but aside from the locals who haunt the bank it is not seriously fished for the salmon. Instead, over the years it has become a popular venue for coarse fishers. Angling clubs along its length cater for a large and active fishing community who use pole and rod to extract roach, dace and pike in good numbers. The river also holds a head of brown trout and there are perch in the river too.

Once upon a time I worked in south county Kildare, just a few miles from Carlow Town. Indeed, I often stayed in Carlow and got to know the town reasonably well at the time. Evenings would sometimes see me go for a walk after work and I used to stand on the bridges, watching the river flowing beneath, wide, deep and coloured. I never did see any anglers though. In my research, I found out that the section of river in the town is actually a good spot for both roach and dace so it is strange that I never came across an angler trying their luck on the town water. The same stretch apparently also holds bream along with occasional pike and perch.

For the purposes of this trip, I eschewed the Carlow Town water itself for a stretch further downstream at Clashganny. To quote directly from the Fishing Ireland website: "The stretch at Clashganny offers coarse anglers the opportunity to try different coarse fishing techniques in picturesque surroundings. Float, feeder and pole techniques all offer possibilities on this superb stretch of river." That sounds good doesn't it? Here I would target the roach and dace which allegedly stalked the weed beds on the bottom. From the images on the internet, it looked like a nice place with the river, a stretch of canal and a lock all possible pegs. The humble maggot and worm would be my baits of choice and it would be a day when the float was going to be my preferred method of presentation. Having only ever caught roach in flowing water by accident on the fly this was going to be an interesting day out for me.

You will all know by now that on these long distance trips I plan for a back-up venue in case my first choice is unfishable or I simply fail to catch anything there. In this case, I figured I would head upstream a bit to Bagnalstown or Leighlinbridge, also on the Barrow. Similar water and fishing for similar species but it would be a change of scene in the event I was still blank in the afternoon. As for tactics I would bring along a swimfeeder rod in case the float did not work so feeders in a range of weights were dug out and tossed into the box. I use smaller feeders regularly but the bigger lads rarely enjoy a dip in the water. On the swiftly flowing Barrow their gravitas might be required.

As always, a humongous quantity of gear came along for the ride. Not being used to fishing in flowing water for roach I was unsure which rod to bring with me, so I brought them all! As I mentioned, my heavy leger rod looked like my best option if I turned to the feeder in the main flow of the river but would my 12 or 13 foot float rods be best suited to trotting a float? I'm used to canals and fishing at close range, what if I had to fish at distance? The Barrow is a big river as it flows through Carlow and if the roach were holding further out I might struggle to present the bait properly. It is also pretty straight with not much in the way of pools or other features where I could easily identify holding areas. The canalisation of the river has removed most features but there are locks both upstream and downstream of Clashganny so these may just be the prime spots to hunt the roach. I needed more clarity of thought. Was I biting off more than I could chew?

Driving to Carlow entails a long and winding journey via Tulsk and Roscommon Town then down to Athlone. Drive east along a stretch of the M6 motorway as far as Tullamore then to Portlaoise. My plan was to stop off in Carlow and pick up some bait from the tackle shop in town. The final stretch is on the R448 down to Leighlinbridge, then the R702. A cool 290 km from home or a 580 km round trip in total. I set off early.

So I pulled up in Carlow Town, already stiff in the joints from 3 hours at the wheel. Barrow Fishing Tackle Shop is on Maryborough street, looking right on to the river. It was immediately obvious that I was in bother as the shop was closed. Twenty minutes past nine on my watch and the website said the shop would be open at nine. A heavy padlock on the door suggested that was not going to happen. A 'self-service' bait dispenser next to the door had a sign proclaiming 'bait 24/7' but it was out of order. It would be good to say I was mildly put out by this turn of events but in point of fact I was livid.

Why would a retail business advertise its opening hours on a website and Facebook page then completely disregard those hours? Now I was stuck with no alternative and would have to make do with the worms and dead maggots I had brought along with me. The dead maggots had been in the freezer for months and were in poor condition, I had planned on just using them up in the groundbait. There was nothing else for it, I drove off again heading for Clashganny, my plans in tatters.

It felt like a very long and tiresome road as I motored ever southwards, down the motorway as far as Leighlinbridge then winding through the khaki-coloured fields of rural Carlow. A very convenient car park close to the water's edge made life a bit easier for me and I was soon taking in my new surroundings. This is a very lovely corner of Ireland, mature trees bounding the brown waters of the river, clipped grass around the neat lock gates, small birds flitting among the undergrowth. I'm sure it is even prettier in the green of summer. Here the river flowed over a weir off to my right with another one a bit further downstream.

To allow small craft to navigate past the obstacles there is a short stretch of canal with locks. The river is high all right, the aftermath of storm Barra earlier in the week but the canal is very shallow here. The strong southerly wind which was forecast for today is absent and the air is pleasantly warm for the time of year.

I had seen an ariel photograph of this stretch but found it hard to get a sense of scale and form so it was only now, when standing on the bank that I could sense what the river 'felt' like. I will try to explain that statement for you. Angling for me is not simply the mechanics of casting/baiting/catching. Sure, technical knowledge, masterly of techniques and so on are vital for success but I have a much deeper feeling for the places I fish. I guess you could say it is a spiritual connection of sorts.

For me, the privilege of immersing myself in the natural world for a few short hours means I can be in a different head space. I am not a neurologist but I suspect I engage different parts of my brain when out in the natural world. So the 'feeling' of a waterway is a major part of how I fish on any given day. The

Barrow noisily tumbled over the weirs above and below me, creating a wall of sound as a backdrop to the session.

The obvious starting point for me was the canal and specifically a swim below the lock where an old boat was tied up. I set up with two rods, the feeder and the float rod. This looked very 'perchy' to me so I tried worm on the feeder rod. Since the sad demise of my old Daiwa Harrier reel I have been using a cheap black one which I bought in Sligo a while back. It even has a baitrunner facility, not that I need that when using it for float fishing but it fits well on the small feeder rod and the baitrunner facility means if anything big does take me it won't pull the whole lot into the water. Balls of groundbait plopped into the water and a short cast sent a worm to the bottom. For the feeder, the waiting began…

The feeder rod could look after itself while I set up the float rod. A couple of feet of mucky water flowed past me so I set up accordingly with an stick float and a size 14 hook. Shotting was simple, bulk shot above the tippet, and a couple of runners spaced up the line. Then I hurled in some more balls of groundbait and loose fed a trickle of the dead maggots.

Having never caught a dace before and lacking any real idea how to target them specifically meant limiting my choices to simply using a small hook below the bulk shot. In reality, I was setting my stall out for roach today instead. I've yet to land one of better than a pound in weight and mostly they are only a few ounces but I still love fishing for the wee silvers.

The float trotted through the swim a few times without being troubled by the fish. The shallow water meant I could see the groundbait lying on the bottom even through the coloured water and the float could be perfectly positioned to cover the exact spot. Soon however it was the feeder rod which gave a small rattle. Dropping the float rod I lifted the feeder and there was a small silvery fish on the end. A dace no less, the first one I have ever landed. It had taken a worm which I found a bit surprising but I was damn glad to see it anyway. Some bubbles on the surface where I had chucked in the balls of groundbait looked like a good omen so I settled into concentrating hard on the float, trotting a worm or a pair of dead maggots through the swim time and time again. Nothing.

Not so much as a nibble. I tried chopped worm, hoping the small pieces would be easy for the small dace to take but they failed to elicit any reaction. I tried a single dead maggot on a size 18 hook but that was no better. The problem with the maggots was not that they were dead, it was their poor condition. They smelled horrible. A hour passed but no more bites were forthcoming so I decided to try my luck above the lock.

The flow was minimal up there and try as I might no bites came my way. I chopped and changed again, going for a lighter float and adding chopped worm to the feeder but still neither method worked for me. Eventually a group of guys with kayaks appeared and noisily launched right next to me. I took this as a hint and decided I needed a change, but where to go? In the end I packed the gear into the car and headed back the way I came and stopped at Muine Bheag where there are some stands on the channel of the Barrow. Three other guys were fishing the pole there and were catching a few roach and dace on (you have guessed it) maggot.

I set up the rods and fished hard for the next couple of hours. Worm after worm trotted through the swim in front on me and never once did the float dip in anger. I knew in my heart I would be catching fish if only I had some maggots but it was not to be and when the rain came in the afternoon I called it a day and packed up.

Returning home I took a different road, driving up the M9 to Athy and reaching Tullamore via Portarlington. I had time to think about what had been a very poor day's fishing. I accept it is possible I would have not caught anything even if I had some maggots but I doubt that. I have seen this before and for me maggots equals fish, it is as simple as that. If I had known the tackle shop in Carlow was going to be shut, I would not have gone fishing there today. I like to be supportive of Irish tackle shops but I am left extremely frustrated and angry by the events of this morning. How hard would it have been to post a on their FB page to say they were closed today?

So despite what was a terribly poor day I did actually catch one fish in co. Carlow, which under the T&C of the '32' project means I achieved my aims. It feels like a very pyrrhic victory though; travelling the length of the country for one small dace was hardly the most exciting day on the bank. At least, the promised high winds and rain kept away while I was fishing.

Poor planning and research on my part was my downfall in Carlow. Having never fished for Dace before I should have read up on them beforehand. Maybe Dace take other baits but I did not bother carrying out any research. Relying on one bait shop being open on a Sunday was also a stupid thing to do. Ah well, we live and learn!

Christmas is but two weeks away and realistically I won't have time to fish again before the festive season kicks in. There are a few days off at the end of the month but it remains to be seen if I will venture out. Today was tiring and disappointing but they can't all be golden days of bent rods and full nets. I know I have now caught one fish in county Carlow and that is all I wanted to do at the outset of this project. Just the one fish was supposed to be sufficient for me but in this case it simply is not. I am left with a hollow feeling after today, a need to right a wrong if you will. Looking back, I am sure that given decent bait I would have done much better so a possible additional visit to that fair county is under consideration for next year. I still have to fish the neighbouring counties of Wexford, Kilkenny and Waterford and they are close enough for me to dart across to Carlow for a few hours angling. If I do, you can bet I will bring a pint of fresh maggots with me!

Chapter 19
Kildare

County number 19

Sunday, 16th January 2022

A new year, will it be any better than the last two? It is mid-January and high time I tried to catch a fish in another Irish county. To the south and east of Dublin stretches the wide flat plains of the Pale. I am no Irish history buff but the term 'the pale' seems to date from the middle ages and signified the area under English control. The borders of the pale fluctuated wildly over the years but Kildare was pretty much always under English rule. Rich farmlands made it attractive and the river Barrow provided a defensible line against the native Irish, those who lived 'beyond the pale'.

Kildare is horse racing country, indeed the nickname for it is 'the thoroughbred county'. Flat grass lands predominate, ideal for the gee-gees I understand. The English based their cavalry here and even today the county is dotted with studs and racecourses. I have no interest in racing but for a fisherman like me Kildare also boasts an awful lot of coarse angling with rivers and canals aplenty. It is very different to some of the more northerly counties such as Cavan or Leitrim with very few loughs.

Monasterevin in particular has a great reputation on both the river and the canal. I have read that there can be good fishing on the Barrow between Monasterevin and Athy but access can be an issue. It's a different story in and around the town of Athy itself where there is ample parking and easy access to the banks on both sides of the river. My problem was that you require a permit to fish at those towns and the tackle shops are closed on Sundays.

With Athy and Monasterevin out of the question, I decided to try further east along the canal at Lowton. I have not read any reports of the fishing around there but I figured roach could be just about anywhere so the stretch at Lowton would be my target. My 'plan B' was to try another stretch of the canal at Prosperous if Lowton was a failure. That was not too far away along a mess of back roads so it seemed to be a viable option.

Waking at silly o'clock in the cold darkness, the usual fumbling around the house ensued as I gathered together tackle, food and clothing under the watchful gaze of the cat who seemed bemused by my antics. Nelson (so christened because he only has one eye) is a creature of habit so me being up at this hour required his full attention as there was the possibility of an early breakfast for him. He was of course right in his supposition and I fed him before leaving.

I know the road to Kildare well having worked there a few years ago. Not a sinner was on the road as I left town then crossing from Mayo into Roscommon and the eastern sky lightened as I cruised through the townlands of Bellanagare and Tulsk. Roscommon was busier of course before the jaunt along the motorway to Athlone. The little village on Allenwood is close to where I would be fishing and I turned off the main roads there on to the narrow towpath.

I felt under less pressure than normal today, it was winter, the fishing would in all probability be hard and so a blank was entirely possible. I could return here in the summer if today was a washout. Okay so this was quite a long journey but I'd be trying for fish I had often caught using methods I am now very familiar with. I planned to simply relax and enjoy being outdoors. Funny how we go fishing in all these different states of mind. I guess that shows us how therapeutic our angling is, we can set off with rod and line in even the worst form but it still lifts our mood. My current negativity will pass and just being beside the water for a few hours will help me so much.

I had brought along a vast quantity of gear (quell surprise), enough to cope with anything the canal could throw at me. Rods bristled out of the quiver, the seatbox groaned under the weight of all the reels and boxes inside. Many miles had been covered already just to get here so I wanted to maximise my enjoyment. My primary target species would be roach as there are vast shoals of them in the canal. Perch should also be active at this time of the year and that is why I had brought along some worms. I felt the big challenge today was going to be finding the fish and then holding them in front of me.

Making my own breadcrumbs for groundbait is something I tried early on in my coarse fishing odyssey but results were pretty poor. The crumb I made was full of lumps and had a soggy texture that clumped together and was hard to mix.

So I packed that up as a bad job and just used shop bought crumb. Last week though I took another stab at it and this time results appear to be much better.

For a change, I dried out some old white bread in the oven before putting it in the blender and this gave a much better consistency with very few lumps in the resulting crumb. When fishing I much prefer a dark crumb, I think the fish can spot something alien when white crumb is used in the natural waters around here.

While I accept the finished product is far from perfect, it will bulk up my groundbait and at the same time use up bits of old loaf which would otherwise go to waste. I have been looking at using 'predator plus' additive when targeting perch but for now it would just be a dash of vanilla essence in the mix today.

Immediately over the old humpback stone bridge I found a parking spot, shut off the motor and went for a reconnoitre along one of the canals. The Barrow line which links the Grand Canal to the river Barrow comes off the Grand Canal here so there are a lot of different spots to pick from. Finding a space between the moored house boats was not easy but there was a small gap on a jetty. Looking into the crystal clear water I could actually see a shoal of roach as they nonchalantly swam by.

That was enough for me and I hastened back to the car to collect all the gear. Of course by the time I got back to the jetty and had set up the rods the roach were long gone and I was left looking into a completely empty stretch of the canal. If one shoal could swim by here, then so could others I reasoned, so I mixed up some ground bait. For me, at any rate that means some hemp in the groundbait and I mixed up a big bowl to start with. My crumb, hemp, ground pellets, oats, a few drops of vanilla and some dead maggots were all blended together and I fired 4 balls into the swim.

For once, I could watch as the balls dispersed on the bottom and lay there in full sight. Thankfully the balls dispersed perfectly as they hit the bottom, something that always concerned me when making up my groundbait. Was it too sloppy or too thick? Did it disintegrate when falling through the water and disperse too soon? On the usually cloudy natural loughs and local canals I never knew, but here in the sparkling clear waters of the canal it was obvious the balls were behaving perfectly. The question now was would the roach appreciate my efforts?

The light leger rod seemed to be a good choice given how fine I would be fishing today so I set the ten footer up with a simple link leger of two swan shot and a tippet of one pound breaking strain mono to a size 16 hook. A pair of maggots were sent out and I next set up the float rod. A reel of six pound mono was the lightest I had which I felt was far too heavy but with no other options it would have to do. A small waggler shotted at the float with some dust shot at the loop to a one pound tippet and a size 20 hook felt about right.

I plumbed up as normal and found around 5 feet of water in front of me. For a few casts, I fiddled about with the float trying to refine the depth to get the maggot riding an inch or so above the bottom. This was because the shoal of roach I had seen earlier were moving and not rooting around on the bottom. I wanted to drop a maggot to them at exactly the right level, hence all the fiddling.

Next on the agenda was a cuppa and a sandwich so I ate while fishing, watching the float like a hawk. The day was still cold at around 4 degrees but apart from that it was a lovely morning to be out in the fresh air. All was quiet for a while then another shoal of roach slowly swam past me.

The water was so clear I could make out every tiny spot on them as they contemptuously ignored the ground bait on the bottom and my cunningly displayed hook baits. I loose fed a trickle of maggots but the little silvery fish wanted nothing to do with them as the maggots drifted down through the shoal. In just a couple of minutes, they mooched off to my left and the swim was deserted again. Well, that didn't work! What had I done wrong this time?

A few houseboats were tied up close to me and a gent appeared from along the towpath with his dog so we got chatting. When I heard his east Lancashire accent, I asked Keith where he was from. This is always a tricky question for a Burnley supporter like me to ask. A fellow claret will be delighted to make the acquaintance of any Burnley supporter but a Blackburn fan might be well offended by the idea of talking to me. Keith was indeed from Blackburn but was not into the inter-team rivalry.

We talked about football and fishing and he asked how I was getting on. Blank so far was the answer. Keith suggested I stop for a break and come on to his houseboat for a cup of tea. I was sorely tempted as Keith was one of those lads who had obviously led a full and interesting life. I declined his offer as there was fishing to be done so he went below deck to have some tea after pointing out some more likely spots to me. A third shoal of roach showed up now, an even bigger shoal than the previous two. Once again I cast baited hooks to the ranks of the roach but once again the humble maggots were ignored and this shoal too swam off in the direction of Dublin.

It was interesting to note how all three shoals were heading in the same direction, none ever came back the other way. They were actively travelling, not nosing about on the bottom looking for food, just swimming in a steady, positive way, like they had somewhere important to be that morning.

Many, many casts later I reeled in and inspected the maggot. He looked a bit tired and so I changed him, mounting a nice fresh red maggot by the tail. Flicking the float out I let the faint current which flowed from my right to left take the float tenderly off. I kept the bale arm open and allowed the float to slowly drift away a bit further. There was a slight tremble on the float, no vertical movement you understand just a faint tremble but I saw it and struck. A fish! Not a big fish but a wee roach and I simply swung him to hand in one swift movement. A quick snap and the hook released from his top lip then off he swam again.

It was a lesson to me as I had not seen that fish despite the clarity of the water. He must have been in the thick weeds which blanketed some areas of the silty bottom. I fished on with renewed vigour under an ever brightening sky. One more shoal swam by but they refused everything I threw at them. I had seen enough by now and I decided to move.

I know this sounds like a stupid thing to do, if I can see fish in the swim surely I should stick it out there. My reasoning was that although the fish were sometimes right in front of me they were not stopping and seemed instead to be intent on travelling somewhere. I packed the gear and set off, back across the bridge and off along the main canal which was by now busy with assorted cyclists, boaters, dog walkers and chatty strollers. Finding a new spot close to a large barge I set up again in a swim which was a good bit deeper than my previous one.

Firstly I cast the light leger as close as I dare to a boat tied up next to me, hoping there might be a perch living under there. Then I cast out the float and it immediately stuck on something solid on the bottom, snapping the slender tippet when I tried to drag it free. A new tippet, still with a size 20 hook attached was soon installed. Losing tackle is just part and parcel of fishing but it is tiresome to lose a hook.

This proved to be a much busier section of the canal. Passers-by often exchanged a few words with me, some to enquire what I was fishing for, others to comment on my bait or choice of venue. Dogs were as usual fascinated by the smells which emanate from by bait box. Most are well behaved but the occasional rowdy customer can cause mayhem and I am always careful to stow away hooks when on a canal just in case an animal gets too nosy.

I plumbed up for the float and found to my amazement there was sixteen feet of water! That is incredibly deep for an Irish canal where anything more than half a fathom is considered deep. To handle the deeper water I took off the small waggler and put a bodied one in its place. A simple washing line pattern of small shot under the bulk at the float was designed to give weight to cast and hold the float but at the same time allow the maggot to gently float down through the water. I started fishing again, the canal bathed in golden sunshine but till very cold.

A few casts in the float plunged down and I struck into what turned out to be an odd catch for this time of the year—a rudd. I always associate rudd with scorching hot summer days, not bone-chilling January sessions. I popped the little lad back and a few minutes later I repeated the exercise with a slightly bigger rudd. Rudd in January, who would have thought it. I have become a big fan of the humble rudd. Yes, I know they can be annoying when tiny ones infest a swim but bigger rudd are such beautiful creatures.

That was it for the day as it turns out. The rudd must have drifted off and of roach or bream there was no sign. It was nice just being out in the fresh air so I fished on for a while but with no signs of fish, the bright sunshine and perfectly clear water it felt there was little hope of further action. I could have stayed on for a bit longer but a good general knows when to leave the field of battle and my race was run for the day (that's enough mixed metaphors for the day too!).

Back along the towpath and heading for the car I bumped into Keith again. He was rounding up the dog who was far too busy zooming around to pay any attention to his master. The battered Land Rover Keith was leaning on looked like it had led a hard existence, possibly no more than its owner. His bare arms were covers with incredibly complex tattoo sleeves and I am willing to guess they told stories of the man's life. We shook hands and agreed that if I was ever back this way I would take him up on his offer of a cuppa on the boat. The long drive home was uneventful and Helen was surprised to see me home again so soon.

In total, I spent three hours fishing and nearly seven hours behind the wheel today and Kildare is nowhere near to being the furthest of the 32 counties from home. The driving is proving to be more of a challenge than I had anticipated and of course the huge hike in fuel prices doesn't help much. My reels and lines need to be sorted out because it was only when I arrived at the venue and decided I had to fish very fine that I remembered the two and four pound lines were on spools for the now dead Harrier reel. Over the course of last season three of my reels broke down and I have done nothing to repair or replace them. That laziness needs to be addressed by me or it will end up costing me fish. As it was, the six pound mono hampered my casting with the float today.

To say the day had been a resounding success would be stretching it a bit but I am more than happy with those three small fish in difficult conditions at a venue I did not know. Three other anglers were also fishing and none of them had so much as a nibble while I was there. By the looks of the tackle, they were using I think they were after pike. Cold, gin clear water and bright overhead conditions made for a challenging day alright. I feel I should have done better when those shoals of roach swam past me and on reflection I should have tried bread on a day like today. I'll take this onboard and have at least a few slices of bread with me in future.

That said, fishing very fine paid off and I landed three fish. The rudd were a complete surprise, I thought they went off and hid in deep water for the winter but it appears that is not always the case. County number nineteen is done and dusted.

Chapter 20
Louth

County number 20

Tuesday, 5th April, 2022

Again, a county I know very little about as I have only been there on business or driven through it. How could I have so long in this country for so long yet have visited so few counties? I thought when I started out on these trips that I was well acquainted with vast swathes of the land but it turns out I am a near complete ignoramus when it comes to Irish geography. Zooming up and down the M1 between Dublin and Belfast had unsurprisingly done little to enhance my knowledge of the angling potential around this particular county. Louth occupies that north east corner of the country between Dublin and the border. I expect the locals would disagree with me but let's just say it is not overly blessed when it comes to angling venues.

Not that is short of anglers you understand, this part of Ireland is teeming with excellent fishers, it is just that they travel to other counties for their angling these days. I trolled the internet for many hours trying to find a likely spot and I can tell you it was bloody hard work. There were a couple of ponds which may or may not hold small stocks of coarse fish but I could find little to recommend them, bearing in mind it is a near 4 hour drive from Mayo to even get to this county. That Louth's rivers used to wonderful fisheries is beyond dispute, the Boyne, Dee and Fane are all examples of previously premium game angling systems.

All of these rivers have seen reduced stocks of migratory fish as well as browns so I felt I was taking a huge leap of faith if I tried my luck on one of them. The thought of driving all the way to Louth only to return having blanked was too much to bear. Come on, there must be somewhere to cast a line?

My dislike of Facebook is deep-rooted and well documented, I never 'got' it. How people can spend their lives posting the minutia of their existence like what they are eating or wearing beats me. Then again I expect most people would regard my posting the details of my inconclusive fishing trips as pretty odd so it just goes to show we are all different. Casting my prejudices aside, for once I turned to FB and hey-presto!

A place called The Grange Trout Fishery popped up in my search. They have a page there which gave some information about the small lake behind a shop in Carlingford. I read every word and admired their photos of impressively large brown and rainbow trout. The rules were helpfully listed and the whole package suggested this was just the place I had been looking for. So I made up my mind this would be the right venue and made my plans accordingly. Louth was very much on!

Three whole months had elapsed since my last '32' trip due to a combination of factors, most of them out of my control. Moments of doubt over the project's completion had crept in over those twelve weeks but now I was feeling a bit better after my brush with Covid and had a chunk of free time to pick up the gauntlet once more. Finding The Grange had been a massive boost, I was just hoping I would not be disappointed. An added bonus was the opportunity to fish for rainbows in a stocked lake. There are very limited numbers of such fisheries here in the Republic, unlike the UK where there seem to be one around every corner.

Even in Northern Ireland there are lots to pick from but as soon as you cross the border the change in attitude to rainbows is very noticeable. With so much fishing for wild brown trout on hand, there is very little appetite for stockies down here. I would never trade the glories of Mask or Conn for a put and take pond of rainbows but as a change from my norm I was really looking forward to this latest challenge.

The road to Louth was a long one. From Mayo on the N5 to Mullingar, then up the N52 (a road that has more twists than an Arizona Sidewinder) to Delvin. I stretched my legs at the service station on the edge of Kells then trundled all the way to Dundalk. From there, I took the Newry road around the town before turning off. That doesn't sound too bad when I write it down but trust me, it was a long enough drive. The Renault huffed and puffed on some hills but it kept going and finally I made it to the Carlingford peninsular. Pulling up in the small car park next to the shop I eased my stiff joints and stretched my legs, looking over the low wall at the lake. 'Lake' is possibly stretching things a bit, the fishery is basically a pond. 'Intimate' might be one way of describing this body of water, it was certainly a big change for me from the vastness of Corrib or Mask.

Just because it was small there was no guarantee I would catch anything, the trout can make fools of us all no matter where they are swimming.

Inside the shop I bought the permit and asked about the fishing but there was not a lot of information forthcoming other than it had not been fished that much of late. Returning to the car I set up my rod and reel. I would use my seven weight 11 footer in anticipation of heavy fish and I paired it with a Hardy Swift mark 2 loaded with a clear intermediate line. I like the Swift reel, it is lovely and smooth as well as possessing an excellent drag. I remember buying it when I lived in London and how it lay unused for a couple of years until I returned to the auld sod. A five pound breaking strain 18 foot leader had a damsel on the end of it which felt as good a starting point as any so I mashed the barb down on the hook and drew the tucked half-blood tight.

With the age of these flies, I made sure to check the hooks thoroughly for any signs of rust before use. A little on the surface of the metal would not do any harm but any deep rust would mean the fly was only fit for the bin. Luckily, most of the flies I examined passed muster.

Fly fishing for stockies is something I'll confess I am totally out of touch with. Blobs, bungs, squirmys and all that malarkey are outside my knowledge so I really did not know what to expect. Obviously my normal traditional three fly cast of peters and dabblers was not going to be of any use so instead I had to rely on some very old patterns fished in what I could vaguely remember as effective retrieves from my past. During the past winter I had reorganised my collection of fly boxes and had two which were still reasonably full of my stockie bashing lures and flies.

Rather than trying to teach this old dog some new tricks I figured these rust tinged old warriors could be relied on for the day that was in it. The damsel pattern was one I have used a lot and it caught me bags of fish in the past. It was a starting point at least. Knots all tested, it was time to make a start. Was that five pound leader going to be strong enough? Sudden doubts rushed through my mind but I calmed down and pushed the gate open.

A path led around one side of the pond but there was no access to the other side. Wooden stands gave a nice platform to cast from and I couldn't help but think how welcome they would be on some of the coarse lakes I fish. All my tackle for today was tucked into an old canvas bag as for once I had scaled down the gear I took with me. Those old fly boxes, a couple of reels and a net summed up the hardware I needed.

This alone was a pleasant change from my normal boat fishing which entails me hauling engine, petrol tank, baler, tackle bag etc. I am sure I could have pared the gear down even further but the few bits in an old canvas bag did the job for me on this occasion. The white and liver spaniel which had been hanging around the car park followed me to the lake, it looked like I was going to be his entertainment for the day.

Selecting one of the wooden stands I started to cast but something was wrong. A quick examination showed I had missed a ring, this time the second top one. I do this nearly every time I go fishing now as my eyesight is getting worse with every passing day. Cutting the leader I re-threaded the line and made a new blood knot, the work of just a few seconds. Finally, I was fishing. There was an awful long drop from the stand to the surface of the water and even with the handle fully extended it was only just possible to be able to net a fish.

I wonder if the level of the pond was lower than normal or if it is always like this. The old line is not as smooth as it used to be but it still shoots well and I was pinging out 25 yard casts no bother. Cleaning my fly lines is a task for the end of the season for me usually but maybe I need to do it more often. Warm soapy water and a soft cloth are all you need to do this necessary job so I don't have any excuses for not doing it more frequently. An occasional fish rose, almost certainly taking buzzers near the top judging by the rise forms. Casts in different directions covered the water and I soon had a rhythm going. Birdsong filled the warm, spring air and I could smell a faint tang of the sea, less than a mile from where I was standing. After the long drive, I was just beginning to relax when the line tightened…

Right away it was obvious this was a good fish. One powerful run after another bent the rod hard over and the reel sang. A couple of times I thought the fish was tired out but he found some more energy and would shoot off again. Five minutes must have elapsed before he slid towards the waiting net. Six inches from the knotless meshes he turned one more time and thrashed the water with his great spotted tail—then he was gone! The hook had just pulled out, he had fought a good fight and won in the end so I had no complaints. It was just a pity to be so close to landing a fish only for it to get away. The Spaniel gave me a withering look of disdain. Was that going to be my one and only chance?

Checking the hook confirmed there was nothing wrong with it so I started to cast again. Coots noisily fought in the distance, a Jay flew past me in an undulating flash of pink and blue. Twenty more casts, maybe thirty, then the line seemed to stop and grow heavy, I was in again! This one seemed confused as to what was happening to start with but it soon woke up and charged around the pond, at one point running out the whole length of the fly line so the joint to the backing chattered as it ran through the rings. The rod bent and I recovered most of the line.

The spaniel lunged at the rainbow as it came close to the muddy bank but I shooed it away and led the tired fish into my net. Thank God, I had one. A fine trout of about three pounds, he was quickly released and swam off strongly after a couple of photos. It was a real relief to land that fish after losing the first one I had hooked. I had forgotten how strongly these rainbows fight!

Hook and leader checked I resumed operations but the pond had gone quiet now and no more offers came my way. Off came the damsel and in its place I tied on a size eight Montana, then a gold head daddy and even a cat's whiskers. These old reliables were all given a swim but without success. It was time for a change of tactics so I tied on a pair of daiwl bach, one brown and the other black. Years of fishing these flies have built a lot of confidence in them, they really are great at sorting out fish feeding on buzzers. Retrieved at a glacial pace a smaller rainbow inhaled the brown lad and put up a good scrap before I netted it. A shade under two pounds was my guess at its weight as I slipped it back into the water. Like the first fish it was in fin perfect condition.

Any thoughts that I had cracked it and more fish would now come my way were rudely disabused and the only action was the inevitable raucous fights between the coots who had brought their never ending dispute to the small island to my right. Time for a break so I sat on a bench and ate a sandwich while taking in the view. Mistle thrushes were busy on the other bank while chiff chaffs, blackbirds and others kept up a chorus which made for a soothing soundtrack to the day.

Fed and watered, it was back to the casting for me. In another change, I took off the black daiwl bach, replacing it with an epoxy buzzer. If my retrieve had been slow before I now slowed down to a barely imperceptible recovery. Inches were gradually drawn in but only to keep in contact with the flies, not to make them move. Buzzer fishing is something I do but can't say that I find especially enjoyable.

Time ticked by with each cast taking forever to be fished out. Finally my line tightened and the third trout of the session put up a hell of a scrap but was enveloped in the meshes of my net in the end. Another nice rainbow with a full complement of appendages. It is impossible to fault the quality of the trout in The Grange, each one was a superb example of the species.

An hour more of casting and slowly retrieving went unrewarded. Somehow I sensed the fish were not going to come back on anytime soon and that it was time to shorten the road home. Packing up, I bid adieu to my doggy companion. Fishing over, it was time to motor back west but this time I took a different route so I could stop off in Carrickmacross to buy some maggots. The shop there closes at 6pm so I made it in time to purchase a pint of red for use later in the week. I am always thinking about maggots these days! From there I threaded my way across Cavan and Longford where I picked up the N5 and the steady cruise home. As you will have gathered by now, these long journeys home are a time for reflection on the day's events.

What is it they say, "a change is as good as a rest." Today had been a change all right, just about as different from my normal angling as it is possible to find in this country. In truth, when I happened upon Grange Trout Fishery the notion of doing something so different was as big an attraction as ticking off another county. This year has been a slow burner for me with very little angling so far due to work and then Covid.

The long journey and day casting for trout was a tonic, an immersion in another world away from the pressures of modern life. To say I loved every minute of it is not far from the truth. I had fretted and worried for so long about finding a nice place to fish in Louth that a sense of relief draped over me as the little black Renault and I trundled homewards that evening, the sun lowering in a sky of pink and gold.

So Louth had been completed now. It almost felt like an anti-climax after I had been putting this one off for so long. Like all proficient procrastinators I can justify this tardiness to myself with a range of half-baked excuses. In truth, I wanted to find somewhere to fish that I could have some confidence in. I knew as soon as I found the Grange Fishery on their FB page that it was somewhere I could have a chance on. In the past, I could happily spend a whole day on a small stocked pond like the grange but three or four hours is plenty for me these days.

I don't know why that is to be honest, maybe the wide open spaces of the western loughs have changed me. All I know is that I had a hugely enjoyable session and landed some lovely trout. What more could anyone ask for?

Here is the pattern for that damsel nymph:

Hook—A size 8 long shank such as the Kamasan B830.

Silk—any colour, I doubt if it makes a difference. Black or brown are grand.

Eyes—Two beads from a sink plug chain whipped on to the top of the hook shank just back from the eye. A drop of glue helps to keep them in place. You can use other weighted eyes as you see fit or even go for a goldhead version that won't sink so deep.

Tail—Olive Marabou, not too long. A couple of strands of pearl flash on each side are a nice addition.

Body—Dark olive fritz for two thirds of the body then light green fritz up to the eyes.

I have tried adding hackles and wing buds to this fly but they made no appreciable difference. Rainbows love this one and can often nip at the fly during the retrieve before a solid hook up. I use the same fly on the loughs for wild browns early in the season fished off a sinking line.

Chapter 21
Down

County number 21

Friday, 6th May 2022

"Where the mountains of Mourne sweep down to the sea"

This was to be one of the big ones, a long and arduous road trip clear across the country from the stormy Atlantic to the Irish Sea. For the uninitiated, county Down lies in Northern Ireland and stretches from the city of Belfast in the north to the border with the Republic in the south. The Irish Sea wraps itself around the rock girt eastern shore while county Armagh kisses its western flank. An area with a rich and often turbulent history, it encompasses just about every type of scenery from industrial wasteland through carefully tended productive farmlands to salty inlets and dramatic coasts.

Country mansions, terraced houses and old farm steadings dot the landscape while the towns of Newry, Crossmaglen and Warrenpoint have their names etched deep on the tablet of the troubles of previous centuries. Of course there is also angling, indeed quite a wide range of it but it was the Newry canal that was tempting me with the prospect of big bags of roach a distinct possibility. There are various sections of this extensive canal system, some of which fish better at certain times of the year as the shoals of roach migrate. I studied the available information and decided the Newry Ship Canal might be my best bet, but I'll confess I could be wildly wrong in my assumptions.

There have been times when I have questioned the sanity of trying to catch a fish in each Irish county. This introspection usually occurs when I am in the throws of planning the longer trips and the reasons are not hard to find. Driving an old car across the country to try and catch (usually small) fish which I return to the water does smack of a certain low level of insanity. For me, a degree of sheer bloody-mindedness plays its part but beyond that I enjoy the challenge and new experiences.

Already I have a wealth of fond memories of the places I have fished on this journey which makes all the effort and expense seem worthwhile. I know it is not everyone's cup of tea but fishing somewhere new to me is such an interesting experience what with each different venue, meeting new people and trying to figure out what will work in a short session. For me there is an intellectual stimulation which is quite addictive, an angling version of doing crosswords I suppose.

For fishing north of the border I required a DAERA rod licence (£5) and a DAERA permit (£17.50 because I am over 60 years old). When I purchased the licence and permit back in January I also bought the Loughs Agency Extension for the princely sum of £1. That final £1 was very important as the ship canal lies in one of the Loughs Agency areas. The canals around Newry are very popular and as such closely policed so I was fully expecting to be asked to produce my licence and permit by the powers that be. I'll admit I find the whole permit system in the north a bit weird and think it could be streamlined but in the end there is a lot of very reasonably priced angling in the 6 counties.

I love the sheer variety of different angling experiences you can enjoy in such close proximity of each other. From what I can gather, many UK and European coarse anglers come to Northern Ireland each year, attracted initially by the vibrant competition scene. Long may that continue, the skills and openness to new ideas these anglers bring is always welcome.

The Newry Canal was opened 'way back in 1742 and closed to commercial traffic only in 1976. The idea was it would link Newry and the hinterland of southern Ulster to the sea, thus boosting trade and in particular the shipping of coal from the county Tyrone pits. I am guessing it must have worked before it stayed open for so long. Those coal mines were worked out long ago, the last one closing in the early 1970s but by then traffic on the canal was virtually non-existent and large sections had fallen into serious disrepair.

The Newry Ship Canal where I planned to fish is the stretch which runs roughly south from Newry town centre to the Victoria locks near the village of Omeath where it reaches the sea. Much wider than most other Irish canals, the Ship Canal must have been quite a sight in its heyday with masted ships bustling to and fro. Only about 3 miles long, there is an impressive set of locks at the sea end but the rest is pretty straight, wide and level.

According to my research roach, rudd, bream and perch all thrive in this canal as well as some excellent pike, so many fish indeed that the canal has been the venue for international competitions before now. In the past, there had been some development work carried out in the shape of angling stands. This was music to my ears as I do love a nice comfortable stand when I am coarse fishing.

The well worn road to Newry was travelled once more with a stop off in Carrickmacross for some bait. I had timed my journey to coincide with the tackle shop opening and that calculation worked out pretty accurately with me pulling up outside the front door of Anglers Choice a scant 10 minutes after they began business for the day at 9am. It was no harm to stop and stretch my legs anyway as I get tired on these trips and stiffen up when behind the wheel for more than a couple of hours. These jaunts just serve to highlight my age, as if I needed any reminding!

Even ten years ago a twelve hour stint behind the wheel was nothing to me but I am more fragile now, muscles tighten and joints seize up all too quickly. Then there are the toilet stops of course! None of us fully appreciate our health until it is compromised, I know I didn't. Aches and pains are now my everyday lot but I am lucky enough to still get around and go fishing when I want. I bought the maggots and some hooks as I was running low on my favourite barbless 12's and 14's.

Back behind the wheel there was some jinking around small roads followed by a short section of motorway before picking up the straight road to Omeath and the canal. Then it was just a case of finding somewhere to park. Nothing in this world is every perfect (except for Debbie Harry circa 1978 of course) and the issue when fishing the Newry ship canal is where to leave the car. A couple of small parking bays on the side of the exceptionally busy main road soon fill up with anglers cars some days and after that it is difficult to find a safe place to park up. Once you have parked up you find there are a number of those fishing stands and these provide lovely pegs for your session.

On this particular day though, there was plenty of space for me and I picked a parking bay which had some battered and rusty signs indicating angling stands almost directly across the road. Fishing here is not quiet, the road is only a few feet behind you so there is a constant roar of cars, lorries and buses in your ears. Two trips across the highway saw me deposit my gear on a stand and I began to tackle up. Would there be fish to keep me busy and forgot about the noise?

A lovely soft day of warmth and light winds meant I could dispense with my waterproof coat for a change. My randomly chosen wooden peg complete with stone seat was spacious and comfortable, the only downside being a fine metal wire mesh which had been nailed on to the timber was in terrible condition and snagged anything that came close to it. This is a common problem on timber stands from what I can see. To make them safer a fine metal mesh is usually nailed on to the flat surface but it soon breaks away and becomes a magnet for the anglers line. With my gear safely deposited on the stand, I took in my surroundings.

Unfortunately we seem to have had anglers who are litter louts fishing here as there were piles of empty beer tins and packaging strewn around. I picked up a few bits and took them home with me in a poly bag but there was far too much for me to clear it all. I really do not understand why anglers chuck litter around. Surely they come fishing to enjoy the great outdoors so why on earth would they pollute their surroundings like this?

As I am only allowed to use one rod here in the north I initially set up with my old 13 foot ABU float rod. I love this old rod with is slightly bashed standoff rings, faded brown blanks and pitted cork handle. Bought dirt cheap on eBay it was supposed to be a 'starter rod', one to see me through my first season's coarse fishing before I bought a new and better model. Instead I have stuck with the heavy carbon rod and thoroughly enjoy using it. Why change just for the sake of it? These old rods and reels of mine are like old friends, we have been through so much together.

While I fully accept these are just inanimate objects, they hold a level of emotional connection to me. The smooth little Okuma fixed spool I put on was filled with 4 pound nylon which I hoped would be sufficiently robust for the silvers. Another reel filled with 6 pound line was buried in the box somewhere if required and in case of desperation the 12 feeder rod had come along for the ride too. Realistically I was not expecting to hook anything big so the fairly light lines should be just fine. Plumbing up, I found there was 13 feet of water in front of me and it was fairly level from about a rod length out. Keeping it simple I rigged a medium sized crystal waggler with a fine insert tip.

Washing line shotting and a 4 pound double strength tippet with a size 18 hook seemed to be a logical starting point. Red maggot was my bait for today and the painful business of hooking them on the small hook was just as frustrating as ever. Specsavers could make a brilliant ad featuring me trying to impale a wriggling maggot.

Despite having groundbait with me, I felt loose feeding might be a better option so I began to trickle in some maggots, feeding a couple of rod lengths out. Early on I missed a tentative bite when the float very slowly slid under but apart from that it was quiet. I didn't really mind, after the long drive it takes me time to adjust and unwind so I was happy to faff about getting everything to hand and taking in my surroundings on this fine spring morning.

The traffic on the far side on the canal could be seen snaking along that road and a heron perched just a few yards away. The colours of the fields, the soft greyness of the high clouds on a duck egg blue background, it was lovely just to be breathing fresh air again. I even forgot about the traffic behind me, isn't it funny how adaptable we humans can be?

An hour or so had passed and I had yet to hook a fish. This lack of action did not greatly surprise or worry me as this is a large body of water was largely featureless from what I could make out. Shoals of fish were in all probability moving around so just getting a few in front of me was the challenge. In the end, I decided to feed and fish a little further out. I can't explain why but I still did not fancy groundbaiting so the catapult was in use firing small numbers of maggots grouped around the float as best I could.

Only the third cast at three rod lengths resulted in a nervous tremor of the float and the strike brought me a small roach. Another roach of similar proportions and a minuscule perch quickly followed then it went quiet again. That was OK with me, I had my fish from co. Down so I could relax even further now.

The bites when they came were all of the same ilk, nervous, mousy little affairs with the float trembling more than diving. I decided on changing the shotting slightly to move the small shot near to the hook. I also changed to a slightly bigger size 16 while at it. My idea was to try and get more positive bites than I had been getting up to now. I had started out impaling one maggot on the size 18 hook but now switched to using two maggots and thought this was more successful. Could it be that the fish here were more selective given the pressure they are under from the competitions?

Maybe twenty quiet minutes passed before the float bobbed a little and I had another roach on the end. The roach/perch mix continued for a few minutes then stopped, a similar pattern as before. My thoughts were the fish were moving and I had the option of ground baiting or switching to the feeder. As I was mulling this over the float disappeared and a trout jumped a couple of yards away. It turned out these events were connected—by my line!

Despite my tardiness, the fish was hooked well and it dashed around as trout do. It was not a big trout but it was a handsome fish once in my hand. I found it somewhat incongruous catching a trout on a float rod, like I was cheating somehow. The trout I am sure did not gives a fiddlers what he fell for, so it just goes to show how conditioned we anglers are about methods.

Another quiet spell ensued then the roach appeared again but now the bites were incredibly hard to spot. Sometimes I struck and there was nothing there while other identical vibrations on the float yielded a small fish. A better angler than I would no doubt have figured out a way to improve their ratio of hook ups but I was enjoying myself as it was so persevered with my rig as it was for a while longer. A different mentality pervades my coarse fishing versus my trout angling.

With the fly rod, I am constantly fretting about fly choice or leader set up or depth or speed of retrieve or any of a dozen more variables. Not so when fishing float or leger, instead I sort of drift along making small alterations and hope the fish will respond rather than me making big changes. I am the first to accept this lethargy is not conducive to improving my catch rate but for me just sitting watching the float is pleasure enough most days.

My game angling pals assume some form of mental infirmity is behind my conversion to bobbing for roach but I like to kid myself that I have reached a zen level of angling where the tiny details of my time by the water are the sources of my deep enjoyment. Bulging bags of fish, trophy sized lunkers or winning competitions don't 'do it' for me these days.

In the end, I opted to try the feeder just for a change. My uneasy relationship with feeders continues and I know that I need to work harder on learning the intricacies of the code if I am to regularly catch more fish on it. Some days I haul out fish with the feeder rod but more often it sits there like an old lover while I canoodle with my new fancy, the float rod.

Breaking down the float rod and setting up a feeder only took a few minutes and I fished a maggot feeder at thirty yards for the last hour. Initial hope soon faded though and for the 60 or so minutes I failed to register even a single bite. Now that could simply have been due to the fish swimming off somewhere else just as much to my ineptitude. Faced with the long journey home I decided to pack up early to beat the horrendous traffic around Newry/Dundalk/Ardee, the purpose of my visit fulfilled. Ten small roach, three very, very small perch and that single brown trout made up the total of my catch.

In truth, like many of my '32' trips it was not much to show for such a long day but I was happy enough. The weather had been kind and I learned a bit more, fished somewhere new and passed another day on this earth in peace and safety (unlike so many others these days).

The end of a fishing session is always a melancholy part of the day. I'm usually left with the nagging question "should I stay on for a while longer?" When coarse fishing I follow a set method of taking down the tackle. I break down one set at a time, cutting off the end tackle and putting that in the bucket for now, taking the reel off and putting it safely in the seatbox then breaking down the rod and slipping the sections into first the rod bag and then the quiver. By adopting the same routine every time, I hope to remember everything and not leave some part of the set up behind me when I leave.

Should I have used ground bait? The answer is almost certainly 'yes' but when I started to fish I felt loose feeding maggots was somehow going to be more attractive to the fish. There is no rational reasoning for this supposition, no great depth of experience to base the approach on. I simply didn't fancy ground bait would do much good. Thinking about this I can see it is part of a bigger issue for me, a lack of faith that ground baits in general are over rated.

I am wary of these sort of ideas which come to me sometimes, proof is hard to come by so I am left with gut feeling and my own gut feelings have proved to be woefully inaccurate over my lifetime. Maybe I just need to experiment more with different ground baits until I grow more confident in them.

My choice of venue might seem strange, given the wide range of possible options open to me across county Down. Wild mountain loughs, turbulent sea trout rivers rushing off the mountains of Mourne, stocked trout fisheries stuffed with rainbow trout—I could have tried any of those and more besides. It is a reflection on my growing confidence with the coarse gear that I plumped for the ship canal ahead of the others, I honestly believed I would have a good chance of a fish there and I was vindicated in my choice.

It is a real pity I live so far from here, so much fishing is just waiting to be sampled in this complex and varied county but the trip is long and increasingly expensive for me. If you do every find yourself in a position to fish not just in county Down but anywhere in Northern Ireland, I'd really encourage you to give it a try. There are so many lovely venues and such a wide choice of angling options.

With 21 counties now completed, it feels like I need a good 'push' to make it to the finishing line. Louth earlier this week and now Down have been long days and that is going to be the same for all the remaining counties yet to be fished. Firm plans in terms of where to fish have been made it now a case of finding the time to fit them all in. It is hard to know what I enjoy most about this project, the planning, travel or the actual fishing.

Each element is a joy for me, taking me physically or mentally to new places. If someone had suggested to me a couple of years ago that I would thoroughly enjoy a session fishing maggots for roach on a canal in Northern Ireland, I'd have thought them quite mad. Yet there I was, loving every minute of watching my float three rods lengths out in the grey waters of a disused canal. Maybe this old dog can learn some new tricks after all.

Chapter 22
Wexford

County number 22

Tuesday, 10th May 2022

Ah, the sunny south east. Wexford both intrigued and vexed me in equal proportions for a long time. Not that there is anything wrong with Wexford, far from it, I think it sounds like a lovely place to live. It is one of the furthest away counties and one which I have never been in before, so once again I knew absolutely nothing about the angling there. This '32' project is making me fish outside of my comfort zone in many ways and I am getting used to setting off for distant places with only the merest knowledge of where I'm going and what I am doing. The only fishing I was even vaguely aware of was some beach fishing for bass that was discussed in an old book I own. Oh, and the boats which head out to the marks around the Tusker rocks for pollack swimming around on the rough ground out there. Neither really appealed to me so I started tapping the keys to see what else was going on down in the sunny south east with rod and line.

What was there for a visiting angler then? Wexford harbour is a large expanse of salt water which appeared to be home to some flats and a few bass but this was all a bit too sketchy for me. The fish could be anywhere and with limited time and no local knowledge it could prove to be a frustrating and fishless journey. Sea angling seemed to be a bit of a dead end to me. Then I happened upon a commercial coarse fishery which looked altogether more promising. Oaklands Lake, which is near to the town of New Ross sounded very well run and full of fish. I figured a day on a coarse lake would be interesting as I have never fished a commercial coarse lake before in my life.

By way of preparation, I watched a few videos on fishing commercials in England where this type of angling is hugely popular. I waded through lots of talk about crucians and F1's, neither of which are present in Ireland as far as I know but there was a lot to learn about carp which was entertaining as well as instructive. My basic grounding in coarse fishing seemed to be adequate for the task ahead.

I am used to turning up on the edge of a wild lough or canal and just doing my own thing but a commercial lake would have its own rules so this would be new to me. Their website stated that sessions at Oaklands lasted from 9am to 7pm, meaning this would be another very early start and late finish for me if I was to avail of a full day. You see it is a four-and-a-half hour drive from Castlebar to New Ross, not a trip to be undertaken lightly when I had a full day of fishing as well. Various other rules around what bait you could and couldn't use plus some other sensible stuff like only fishing from the marked pegs did not appear to be too intrusive so I packed a load of coarse gear in the back of the car and a pint of maggots from the bowels of the bait 'fridge.

Our road system in Ireland is none to helpful when driving from the north west to the south east as I would be doing. The motorways and main roads radiate out from Dublin on the east coast like the spokes of a wheel. That makes sense as it links the other cities like Waterford, Cork, Limerick, Galway and Sligo but also means journeys across this flow require many diversions. Our Dublin-centric planning has a lot to answer for!

A 4.30 am rise is not something that worries me, for years that was my normal start to the working day and a long spell behind the wheel as I crossed the country was fairly common too. I have worked in Donegal, Belfast, Dublin and south Kildare at various times and all of these required early starts and long drives. While I set an alarm, it is rare for me not to awake before it, I'm so used to getting up at that ungodly hour. Luckily I am a morning person, a fresh start to the day suits me down to the ground.

The poor old car was packed to bursting point with tackle. A quiver full of rods, tackle boxes, bags, net and a plethora of lesser gear were stuffed ignominiously into the back of the black Renault, the whole providing a vista of utter disorganisation to the uninitiated. Indeed, it didn't look much better to me and it was I who had done the packing. Due to the small size of the boot in this car the tackle spills over on to the back seat.

Even still, the chances of me remembering everything were not good. As soon as I turned the engine on I could hear there was a problem, a very noisy exhaust! It would have to last today so I set off with a throbbing rumble emanating from the rear of the car. A job for this weekend no doubt. Oh the joys of owning an old car.

As I drove south I mulled over the coming day. The lake was stocked with bream, rudd, roach, tench and carp. Yes, carp! It is unusual to see these fish here in Ireland so I pondered whether to set up one rod specifically to try and tempt one. They are a big, powerful fish but like the pike, I find little attraction if fishing just for them. Is that odd? I mean most anglers want to catch big fish but I lack that need in my make up.

For me, perhaps setting up a feeder rod set up for carp and the float rod for all other species was as much as I was prepared to try. I know very little about catching carp, to date it is a branch of the sport which has not appealed to me. Three days living in a tent waiting for a run does not sound too great to me but if one happened along today I would be damn glad to see it.

Weather wise it is normally much better in Wexford than we get in Mayo. Sheltered away from the Atlantic, they enjoy more sunshine and less battering in the wind and rain. It was breezy when I left Mayo with low clouds scudding across the sky and sudden downpours of rain. By Athlone, the weather had dried up and as I pressed on south the sun came out and it got very warm despite the strong wind. Almost exactly four hours after pulling out of the driveway I turned into the car park outside Oaklands and shut off the embarrassingly noisy engine.

The tackle shop on site is crammed with a plethora of angling goodies but I am not tempted and instead chat with the owner and one of the staff. I explain my reason for being there today and assure me the lake is stuffed with fish and I will surely catch some today. Fees paid, net dipped in disinfectant, it was time to select a peg. With only a couple of other anglers there, I had free range and decided on peg 7 which was about fifty yards along from the shop. Would it be lucky for me?

A small island sat a few yards out from the bank provided a nice view. Some ducks quaked and flustered around as I set up on the roomy stand. Mixing some brown crumb, Sensas Lake, a little hemp, a small tin of corn and some dead maggots, I rolled six small balls and set them aside. Next I fed a swim one-and-a-half rod lengths out with a scattering of maggots and a couple of small balls of groundbait then set up the 12 foot feeder rod. Would the six pound line on the old Okuma reel be strong enough if a carp happened along? A 20 gram cage feeder packed with groundbait plopped into the green water a few yards out and I was fishing at last.

As I was putting the float rod together I missed a hard knock on the feeder, a very encouraging sign indeed! Setting the green waggler at slightly over the nine feet I had plumbed, I baited up a size 12 barbless hook (as per the rules) with four maggots then settled down. The wind was blowing from right to left and a strong sun beat down from above. It felt really good just being here, experiencing something new. Of course I badly wanted to catch something but a great sense of relaxation flowed over me as I sat there watching the red tip of my float.

Here is the attraction of coarse fishing for me. It looks to the uninitiated as if I am doing nothing but in fact I am thinking all the time while at the same time watching what is happening around me. Immersion in the detail of the day distracts me from any other thoughts and steals me a way to an altogether quieter, more serene place. Of course I enjoy actually catching fish, what angler doesn't? It is the whole experience that I enjoy though, every aspect has an attraction for me, the sights and sounds, the smells and feelings of the day just make me happy. It is strange how I arrived at this branch of the sport so late in life and from the obtuse angle of my 32 project. Without that inspiration I would never have considered the world of maggots and roach, let alone find myself sitting beside a commercial pond in Wexford.

If I was to detail all the fish I caught, we would be here for a long time so I will just go over some of the highlights. Right from the off skimmers of up to a pound or so were constantly biting, coming to both float and feeder. Strong gusts of wind swept up the lake so I had the float shotted well down and bites were relatively easy to see. The fisheries cat kept me company as I reeled in fish after fish.

These skimmers were in lovely condition and not nearly as slimy as most snotties are. That being said, catching a few of them inevitably meant absolutely everything received a coating of goo. The fishing was steady and I rarely went more than a few minutes before the tip of the feeder rod pulled over or the float disappeared. About an hour in the float dipped and I lifted into a solid fish which ran off to my right and took a bit of battling to get back in front of me. Although it didn't show it was obviously a carp, the bend in the old rod suggesting it was no monster but still a decent fish.

The carp stayed deep and put up a dogged fight but I eventually it rolled on top and I slid it into the net, a beautiful fish of about six pounds. As near as I can recall this was my first carp since 2008 when I caught some in the UK. It was a bit of a tight fit getting the carp into my meagre net so it might be time for me to think about investing in a larger model, it would be handy for my tench fishing too. There is always something for us anglers to buy, isn't there?

Some tiny rudd and perch kept the count ticking over then a shoal of roach camped in the swim for a while, sitting in mid water so the bites were mainly seen as the float lying flat instead of cocking. A second carp, maybe a pound lighter than the first one came along and fought hard under the beaming sun before sliding into the waiting meshes. My companion the cat, who had been sunning itself next to me, pounced on a small roach which came off the hook as I swung it in, a trick I am sure it has performed many times before.

All the time I was trickling maggots and small balls of groundbait into the swim. Just knowing there are a lot of fish in front of you is lovely feeling for any fisherman and here at Oaklands there are plenty swimming around. The fishing here had such a different 'feel' to it compared to the wild loughs of Leitrim or Roscommon. It is very hard to describe this exactly but maybe just knowing the fish are there makes a big difference.

Next were three quick hybrids, scrappy little fellows. My float quivered and on striking found myself fast to a lovely rudd which fallen for the maggots. I do love a nice rudd and this one was a beauty of well over a pound in weight. More skimmers and lots of missed bite kept me busy then a late bream made up the balance of the catch. I kept count and during less than three hours I had landed 17 skimmers, 11 roach, 3 rudd, 3 hybrids, 2 carp, 1 bream and a perch (38 fish in total).

I'll confess I fished very lazily and with more effort I think I could have doubled that number. The float accounted for most of the catch, including both carp. If I had made some adjustments to the feeder set up, I am convinced it would have caught more fish but I didn't bother. With fish coming steadily to the float, the poor old feeder was left to its own devices, something I do far too often out of sheer laziness. As it was I just enjoyed the fishing and the peace of the fishery. Being outdoors on a warm summers day and steadily catching a few fish was such an enjoyable experience for me.

Maybe it is because I am getting more practice but I am finding unhooking easier and quicker than I did before. Keeping the line tight was a major step in the right direction for me but I am now quick to slide the disgorger in and twist the hook out without harming the fish. Locating the cheap plastic disgorger in a little pocket on my waistcoat has proved to be a good move and saves me from hunting around for it like I had been doing.

The sum total of all the little details of how I fish are gradually making me a slightly better coarse angler but I still have so far to go. Other fishers catch much more than I do, especially the lads using the pole. I wish I could say I fancy trying the pole but I am afraid it holds zero attraction for me. That it is a super-efficient method of catching fish is beyond question but it is just to mechanical for my liking. Anyway, I have more than enough gear as it is without adding any more.

Oaklands is a lovely fishery with high stocks of quality fish in a well maintained setting. There is an impressive tackle shop on site and all the facilities you could possibly ask for. It is a pity this fishery is so far away from where I live, I would love to have somewhere like it closer to me. We humans are never happy, are we!

On the way down, I had eaten most of my sandwiches but had saved one for lunch and decided to eat it before packing up. Reaching down into the plastic box a movement caught my eye, a bloody spider was in there with my last egg sambo! I am fascinated by most small critters but not spiders, they give me the creeps. Both sandwich and spider were unceremoniously flung into the bushes and I went hungry for the remainder of the day.

All good things must end so at 1pm I packed up the gear and headed back to the car. It sounds odd to drive all that distance only to pack up early even when the fish a biting but there was method in my madness. Another angler was fishing a few pegs down from me and we chatted as I headed for the car. He was a regular and came to target carp. With a proper seat, all the equipment you could possibly think of and even a barrow for transportation he cut a very professional figure despite being a pleasure angler like myself.

I try to be as minimalist as possible but I find lugging everything on my shoulders to be the most tedious part of my coarse fishing. If I had money, I could easily spend a lot on similar gear but for now at least I will bumble on with my old kit. Justification for any additional expenditure on fishing tackle is hard for me. I already have a ton of gear, most of which rarely gets used these days so to add even more feels like a stupid waste of scarce resources. On the other hand, I am not getting any younger so a smallish barrow could be a good move for me in the future. I could have stayed and enjoyed a lovely afternoon at Oaklands, indeed that was very tempting, but I had another plan.

Wexford can now be emphatically crossed off the list. The long drive had been worth it in the end and my first ever session on a commercial coarse fishery had been hugely enjoyable. I know that if this type of fishing was all that was available to me I would quickly tire of it but for a change it was a wonderful way to spend some time catching different species. What I had not been prepared for was the very pretty scenery in the south east. Rolling hills, sleepy villages, clear blue skies—it had an awful lot to offer a visitor.

Chapter 23
Kilkenny

County number 23

Tuesday, 10th May 2022

So there I was in New Ross, Co. Wexford on a fine spring day having caught a load of fish at Oaklands. It was 1pm and I had options to consider. I could spend the remainder of the afternoon fishing there (very tempting), drive back to Mayo and get home at a decent time for a change or I could try to fit in another county. From all my previous research, I knew where I could fish in co. Kilkenny which was not too far from where I was sitting in the warm sunshine. I had tried to squeeze in two counties in one day before but had not worked out, would today be any different? Hell, I'll go for it. Swiftly packing up I said my goodbyes to the staff at Oaklands, rammed everything into the car and headed off, picking my way through roundabouts which surround New Ross until I found the Kilkenny road.

Kilkenny is a popular city for visitors from around the world and the county is famous in Ireland for their hurling team who play in black and amber stripes. The city used to be a big brewing centre but that industry has closed down since the work was transferred to Dublin. Strangely, I had never been to Kilkenny before, somehow my wanderings had never led me to the Marble City. Back in 2017 I almost went there to look at a machine the company I was working for at the time was thinking on buying but they pulled out of the deal at the last minute so I never made it to Kilkenny. On this occasion, I was not going to visit the city itself but it was time to find out what the county had to offer a game angler.

One venue seemed to stand out above all others, the river Nore. Formerly one of the great salmon rivers of Ireland it is now better known for its trout angling. There is a lot of water available to fish on day tickets but I figured the club waters at Thomastown might be my best bet. The timing this trip was a bit too early to coincide with the famed hatches of Blue Winged Olives, June and July normally being good months for these small upwinged flies that the trout love so much. The river also supports a wide range of other trout food so I was hoping there might still be a few fish around.

My target species this would once again be brown trout. Further downstream the Nore is a first class coarse fishery but the runs and pools around the city are perfect trout water. The famous Mount Juliet stretch is just up river from Thomastown but I would be fishing the local club water, an altogether cheaper option! There could well be a few dace or roach in the stretch I planned to fish and either of those species on the fly would be welcome too. River fishing for wild brownies was where I started my angling so this was going to be a bit of a trip down memory lane for me.

The road from New Ross to Thomastown wound through lovely scenery and I arrived in the pretty village around 2pm. My first job was to buy a permit for the afternoon. A couple of outlets in the village sell them and I rocked up to Treaceys Hardware shop, not far from the river. For old codgers like me, a country hardware shop is a wonderful place full of interesting items arranged in a glorious muddle. I could have contentedly spend hours searching through the tools, materials and oddities in these shops. So much more satisfying than perfectly ordered soulless superstores in retail estates on the edge of every town and city.

Once in there I was furnished with a permit and pointed in the direction of the hurling park where I could park in safety and fish for three miles downstream. Leaving the shop I dawdled on the bridge high above the sparkling water for a while, taking in the views of the old buildings of the village on one side with the huge bulk of the church in the distance and mature trees on the other. I could have spent longer just gazing over the parapet watching the ducks and swallows go about their business. It occurred to me how much of my life I must have wasted gawking from bridge parapets. There is always so much to see (or is that just me being odd again).

The engine clattered into life and I picked my way along tree lined streets, through a council estate and down a rough track to a voluminous gravel car park next to an impeccably maintained GAA pitch. God bless Kilkenny hurling! A couple of dog walkers said hello and we exchanged pleasantries as you do. A big man sporting a fine example of a farmer's tan bid me good luck.

The red-haired young mum with boisterous child and yappy terrier in tow hoped I would catch my dinner. We take these minor interactions all too casually here in Ireland, that people want to make the effort to communicate is something to be treasured. Having lived in London where nobody ever made the effort to talk to a stranger I appreciate the Irish need to say something to people they have never met.

The Nore here is a wide river which reminded me of the Aberdeenshire Don where I learned to fish all those years ago. Low, clear water and a strong upstream wind under bright sunshine were far from ideal conditions but I've caught trout in similar conditions before so I togged up in a reasonably confident state of mind. Climbing over a stile a narrow path took me past the pitches and down to the edge of the water where the Nore flowed lazily through a big, wide pool.

Here the bank was high, affording me the ability to peer into the clear water and look for signs of life. Thank God I had remembered to bring my sunglasses, they made life much easier on a day of glaring sunshine reflecting off the water. It quickly became apparent the river was stuffed full of fish, I could see them in the crystal water holding near the bottom. At first, I thought they were roach or dace but no, the fish I saw were definitely brown trout. I had not expected to see so many fish and I watched them for a while, fascinated by the way they moved around then settled in one spot for a while. It didn't look to me like these fish were feeding.

My venerable five weight Orvis matched with a nice little Pflueger reel and a floating line is my preferred set up for this style of fishing, it has served me well for many seasons now. Very much an 'all-round' sort of rod it does most things well enough without excelling in any particular code. A pair of weighted nymphs on a fine leader appeared to make a logical starting point so I tied on a size 12 Pheasant tail and a size 14 Hare's Ear Goldhead. A strong upstream wind making it hard to be precise with my casts but I stuck at it. Fishing down firstly the pool and then a long slow run failed to meet with any success so I swapped my nymphs for a pair of partridge hackled spiders and fished down a faster run but again, without so much as a pull.

The river felt lifeless with no signs of fly life and I was beginning to think this had been a step too far for me. I had arrived too late for any lunchtime activity and too early for the evening rise. Changing flies again I put a black spider on the dropper and a beaded PT nymph on the tail before moving a bit further down the river. This changing of flies is about normal for me when fishing on rivers. My own experience has taught me that just flogging away with the same flies all day is rarely the right approach so I give each fly as spell on the leader and if there is no response to it I take it off and tie on something different.

So strong was the wind that it lifted the cap off my head at one point and I was lucky to retrieve it before the river washed it away. A good few of my hats have disappeared into the water never to be seen again over the years. Sunglasses too have met a watery end in the past and that is why I have never invested in particularly expensive sun specs. I fished on bare-headed, reddening as the afternoon wore on. I moved further downstream to where a fast run looked inviting.

I fished the creases methodically, changing angles to suit the flows and mending the line frequently to control the speed and depth of the flies. No stir. Not so much as a pluck from a small lad. Time for another change of flies and on went an Olive partridge spider and a Greenwells, both of them tied on little size 16 hooks.

More wading, only knee deep but on a slippery bottom so I used my staff for support. With each step downstream, I tried 3 or four casts, still altering the angles and length as I sought to fish the flies at varying depths and speeds. This was a lovely stretch of river to fish with lots of likely lies to cover. Still no joy so I went back to the black spider/PT nymph. Cattle were in the river below me but they nosily left the water as I approached, eyeing my suspiciously as I entered the next run and slithered into knee deep water.

When confronted with tough conditions, I like to take my time and observe what is happening around me, tune in to the river if you like. The cool water swirled around my legs as I leaned on my wading stick, the Orvis in my hand. My rod and my staff. Who knows how long I stood there silently observing the watery world, melding with the ancient river, becoming part of her.

There! Under the far bank in a back eddy I saw a rise. Almost a sense of disbelief at first but no, I was sure it was a trout rising. That lie was too far to cast to but perhaps this was the beginning of some action. At the very least, it was hugely encouraging to see a fish on the surface. Minutes passed, me still motionless in the streamy water, the cattle lowing on the bank behind me. Another fish rose nearly directly below me but thirty yards away, quickly followed by another this time within casting distance. Knots and hooks checked, I started to cast, my concentration levels at their highest.

Cast and mend, cast and mend. Judging the different flows between me and where the fish showed, adjusting my casts as I felt necessary but doing so in an unthinking manner. After all these years, it just comes naturally. A pluck but no solid contact. More fish are rising now and I can see a very small dun on the water, probably a BWO. There is no time to catch one and do a proper identification. I spot a fish rising maybe 15 yards away, slightly down river from where I am standing.

With more line pulled off the reel, I switch the line upstream then lift into an overhead cast. The line alights just where I want it (for a change) and I flick a small mend in the line. Finally a solid pull, some light wriggling at the end of the line and a small trout comes to hand! I breathe a sigh of relief, over an hour had passed before I had eventually landed this small fish but it felt like a triumph in these conditions. It is a gorgeous fish, dark spots on a bronze background and golden belly. The small spider is in the corner of its jaws and is easily flicked out without causing any harm. A photograph, a memory created then it is back into its watery world once again.

When fishing wets like this, I vary the direction of my casts as required, sometimes sweeping them down and across, sometimes flicking them upstream. You might think that I should have switched to the dry fly when the fish started to rise but in my experience these afternoon rises can be over just as fast as they began and I felt the time taken to change to dries and then find the right pattern was too risky. Also, most of the trout I saw on the surface were below me, meaning I would have to come out of the river then re-enter some distance below. That would take time and risk disturbing the fish. So the wets stayed on and did the business for me.

It felt like the years had rolled back and I was fishing the way I used to. Casting to rising fish is an intoxicating pastime and I became utterly absorbed in spotting a rise, making the cast and hooking the fish. Gradually I worked my way down the run, a stand of willows behind me forcing me to be inventive with my casting. Some rolls and even some single handed speys were pressed into action. I loved every minutes of it.

The trout seemed to move around and were not holding station, meaning throwing the flies to the exact spot where I had seen a rise rarely produced a take. Takes were usually positive and because this was a fast stretch of water even a small trout could pull hard. Of course many threw the hook during the fight, especially the ones hooked downstream of where I was wading. I didn't mind, for me the take is the high point of my angling. What is it they say "the tug is the drug," how true that is in my case!

As is often the case the rise did not last long. Fewer and fewer fish showed and the number of naturals in the air reduced from not much to start with to none at all. A couple of trout still rose steadily in a backwater under the far bank so I waded over towards them. Deeper and stronger flowing water barred me from getting too close so I fished for them from about twenty yards, throwing ridiculously big upstream ends to counter the fast flows between me and the fish.

The rise forms suggested they were taking flies off the surface and so a dry fly really should have been used but that was not an option for me given the trout were slightly downsteam of me as well as across a heavy current. I plugged away with my pair of wets and in the end I pricked both of them but failed to hook either. I tipped my cap to them and left them in peace.

Over the course of that hour when I was up to past my knees in the sparkling Nore I lost more trout than I landed. Never the less, by the time the short lived rise had petered out eight gloriously spotted browns had fallen for my flies. None were better than 12 ounces I suppose but that didn't matter a jot to me. Each fish was perfect, beautifully coloured and glowing in the afternoon sun. In the end, it was honours even with roughly the same number of fish on the wee black spider and the PT.

Turning back I waded up river, leaning heavily on my staff. Pushing against the primeval flow I came ashore in the midst of the young cows who mooed loudly with indignation at being disturbed once again. It was 4pm by now and the river which had been pock-marked with rising trout a few minutes ago was deathly quiet once again. There was much more fishable water further downstream but it felt like it was time to go so I wound in and bid the river adieu. Walking back to the car I mused over the afternoon. To be honest it had exceeded my expectations by a long way.

Under the still hot sun I relived the takes, fish landed and fish lost. Thoughts of what I could have done better were tempered by the knowledge I had at least tempted a few fish. Legs heavy and damp with sweat after being encased in waders, over one last stile and then the familiar and very welcome the 'click' of the central locking as I gained the car.

Tackle dismantled and tucked back in the noisy Renault. Flopping into the driver's seat I called home to give an ETA then swung out of the gravel car park on headed for the long road to Mayo. I sweltered in the car as I gradually worked my way home across the midlands. There was heavy traffic around Kilkenny and Athlone but the roads became quieter after Roscommon town. It had been a very long day but I was a happy man. For me, fishing is not about big bags or huge fish, it is the experience of the outdoors, that connection with nature which is the drug I crave. That inner peace a fly fisher feels after a rise is surely one of the great emotions angling supplies us with.

It had been a long day but one I will remember for many years to come. Our short lives are often filled with troubles, real or imagined, so days like this are to be appreciated and enjoyed. Sinking into bed that night I closed my eyes and could hear the soft burbling of the Nore in my mind. I hope I can make it back there again one day.

The Nore at Thomastown is a wonderful piece of river and if you are ever in the area I would urge you to give it a try. In fact, the whole of this area of southern Ireland is a fantastic place for a trout angler to visit. We tend to think of the wilds of the west when to comes to Irish game angling but there is something special about fishing the clear, cool rivers of the south lands. They teem with trout, mainly small ones I'll grant you but there are bigger fish there too.

Chapter 24
Derry

County number 24

Tuesday, 17th May 2022

A week since my last trip and with some free time I am cramming in as many counties as I can now. Another long journey for me to and from this northern county and another chance to cross the border into the UK. I know that political correctness demands that this county is referred to as Derry/Londonderry but I can't be bothered typing that in all the time so Derry it is for the purposes of this post. County Derry stretches all the way from the border with Donegal and Lough Foyle in the west to the shores of Lough Neagh and the river Bann in the east. The hugely popular north coast is home to internationally famous golf courses and miles of beaches for the summer visitors. There is a lot going on in the county these days.

Once again this is a county with a troubled past which stretches back into the mists of time. Murder and mayhem were everyday occurrences in Derry over the centuries but thankfully these days it is a peaceful part of the world and long may that continue. The city of Derry has become a tourist destination and the county boasts some gorgeous countryside.

The main fishery in the county is the mighty river Foyle which meets the sea at the walled city which carries the county name. The salmon fishing which the river was famous for is but a shadow of what it used to be, so instead I searched for somewhere to do some trout fishing. That was when I happened upon an amazing wee lough called Binevenagh.

60 odd million years ago lava from volcanos flowed across what is now Antrim and Derry. The lava cooled and the western extent of that flow was here at the rocky outcrop which is now called Binevenagh. So the rocks I would be walking over were created by volcanic action around the same time that big rock

hit the earth and wiped out the dinosaurs. I find that amazing. The outcrop has been weathered over the years into the rugged shape it is today. This is now an Area of Special Scientific Interest as well as an Area of Outstanding Natural Beauty.

What first caught my attention when researching for this trip was the photo I saw on a website somewhere, a marvellous picture of a small lake perched atop a rocky crag. It seemed like something out of film, you could imagine Indiana Jones up there looking for treasure. Or is it the escarpment from the Tarzan movies. Binevenagh lough sits high on the top of the rocky hill with stunning views out over the northern coast.

Not a natural body of water, this lough was created by damming a small stream before it plunged off the edge and into the valley below. With no naturally occurring fish in there, it is stocked with a few rainbow trout each season and my plan was to try and catch at least one of them. That sounds simple enough, doesn't it?

NI Direct helpfully publish the numbers of fish stocked in each of the loughs they control. In 2021, they put 2,000 rainbows into Binevenagh, 1,000 during February, another 250 in April, 250 in May and a final 500 in August. That may not strike you as a big number but bear in mind this is a small fishery and there can only be limited feeding for the trout so putting in any more is not a good idea. I was working on the assumption that a not dissimilar stock density and timetable would be planned for 2022. I checked at the beginning of May but it looks like the stocking policy has changed.

Only 500 fish had been stocked in February 2022. I had hoped to see a much higher number and considering nearly three months had elapsed since the lough was stocked I was worried there would be no fish in it now. Maybe they did put a few rainbows in early this month, only time would tell. In the event, I blanked on Binevenagh I had a backup plan to try a small commercial fishery at the foot of the hill called Duncrum. It too was stocked with rainbow trout.

Binevenagh is small and I wanted to be able to walk all around it in search of fish so I packed my gear accordingly. An old Hardy 11 footer and some no.6 lines on an even older Leeda LC80 reel would do and a couple of boxes of flies stuffed into my waistcoat. My trusty wading staff and a small net were all that I required. Some more gear could wait in the car if I had to go to 'plan B' and fish for the bigger trout swimming around in Duncrum.

I still enjoy using those old fly reels, even the cheap LC series. They are simple and robust and do anything I ask of them. I have to admit to a healthy distrust of some modern fly reels made of space age materials and as light as a feather in the hand. I need tackle I can drop without breaking!

Another early start for me saw me hit the road at 05.45 am. That clear early morning light as I put the last few bits into the back of the car, the familiar wheezing and clatter as the old engine burst into life and the cool, damp air smelling of groundbait and wet jackets which is so comforting in every fisherman's car.

Through the still slumbering town to the bypass and then the open road, sipping hot coffee from my small green flask, head full of anticipation of the day ahead. The very epitome of optimism is surely an angler heading to fish a new lough. A long road stretched before me but I held my speed in check to reduce fuel consumption. The familiar roadside vistas passed by and I pressed on, heading for Donegal first and then the border.

I used to work in Donegal years ago so the road to Letterkenny was well known to me. From there, I struck north and was soon across the border, through the outskirts of Derry city and on to the A2 for Limavady before turning up the narrow hill road and the climb up to a turn off on to a dirt track. The forestry track was more suited to a Land Rover than an old Renault but after a mile or so of climbing on the rutted gravel the lough suddenly came into view. A campervan was parked up but other than that I was alone up there. Parked up, I shut off the engine, now all of 260 km from home in Mayo.

I knew when I decided to fish here that the exposed nature of the lough meant that in all likelihood the wind was going to be a major factor on the day. As it turned out a gale was blowing towards the dam wall and would make casting a challenge but that would be preferable to flat calm. Having said that I have found over the years that it is possible to catch rainbows when the surface of the lake is like a mirror, brownies are a different story though.

The winds which had blown down our washing line yesterday remained and it would be a physical challenge just to get the flies out to the fish! My normal plan would have been to fish from the dam wall but in this wind that was a non-starter. Anyway, before I started to fish I wanted to have a look around this place.

An ugly plantation of spruce blocked the views to the west of the dam. On an island so denuded of trees, these plantations are an abomination, just tax breaks for the rich. A wild wood featuring some oaks would have been much more appropriate here in the oak leaf county. A short walk from the car park brings you to the edge of the escarpment. The views to the North are breathtaking, simply stunning! I wish my photographs did them justice but they do not. I can only implore you to make time and visit this spot, it will do your heart good. Sightseeing over, it was time to tackle up so I battled back against the wind to the gently rocking car. Thigh boots and a heavy waterproof jacket over a fleece were soon donned and I was ready for the battle.

There is a four fish limit for taking trout from this lough with a minimum size limit of 25.4cm (10 inches in old money). This suggested to me that the stockies were not going to be of huge proportions and given the exposed nature of the lough the chances were that not too many rainbows would over winter. I scaled my leader to match those expectations and had made up 3 fly leaders from five pound nylon. Although I didn't carry a lot of gear with me, I had a range of nylon of different thicknesses to cope with different conditions but the five pound was at least a starting point.

My choice of fly line was dictated by the wind too. Usually I would have started with a floater on a lough like this but in these gusty conditions I opted for a fast glass, the idea being to get down a little and at the same time have a fairly heavy line to combat the wind when casting. Over the course of the day I think that plan was a pretty good one.

When starting to fish a new water, there is always that trepidation regarding what flies to use. Lacking even the merest shred of local knowledge I plumped for three proven rainbow trout patterns, a Montana on the tail, a Silver Invicta in the middle and a Wickhams Fancy on the bob. With the wind whipping up the surface, I commenced operations from the stand in front of the dam.

It soon became apparent the wind was stronger than I had anticipated and just getting a cast out was something of an achievement. On only the third or fourth cast, a small rainbow slashed at the bob fly, missed it completely then made a second attempt and I pricked him without setting the hook. This was hardly surprising what with the huge bow in the fly line but it felt like a blow to rise a fish this early but not land it.

Buoyed by the sight of a fish though I pressed on, fanning casts out as far as I could, dropping the point of the rod into the water for the retrieve and roll casting when the gusts were too strong for conventional overhead casts. No more offers were forthcoming so I changed flies, trying a claret bumble, a deerhair sedge and a viva on the point. Still no joy. I kept casting…

I stuck at this up for the better part of an hour, changing patterns and trying different retrieves but the fish were just not interested. Forsaking the solid footing of the stand I walked up the shore a ways, finding a sheep path through the heather and hissing rushes to the water's edge above a small reed bed. Here a shoulder of rock and bog behind me provided a degree of shelter from the wind. I was only about 150 yards away from the stand where I had been fishing but there was a noticeable reduction in the ferocity of the wind, the gusts were much less powerful and this allowed me to cast a bit further out.

Time for yet another change of flies, this time I put a gold-head daddy on the tail and started casting again, gradually moving to my left a few steps at a time. The edge of the lough was rough with lots of dips and puddles of water, so I had to watch where I was putting my feet. Line which I had retrieved would often snag on the heather or rushes, another joy of fishing wilder waters. I stuck doggedly to my task, experience has honed my ability to just keep fishing despite being faced with what looks like an empty lake.

Another cast, start the retrieve, keep that rod down low. A take! The fish swirled, ran a few yards then it all went sickeningly slack. Check the flies—all OK. Start casting again. You can't let yourself be too disappointed when things are not going your way, just get back into the rhythm once again and concentrate. Some more steps along the rough and soggy bank, the line hissing as it shoots through the rings. The fast glass is a lovely line to fish with, especially in these conditions. It flies though the air and any lack of subtlety on landing is lost in the waves.

More steps, more casts into the void. Suddenly the line goes taught and I lift into a fish once again. Head shaking, this fish moves away from me as I wind the slack line on to the spool. I hate having line lying around when playing a fish, it is just asking for trouble. I could easily stand on it or the line could snag on a root, either spelling disaster. Off he goes at lightening speed, a feature of how rainbows fight.

He dashes away to my left and leaps, then repeats the aerobatics. The hook holds and I play him out in a couple of minutes. Beaten, he slides into my waiting net on his side, a nice rainbow of a bit better than a pound in weight. The freezer is a bit empty right now so I had decided previously if I caught anything today I would bring some fish home. I quickly dispatch the trout and return to my casting.

It goes quiet again so I change the flies on the droppers while making steady progress along the bank to the top of the lake. On go a fiery brown in the middle and a butcher on the bob. Here a reed bed stretches out in to the water and I fish hard around the green reeds, getting one pluck at the flies without making solid contact. Hunger pangs drive me back to the car where I devour a sandwich and drink some water. The calmness inside the car is lovely after the buffeting I am getting outside but I can't sit there all day and so I cut off the leader when I find a wind knot in it. A new leader is soon made up and I tie a size 10 Claret

Murrough on the dropper, one of those with a greenwell head hackle I like so much.

Trudging through the grass and heather into the wind I select a spot to start again. There didn't seem to be much happening at the top end of the lough so I begin close to where I caught the fish earlier. Stopping for something to eat was a good idea and I feel much better with some food inside me. Like a lot of anglers I tend to forget or put off eating while I am fishing. That sounds crazy I know but it is so easy to get so focussed on the fishing everything else is pushed to the back of my mind. Unhooking the tail fly from the keeper ring above the handle I strip off some line and begin casting again.

Only a handful of casts later there is a tweak on the line and I lift into a small trout which is quickly subdued and netted. Another one for the goldhead daddy but this fish is only about ten inches long so I pop him back in the water. Rain starts to fall, not too heavy to begin with but enough to make it feel unpleasant. Starting to edge back to the car and some respite from the elements I hook and quickly lose a fish before another solid take results in a hard fight with a second takeable trout. This one had my Murrough in his scissors. This one too goes in the bag just as the heavens open and cold rain pours down. Sod this, I am off to the car again!

Thirty minutes or so sitting in the car while the rain beats down then I spend a fruitless hour casting in the wind at the dam again. To me that looked like the spot where trout would gather in this wind but of course the fish prove me wrong (again). It feels so good when one of your hunches comes good and you catch a fish but often your instincts just don't produce the goods as expected. That's OK, it's just part of the game. I break down the rod at 3pm and pack up, the long drive home curtailing the day somewhat early. The wind is still as strong as ever.

When winding in my old fly reel was a bit tight and later on inspection at home showed the spindle looks a bit worn. It have greased it again and will try it out next time I am fishing but at well over 40 years old I suspect its days are numbered. I do wonder if some of today's hi tech reels will last so long?

I disrobe at the car, wet and now a bit cold but the heater will soon sort that discomfort out. The old fleece which I keep on the back seat for days like this is most welcome. Back down the gravel track I bump, slithering on the now wet surface. Steamed up windows are wiped so I can see where I'm going and I slip a CD on as I reach the main road, swinging right and pointing south. I decide to take a different way home and head for Enniskillen instead of Letterkenny simply for a change.

When driving through Omagh, I take a wrong turn and ended up on a road I didn't recognise. Heavy traffic and rain didn't help much but I found my way to Enniskillen then got snarled up in more queues of cars there. If you would allow me to build a bypass for only one town on the island, it would be Enniskillen. I am guessing that the need for multiple bridges across the Erne and its backwaters is the reason for avoiding a new road around the town. Unless you hit the town very early or very late there will inevitably be a traffic jam somewhere in the town.

What to make of the day then? Perhaps on a less windy day I would have done better but I thoroughly enjoyed my few hours in co. Derry and am more than happy to have landed three rainbows. The views from the top of the hill, dashing little trout that responded to my flies, the fresh air and solitude made for a memorable day out north of the border. Binevenagh is a lovely spot to spend an hour or two with a fly rod so if you ever find yourself in the area I can highly recommend you try it out.

This has been a good month for my pet project and only eight counties remain to be successfully fished. The coming weeks look very busy for me so I fear another hiatus is on the cards. Pity, I am really enjoying these trips!

Here is the dressing for my Claret Murrough:

Hook: 8 to 14 wet fly hook.

Tying silk: brown.

Rib: oval gold tinsel.

Body: claret fur. I tie this fly in a range of shades of claret from light to black claret.

Body hackle: red game, cock or hen.

Wing: dark brown squirrel tail hair.

Hackle: a long fibred Greenwell hen hackle tied full in front of the wing.

Chapter 25
Tyrone

County number 25

Tuesday, 31st May 2022

Slap bang in the middle of Ulster lies the old kingdom of Tir O'ne, modern day Tyrone, the largest of the Northern Ireland counties. The O'Neill clan ruled these lands for many years until the flight of the Earls in 1607, marking the end of Gaelic lordship in Ireland. This is archetypal Northern Ireland countryside with neat, well-tended fields and impressive farm buildings. Bustling towns, some bedecked with flags of one tradition or the other, are complimented by serene little villages amid the greenery. I have visited Omagh and Dungannon in the past but can't claim any great in-depth knowledge of the angling in Tyrone.

I vaguely recall stopping off in Dungannon many years ago and catching a couple of rainbows in a lake which was set in a park but don't ask me what it was called. For the purposes of this project, I am going to disregard that minor success of long ago and set out to catch a fish in Tyrone using any legal method.

These are once again uncertain times in the North, Stormont is unable to sit as the DUP want the border down the Irish Sea to be re-negotiated. My personal opinion is that Brexit was an unmitigated disaster for everyone, there were no winners on either side. I don't for one minute believe anyone on mainland UK gave two hoots about the Good Friday Agreement or peace in the North of Ireland when they voted.

The consequences of the UK's exit from Europe will rumble on for years and have the potential to degenerate into violence once again on this island. Shifting demographic sands, loosening political allegiances and the new realities of European relationships are destabilising an already volatile society and nobody can predict where we are heading. I would dearly love to be more positive as I have an abiding affection for Northern Ireland. It both inspires and appals me in equal measure but I find it utterly fascinating.

Today would be about hedging my bets. In south Tyrone, there are two small lakes close by each other, one a trout fishery and the other full of coarse fish. Creeve is the coarse fishing sister to Brantry which has the brown trout swimming around in it. The loughs are of similar size and have both been developed for angling with car parks, fishing stands and paths around them. I figured if I could not catch a fish on one I could try the other. These loughs lie in the lush countryside which straddles the border where twisty wee roads squeeze between undulating fields and quaint hamlets. These borderlands are quiet now but are still bisected by an unnatural division created to address a century old imagined disaster, created with no thought of a changed future.

So with that unusually well-constructed plan in mind I packed and set off for the border early on the last day of May. Quiet roads meant my journey along those oh so familiar roads was uneventful. When making my plans, I had toyed with the idea of taking a scenic route through Cavan but decided in the end to take the main road and not dawdle. There was a quick stop in Enniskillen to get some bait. As is my want, I bought far more maggots than I needed for the day but I planned on fishing again this week so stocking up on bait made sense. The array of coarse tackle on display in the shop was dizzying. Much as I love my coarse fishing there is no way I could ever get to the point where I'd part with over a thousand pounds for a pole or a similar amount for a fancy seatbox. I am altogether cheaper than that and a couple of second-hand rods with ancient reels will do me. I invest in good quality line and hooks mind you but these items will hardly break the bank. Despite my frugality, a couple of small items found their way into my basket and I chatted to the staff in the shop to find out how the fishing had been around Fermanagh and Tyrone recently. Back into the stream of commuter traffic through the town and then a toddle along the road to the huge roundabout at Ballygawley where I peeled off for Aughnacloy.

I turned on the radio and tuned into the national news as I drove, something I never normally do. Propaganda is all I hear but I think it is important to listen to all sides and then make up my own mind about what is going on. The miles slip by as I listen to a debate on government (or lack thereof) in the north. It seems to me that entrenched views on all sides show no signs of easing any time soon. Enough of that, I switch off the radio and think about the fishing which is now only a scant few miles away.

The only question for me was which lake to start with but in the end I plumped for Brantry first. Fishing the fly is still the method I am most comfortable and confident with. Guarantees don't exist in any form of angling though and that's why the coarse option hovered in the background. It is hard to make exact plans when fishing but I figured if I was still without a trout by 2pm I would up sticks and head a mile down the road to Creeve and try for a perch or roach. I know there are much more scenic loughs in this county but my express intended outcome was to land a fish so this seemed to be my best bet. With time limited good access and easy, fishing are key elements to these 32 trips, I don't have the luxury of taking hours to size up a fishery.

The car park, commodious and none too busy, was easy to find and I parked up in the light rain a few minutes just before ten o'clock. 'Scattered showers' the forecasters had said and sure enough since the border the windscreen wipers had been used a couple of times. Thankfully it was drying up a bit now, the rain easing to a fine drizzle. Parking beside the only two other vehicles there I got out to have a look around.

The lough, about 20 acres in size, is edged by tall trees all around but a number of angling stands have been built to allow access. A good path circumnavigates the lough making it a popular spot for joggers and dog walkers. A lady is walking an arthritic terrier and we chat for a while, she interested why anyone in their right mind would drive all the way from Mayo just to go fishing here and I ask about the old dog who has kindly watered the front wheel of my car. We part and I get on with the serious business of the day.

The 11 footer and old System 2 reel came out again and a yellow floating line ending in a light cast of three flies was soon rigged. On smaller waters I tend to favour small flies unless I see something bigger on the wing so I opted for a size 12 Welshman's Button on the bob, a size 14 Silver March Brown in the middle and a Black Goldhead dressed on a size 12 long shank on the tail. Maybe not the most obvious selection to many of you but three flies that have done well for me over the years in the month of June for stocked browns. Now it was time to investigate my watery surroundings.

The nearest stand was actually at the car park so once I had rigged the rod I grabbed a sandwich and walked to the end of it to have a look around. Milky coloured water was fringed with reeds and ruffled by a steady wind coming out of the north east. Worryingly, try as I might I could see no insects on the water or in the air. While munching on the last bite of the sandwich (egg and cucumber if you must know), a big fish splashed the surface forty odd yards out in directly front of me.

I didn't see the fish properly but the commotion suggested something heavy. Lacking any better ideas I decided to start right there on this stand. A vast bank of reeds grew well out into the southern end of the lake and from this stand I could reach the edge of them with a good cast. So back to the car, grab rod, bag and net then I was set to go.

That wind was at an awkward angle for fishing towards those reeds. It was coming on to my right shoulder meaning the cast had to be timed to perfection, any slovenliness would result in the line wrapped around my ears! My first cast was a bit short but I fished it out and re-cast, this time dropping the flies a foot from the reeds. Short, sharp pulls to get that goldhead working just below the surface. Lift off, one false cast then the line shot out again. A few pulls then wallop!

Well that was an unexpectedly good start to the day. A heavy fish dived before leaping a foot in the air, flashing silver and pink—a rainbow. More runs that made the old reel screech, two more jumps as well but soon the trout tired and came close to me. Played out, I slipped the net under him and my prize was safely ashore. What was a rainbow doing in here, I had read this was a brown trout fishery?

That old reliable black goldhead was in the corner of his mouth. You can keep up to four fish on this lake but I slipped the 'bow back into the water once the hook had been fetched from his scissors. It ran through my mind to kill this fish so I could have a look to see what it had been feeding on but that felt like a pretty pointless waste of a life. The black goldhead is a general pattern so the trout could have taken it for any number of different things. Well, that was a good start anyway. Back fishing, maybe twenty casts later another solid take saw me into another fish and yes, it was another rainbow.

A wee bit smaller than the first one it was still a nice trout but he too was carefully returned. This was all feeling a bit surreal, a few minutes ago I was driving and now I had caught two fish in my first few casts. That wind was tricky and I had to pay close attention to my casting to prevent any tangles. Searching the water to my right produced a strong pull but that fish didn't stick around. More casting as I searched the water around the stand. I tried letting the flies sink a bit deeper and that worked as soon yet another hard pull resulted in a third rainbow, all three trout hammering the black goldhead. All were fully finned fish in great condition. What a lovely start to the day.

An occasional small fish showed far out beyond casting distance and I began to consider my options. Stay here or move to another stand? Casts at different angles and different retrieves were tried before a nice morning was rudely interrupted by a phone call from work. I hate my current job and the call, innocent and well meaning, never the less upset me greatly. This was the last day of my time off and here I was forced into thinking about work again.

In an instant, I had gone from immersed in the fishing to worrying about work. I tried to fish on but could not shake myself out of this gloom, so I decided to pack up and head for the other lake, Creeve. Rod disassembled and reel safely tucked away, I picked my way along the winding minor road I had driven up a scant hour before. I have to confess I was not in good humour.

Only a mile or two south of Brantry, Creeve is a very similar looking lake. It's a tad smaller and rounder maybe but has similar facilities, the only difference being the occupants. This lough has pike, perch, bream and roach in it and I planned to float fish for the latter three species. Creeve has suffered greatly in the recent past with blue-green algal bloom which are dangerous to humans and animals alike.

It was my hope this affliction would not be present this early in the year and a careful search around the edge turned up no signs of the deadly algae. Mine was the only car in the car park when I got there so I knew I had the place to myself. Was that an indication of how this lake had been fishing of late?

I tackled up with the 12 foot general purpose rod so that I could switch easily to feeder if necessary but I started with a bodied waggler to a size 14 hook fished over depth. The swim was only one rod length out, the wind being too strong for attempting anything further out with the float. Groundbait and a steady trickle of loose fed maggots went in and I tried hard to settle in to the fishing but images of work haunted still me. Mature trees gave me cover from the cool wind but also made casting a bit of a pain.

A couple of times I stuck the hook in a branch which just further lowered my mood. A pair of ducks swam down the lake to investigate who was in their patch and then went on to spend the rest of the session tormenting me, swimming close to the line and even pecking my float on a couple of occasions. All in all it was a session to forget, the only highlight being a solitary perch which pulled the float under after an hour or so of work/duck/wind stress.

Normally I would have made some changes and possibly switched to the feeder by my heart was not in it now. A couple of hours slipped past but that one lonesome perch was all I caught. Clouds darkened and rain threatened so I cut my losses and called it a day. Briefly, I toyed with the notion of going back to try for more rainbows on Brantry but my mood was very low so instead I broke down the rod and packed away the tackle in my seatbox.

Back along the track under the sighing trees to the solitary black car I trod and after a quick divestment of my waterproof clothes I was back behind the wheel. Then I pointed the car for Mayo and set off back down the twisty road to Aghnacloy. Heavy showers chased me across the border but they petered out by the time I was past Manorhamilton in Leitrim.

I consider myself to be fairly logical and stable but that perfectly innocent phone call from work really shook me and has opened eyes to a big underlying issue for me. For quite some time now, I have been struggling to justify working in a job that I hate but have pushed those thoughts down and 'just got on with it' like so many of us do. My reactions on the banks of the wee loughs in Tyrone appear to be out of proportion but in truth it felt like some sort of mental pressure valve had been released. Big changes are now afoot and I feel much better now I am taking action instead of fretting and worrying.

It had been a day of pluses and minuses. Three rainbows were unexpected but very welcome and my short time fishing Brantry had been really enjoyable. That wee black goldhead is a great fly when you have no idea what to try on a new water. It works just as well for stocked brownies as rainbow so it is good to have a couple in your box, so here is the tying.

Materials List

Hooks—all sizes. 12 long shank is my favourite.
Black tying silk.
Rabbit fur on the skin, dyed black.
Gold bead, 2.8–3.3mm depending on the size of the hook.
Hen hackles dyed black.
Something for the rib such as oval tinsel.

Method

Take one of the beads and thread it on to the hook. Put the hook in the vice and test it. Now push the bead up against the eye and start the tying silk behind the bead, building up a dam to hold the bead in position. You can add a dab of superglue if you want. Prepare and tie in a black hen hackle then run the silk to the bend to create a bed for the tail. Take a pinch on rabbit fur, stroke out the shorter fibres and tie this in as a tail. The tail should be about the same length as the hook shank. Now bind the butt ends of the fur down with turns of silk as you wind back up to where the hackle is tied in. Remove any waste fur.

Catch in a length of your ribbing material and wind back down to the tail. Take another pinch of the black fur and dub enough for a body on the silk. In practice, the short fur you combed out of the stuff you used for the tail will make the body. Wind this rope up the shank. Now rib in open turns, tie in and cut off the waste.

Wind the hackle, two or three turns is all you need. Cut off the waste end of the hackle. Make a whip finish between the hackle and the bead, cut off the silk and carefully varnish.

Back at home I checked the NIDirect website and here is what is says about Brantry:

Nearest town	Benburb
Area/length	24.3 hectares
Species	**brown trout**
Season	1 March to 31 October
Methods	fly fishing only from boat and shore
Daily bag limit	four trout per rod
Size limit	minimum takeable size 25.4cm

As you can see there is no mention of rainbows but I guess the stocking policy must have changed. It just shows the value of trying a general fly pattern like the black goldhead, it will trick any stocked trout, be they brown or 'bow.

The afternoon was one to forget. I can't blame anyone or anything else on my performance on Creeve, I simply fished very poorly. The wind was tricky but there was nothing to stop me heading over to a different peg with some shelter. With no bites forthcoming, I should have changed tactics but instead toughed it out and wasted my time watching for bites that never materialised. While it is easy to say, I was just not in the right head space on the day I was still out fishing and should have just relaxed into a quiet afternoon in the fresh air. I just was not thinking straight.

Sitting at home now and reflecting on the day, there is a degree of satisfaction that I have now caught a fish in all of the six counties which make up Northern Ireland. That alone is a nice little achievement. I'll admit I really enjoy the angling in the North, there is such a range to pick from and the other anglers I meet up there all seem to be very accomplished with rod and line. I have made a mental note to fish some more venues across the border next season.

Realistically, if I put all my efforts into completing the 32 this year I will have little time left for anything else during 2022. Only seven other counties in the Republic remain on the rapidly shrinking 'to do' list but they will take a fair bit of time to organise and complete. By my dodgy maths that means close to 80% of the total have been completed to date. These last few will all be very long days of tiring journeys to the far corners of the island of Ireland but I can almost see the finish line now.

Chapter 26
Cork

County number 26

Monday, 6th June 2022

Lough Bofinna. I have no rational explanation why this secluded little lake sang to me but as soon as I read about it I decided I simply had to fish it. Cork is a big county with countless opportunities to fish so quite how my brain fixed on this far off lough will for ever remain a mystery. Close to the tourist trap of Bantry in the far south west, it was going to be a long, long journey for me but I didn't mind, indeed I was excited by the challenge of the day. Little did I know how great that challenge would be.

Bofinna is an unusual place to fish, tarred roads run along two edges of the triangular shaped lough. Trout, a mix of browns and 'bows, are stocked at intervals and some rudd live in there too according to the IFI website. Fishing is by all legal methods so I could fish fly (preferred), worm (might for an hour) or spin (desperation). My research suggested this was a very popular fishery so the usual pressures on hard fished stocked waters would probably apply.

You are required to buy a permit to fish this and the other SW stocked lakes but it can be bought online easily enough so I had previously parted with my €20, printed off the permit and tucked it into my jacket pocket. A dozen or so small worms dug out of the compost heap in the garden were in a bait box which came along with me in case things got desperate.

The journey seemed to go on and on and on. By Limerick, I was barely half way there, the roads worsened and narrowed as I travelled deeper and deeper into Munster. No direct road brought me to Bantry so numerous junctions and turns took me along lesser byways, but I got there in the end with only one slight detour when I missed an unmarked junction on a bad bend. In the grand scheme of things, I figured one small mistake was not too bad.

This was the longest trip for me so far on the project, even Wexford and Antrim were marginally closer to home. The countryside changed as I drove becoming more rugged and unkempt. Hills rose around me then receded in the distance, the road signs changed from English to Irish and the fields shrank in size.

Finally, the lough hove into view just after a water pumping station by the side of the road. By now, it felt like I had been driving for days, not hours. Turning left and driving up the narrow tarred road on the far side on the lough I came to a small parking space where an impressively large motorhome was parked. Reversing into the remaining space I got out and took in my surroundings while at the same time I tried to massage some life back into my stiff legs.

With little wind to ruffle the surface, I peered out across the lake hoping to spot an odd rise but there were no signs of life. Ah well, I had the whole day ahead of me and the fish could waken up at any time. Time to get togged up, the rear door of the car creaking as I opened it up. A couple of new struts would not go amiss but are unlikely to be done this year. Thigh boots and jacket on, I was threading the line through the rings of the 11 footer when the door of the motorhome opened.

"I have got some bad news for you," his thick Devonshire accent was a bit unexpected here in deepest Cork. Tall, bearded, about my own age and weather worn, the owner of the huge white vehicle had my attention. "What's that?" I retorted. "There are no fish in this lake" he said in a voice which clearly demonstrated he was not joking. Now when you have just driven the length of Ireland to go fishing this is not the kind of statement you want to hear. Stopping what I was doing I turned to listen, my mind whirring as I tried to comprehend what was going on.

What unfolded next was a sorry tale but sadly not an unusual one in present day Ireland. My new acquaintance came to fish here every season from the UK and had caught many fine trout from the lough over the years. This past three days he had fished hard but had not even seen a fish rise, let alone catch one. Locals he knew and trusted had told him the lough had recently been poached by a gang who came under the cover of darkness with small boats, nets and huge plastic containers on a truck to transport their illegal catch.

This type of almost professional poaching is rife across the country and no fishery is completely safe. Somewhere like Bofinna was a poachers dream with easy access right up to the water's edge.

My man explained that nobody was bothering to fish the lough now it was empty. Word had obviously spread quickly around the local area but I had not heard or read about the poaching, what with me being so far away up in Mayo. We chatted for a while but it was clear there was little hope of a fish from Bofinna today.

"Look," I said, "I am here now so I will set up the rod and take a walk down to the water." A shake of his head told me this was little short of madness in his opinion but as I tied up a leader with some flies he said he might join me later on for a few casts.

So here I was, miles from anywhere and without a plan 'B'. Mulling it over I decided to give it an hour or so since I was here. At least, I would be fishing as I tried to hatch a new plan and figure out where else I could try. An old leader from my last outing was on the reel so I removed it and made a new one to which I knotted three flies, a black goldhead on the tail, a daiwl bach in the middle and a small claret deer hair sedge on the bob. Now I had to decide where to actually fish.

Through some trees I could just make out a clear part of bank off to my right near the top end of the lake. Across a small slatted concrete bridge over a dried up stream to a path which led to a shelving gravel bank at the head of the lake, I strode. Alder and willows grew close to the water's edge but there was just enough room to cast. This looked to be as good a place as any to try.

There was virtually no wind to speak of and the surface of the lake was flat calm as I started to cast. My slime line got the flies down off the surface and allowed me to fish without leaving a wake, something I think is important on days like this. Short casts to cover the shallow water near at hand then longer throws out to about twenty yards or so, fanning from right to left so I was covering as much water as possible. Over the years I have caught many trout in water only a few inches deep and within a few feet of the shore.

At one step per cast, I was soon up at the far end of the small bay so I wound in and went back to where I had started but this time I waded out a bit so I could reach out into deeper water. I didn't chance going in too deep what with the slippery bottom and my dodgy sense of balance. Bad enough there were no fish without me getting a ducking. Maybe 30 or 40 minutes elapsed and no signs of fish had caught my attention even though I was watching the surface intently. Fly life, in the form of buzzers, small ginger and dark brown sedges and a sprinkling of olives dotted the surface but nothing tried to eat them.

Chaffinches tweeted noisily in the bushes behind me but all was eerily quiet apart from them. By now, I was back at the head of the small bay, thigh deep in water slightly clouded with algae. A change of fly was on my mind now as there had been no interest in the three currently on the leader. I turned to make my way back to where I had entered the water—then it happened.

Perhaps it was because I was paying such close attention to all around me that the rise, when I saw it, seemed almost surreal. I was looking back down the lough when a fish broke the surface about 15 yards from where I was standing in the greenish-grey water. One of those swirling rises as a fish turns to take something on or near the surface. A confident rise of a feeding trout. The sight of that swirl transfixed me. It really was almost unbelievable. After all, I had been told about the total lack of fish in here a trout was close to me and feeding. I had a chance.

My line was in the water, about ten yards of it was out to my left, unseen a couple of feet below the mirror-calm surface. Stripping in with my left hand I felt the weight of the line on the rod and judged when to sweep up to lift the line out of the water and into the air. Two false casts, the first to change direction, the second to increase length. Out shot the line, the flies turning over nicely in the air and the whole alighting gently close to the slowly disappearing ripples of the rise and a few inches to the left as I looked at it. I let the flies sink for a couple of seconds, aware of my heart thumping in my chest, then started the retrieve—slow, short pulls. BANG!

Some head shakes followed the electrifying take then the fish ran out towards deeper water, putting a good bend into my rod which I was by now holding high to stop my line getting drowned. I let him go off on the run and at the same time I wound the slack line back on to the reel. Just as I got the last of the line on the spool he jumped and I could see he was a nice fish but nothing special in terms of size. Another short run then he thrashed the surface, throwing spray around in an unpleasant way.

I am not a religious man but trust me, invocations to an unspecified deity were being muttered under my breath as that trout fought well for those couple of minutes. He tired though and I reached for my net, which was conspicuous by its absence. Damn! I had left the net on the back seat of the car. Lady luck was smiling on me though as the gently sloping gravel made a perfect place to beach the fish once he was properly tired out. Exhausted, my prize was easily led on to the beach where one very relieved Scotsman picked him up and applied the coup-de-grace. I had caught a fish in the Rebel county after all.

The size 14 deerhair sedge was firmly in the scissors, where we all like to see our flies. In the long grass, I laid the fish while I sorted out the leader and checked the hook point on the sedge. Re-organised, I waded back out and started to fish again when my new friend appeared, rod in hand. "I know there are no fish in here but I will give it a try anyway" he told me, started to cast a beautiful line just where I had hooked my fish.

"I have one," I said, trying to find a tone which did not sound overly triumphant. I am not sure I succeeded in that though. He looked at me as if I had just informed him of an alien encounter. "What?" Picking the fish from the grass where it lay I proffered the corpse to validate my claim. The poor man seemed utterly stunned. With lots of similar deerhair sedges in my box, I took one out and gave it to him, then resumed casting a few yards along the bank. We fished on for a while, the details of the take and fight being dissected in the minutest detail. His casting was exemplary, a joy to watch. Each throw landed like thistledown and he fished like the expert he obviously was.

An hour passed without any further action, despite increasing numbers of natural flies on the water and almost perfect conditions. I feared the story of the poachers was true and that this lough had been all but emptied by the gang. By some fluke, I had run into one of the few fish remaining there. Any hope I harboured that there would be some more rainbows still swimming around in the lough gradually evaporated as time passed. Flies were changed a couple of times but all to no avail. It was decision time, did I stay here and keep flogging, did I cut my losses and head back to Mayo, or was there a third option?

Just after midday I reeled in, waded back to the gravelly shore and walked back across the wee bridge to the waiting car. A strange mixture of elation and disappointment hung over me and even then, as I took my rod apart and unscrewed the reel, I felt a need to return to Cork at some point in the future. There is so much fishing all across this vast county I have yet to sample and I am not going to let a gang of poachers colour my feelings for the place.

I would go as far as to say I would come back to Bofinna again. It looks like a very interesting spot to fish when there are some trout in it so who knows, I might make the long trek here once more.

A new plan had been hatched, one that would take me somewhere new.

I have had time mull over the few seconds which defined my trip to lough Bofinna. I believe there are lessons from that short period of time which will stand inexperienced anglers in good stead.

1. Keep fishing. I know this sounds obvious but as long as your flies are in the water you have a chance. I could have easily not bothered setting up, so devastating was news of the poaching. Instead I figured there might but an odd fish left so I might as well make an effort. This time it paid

off for me. It does not always work out that way but the basic credo of keeping on fishing is one to bear in mind on the toughest of days.

2. Look for places where fish could potentially be found. That gravel bank shelved quickly, creating a drop off which fish love. Headlands, around islands, underwater rocks, weedbeds etc are all potential fish holding areas so concentrate on them when the fishing is difficult.

3. Keep your eyes peeled! Even though I had been told there were no fish I kept looking for any signs of one. I scanned the lough for anything that might be a fishy movement. I was very lucky that when I did see a fish it was within casting distance. If it had been further away, I would have quickly moved to cover the fish rather than wait to see if it would swim towards me.

4. Work on your casting until it becomes second nature to you. I had one shot today, if I made a mess of my first cast the fish would have spooked and be gone in a flash. Remember, good anglers are invariably expert casters. If you are struggling, there are lots of casting tuition options out there.

I have to confess I was very disappointed the fish had nearly all been poached from the lake. It was not just the long journey but I had been really looking forward to spending the day exploring the lough, trying different flies and hopefully catching some nice trout. I had rejected so many other options so I could fish here and my plans had all gone up in smoke. I had even been looking forward to trying the worm for an hour just for something different. Instead I felt cheated by the thieves who had just wanted to make money.

It is impossible to police every lough in the country but government money had been spent stocking this lake and may be it is time to think about better security such as cameras by the water. This approach has worked to greater or lesser degrees at other venues and led to successful convictions. These types of criminal operations are not just someone taking one or two fish for the pot, these are dangerous people who will use violence if anyone gets in their way. As a society we should not tolerate such felonious behaviour.

The fly that caught me the only fish of the day was a Deerhair Caddis. Tying is simplicity itself. Although today one was tied on a size 14 hook, I find that I use size 12–16 hooks for here in Ireland but you may decide to go bigger or smaller to match your local hatches. Dark 8/0 silk (black, brown or olive all work) is started at the neck of the hook and run down to the bend. Dub a fur body and run this back 2/3 of the way to the eye (fiery brown fur was used on today's one).

Now prepare a thin noodle of deer hair, either natural or dyed as required. Align the tips of the hair using a stacker and position the hair on top of the hook with the tips in line with the bend. A couple of loose turns with the silk are taken first then more, tighter wraps to firmly secure the deer. Now remove the waste ends of the hair. You can use the fly like this or you can add a hackle. A cock hackle can be tied in front of the wing, a couple of turns is usually sufficient. I used a coachman brown coloured hackle on the fly today. Form a head and whip finish before varnishing.

Chapter 27
Kerry

County number 27

Monday, 6th June 2022

6th June, D-day. I was stood up to my knees in Lough Bofinna in county Cork trying to decide what to do when it occurred to me that Kerry was not so terribly far away. With little hope of adding to the one trout I have in the bag the notion of fishing a second county today held a huge appeal for me. There is a stocked lough called Barfinnihy which lies high up in the hills on the ring of Kerry, very close to Moll's Gap. An hour's drive should get me there and I could spend a while attempting to winkle out a trout or two. Reeling in I bid adue to Bofinna then stowed the gear away, well, chucked it all willy nilly into the back of the car really. I bid farewell to Bantry then took the tortuous route north along the N71 via the hustle and bustle of Kenmare.

All of my hard work researching possible venues across the country had paid off and I had read about this place before. Barfinnihy is another one of the lakes covered by the SW stocked lakes permit system, the permits being available locally or online. As I already had one in my pocket for today I could just rock up and commence fishing. From what I could gather, this was a very popular place with the locals. Would this lake be devoid of fish too? It felt like a gamble worth taking.

Kerry is beautiful but crowded during the summer as it fills with visitors from all over the world. The beaches used to be a great spot for bass fishing in the winter and dedicated bass anglers travelled here to hurl baits past the third breaker on the lovely, lonely strands. Those bass are rare now and the anglers tend to come more for the rays and conger which are still there.

I am no stranger to the kingdom of Kerry, it used to be one of my favourite places to fish. Back when I lived in Scotland I would drive all the way from

Aberdeen to Fenit or Valentia Island to fish the rich salty waters for bass, rays and wrasse. In those far off days, I loved nothing better than riding my bike, wild camping and fishing in the most difficult to reach places. Happy days indeed but it has been many a long year since I have partaken of any of those pastimes which were once so dear to me.

Life seems to slither away so damn quickly, one minute you are young and strong and carefree and before you know it the grey hairs, aches and fears over take you. My motorbikes are long gone and the treks to Kerry stopped around the same time. Somehow there just never seemed to be time to go back to do some fishing there. Apart from a flying visit to Tralee with work in 2017 I had not visited Kerry for nearly 40 years. I used to know my way around the county but that knowledge has long since faded and I strongly suspect the sea angling has similarly declined.

There would be no return to the smell of two stroke engines nor the thrill of scaling 100 foot cliffs on my return to Kerry in 2022. Those days are past now and in the past they must remain. For those of you unfamiliar with Ireland, county Kerry lies in the south west of the island. There are a few towns but this is largely a rural area with stunning scenery and a rich history. A haven for visitors, Kerry has an economy based on agriculture and tourism. Football (the GAA variety) is a passion in the county and many fine players have togged out in the green and gold colours over the years. Of course there is always a healthy rivalry between Kerry and their next door neighbours, Cork.

Right from the get go the road was a series of bends and hills. The gearbox on the old car got a good workout and the same went for the brakes. Once past Kenmare, I pointed the car north along the N71, surely the most scenic route in the country. Steep climbs with sheer drops a few feet away, tunnels just wide enough for one car to pass through and views across the glens to die for. On this June bank holiday weekend, it was jammed with every conceivable form of transport but in little over an hour I turned on to the road for Sneem and rounding a bend spied the lough below me.

I found a parking place across the road from the lough where a few other cars and vans were already sitting and shut off the poor overworked engine. This lough is set in a natural dip between the hills so the faint wind was barely sufficient to ripple the surface. Mist hung in the damp air as I got out of the car and went over to have a look at the water from above, quickly spotting a few other anglers already hard at work.

Even at this distance some fish could be seen rising far out in front of one chap at the western end of the lough beside an island. I could make out he was busily chucking a large bubble float at the rising trout and as I watched he hooked and landed a fish. From the casting motion, he was using it looked to me as if he was fishing bait and not flies on the bubble. The hapless trout was clunked on the head and disappeared into a grey coloured holdall. Well, that was encouraging at least! Back at the car I re-assembled the fly rod and retained the same leader of flies, as good an option to begin with as any others.

Deciding where to start occupied my mind as I tackled up. The lough was roughly oval in shape with one island close to the roadside shore. I could not see any great amount of reeds or weeds around the edges so access appeared to very good, always a plus in my book. The idea of heading over to the far side was initially tempting simply as there was nobody else on that part of the bank. The rough nature of the bogland put me off that notion and instead I would slot into a big gap between the anglers below me. Gear checked, I was ready to go. Then it was across the damp tarmac and down the steep slope.

Steep slopes are difficult for me, what with my arthritic joints and dodgy balance. Slowly and inelegantly I picked my way down through the boggy ground to the edge of the water. It was slippery underfoot causing a few wobbles and increasing my heartbeat but I made it to the shore without mishap. Only when I was there did I realise that I had done it again—left my bloody net in the car. Twice now in one day I had made this schoolboy error. The notion of climbing back up the slope again lacked any appeal for me so I started to fish without a net, an act of bravery or foolishness, I will leave you to decide.

That old net has a long history and has been in many scrapes over the years. I bought it as a youngster and the very first time I used it was when fishing the tidal beat of the river Ythan at Newburgh in Scotland. For some reason, I had taken it off and laid it down on a shingle bank, then forgot about it. Of course the tide came in and my shiny new net disappeared. This was in my pre-motorbike days and my late father came to pick me up that evening only to find his only son distraught at the loss of his net.

I got an earful for my carelessness as we drove home but the auld fella woke me early the next morning and he drove me back to Newburgh to search for my lost landing gear. It was now low tide and almost unbelievably there was my net, still where I had so carelessly left it the previous day. Funny to think I still use that net but my father left this world over twenty years ago.

Two chaps away off to my right were float fishing worms and in short order they pulled out a brace of trout. Their gear looked to be on the heavy side and the trout came in rapidly as the handle on the big reels were cranked. The fish would have had more chance if they were being pulled in on the end of a Grimsby trawler's winch. Each to his own I suppose.

A perfectly adequate spinning rod nestles in the back of my car on a permanent basis but it very rarely sees the light of day. It is there as a backup should I feel the need to chuck ironmongery about in an act of sheer desperation. Knowing I had the option of both spinning and even worms was of some comfort to me but I hold the opinion that rainbow trout will take a fly just as willingly as they will the humble worm. Here was the perfect opportunity to prove that theory.

The road behind me was busy with holiday traffic but down here the sound of engines was just a mummer in the background. Once I reached the water I found the rough and very wet path of sorts led off in both directions. Big boulders were strewn across the bank while deep holes were hidden under ferns and straggly grass to trip the unwary. Rivulets of water trickled down through the heather so I was glad of my sturdy wellies and over trousers. My trusty wading stick came in very useful here, how often have I said that over the years? I can recall buying this stick all those years ago and thinking it would rarely get used.

Little did I know how unstable I would become and how reliant I'd become on that rough shaft of ash.

The chap on my left was staying put and I didn't blame him as there were fish still rising in front of him. Unfortunately there were no signs of fish in front of me though so I started to cast at 90 degrees to the bank. With each new cast, I took another step along the shoreline, methodically working my way to the east. Just casting is in some way justification enough to go fly fishing. The fluid motion, that control and split second timing are almost meditative to me. Those nearly imperceptible alterations and corrections to accommodate the wind must be performed by tiny brain functions we are unaware of. A rhythm develops, lulling us into a quiet space so familiar and comforting.

The line sings softly through the rings then tantalisingly hangs just for an instant before dropping on to the surface of the lake. There is beauty in many places but for me it is easy to find in the gentle curves of a fly rod. I kept moving and casting, moving and casting. Still no signs of rising fish close to me though. After a while, I came to a huge rock which barred my path so with some huffing and puffing I got up on top of the immense boulder and once I had caught my breath started fanning some casts out from my lofty perch. No doubt it had been deposited there by some retreating glacier after the last ice age and here was a fishless and rapidly tiring Scotsman standing atop it in the damp Kerry air. A very inviting faint ripple off the my right was unfishable to me as the wormers were set up there. I kept casting.

Time passed by on the edge of the steely water, the mist came and went leaving me damp and chilled but I stuck to my task. A temptation to move again was resisted, I had a birds-eye view of virtually the whole lake from my mossy boulder. Finally, from atop my rocky outcrop I saw a fish rise about 10 yards beyond my casting range. With little to lose, I pulled another couple of yards of line off the reel and aimed my next cast in the general direction of the fish, repeating this three times. Around 25 yards of fly line were in the air, about the most I can arialise with this rod.

The weight in the goldhead on the tail helps to turn over the leader and my casts are flying out without a hitch. I inch the flies back in short, sharp pulls trying to give the flies a bit of life. By some trick of the light, I saw the fish turn under the water a split second before my line gave that longed for jump and I was into a trout. Like most rainbows this one fought well, finding the energy for one final run just when I thought it was tired out.

As I played the trout I picked my way down from the top of the boulder to the edge of the water. With no net, I had to guide the fish into a tiny sandy space between some rocks where I could then pick it up but soon I was clutching my prize. It had absolutely nailed the black goldhead.

I tapped the fish on the head and admired my catch, stockies can be poorly formed sometimes but this lad was a well-shaped fish of about a pound-and-a-quarter. The goldhead was well down the gullet and took a bit of retrieving. The hook was checked and found to be in perfect order so I was good to go again once I had washed my hands in the cool water of the lake. The decision to try here was fully vindicated and I could fish on now with no pressure.

With one in the bag, I was hungry for more so I resumed operations but this time from a lower perch near the base of the mighty rock. This made casting a little harder because I was closer to the rough ground behind me but the flies were still getting out a fair distance in the cats paw of a breeze. Half-an-hour slipped past in no time, I was just enjoying casting and fishing the water. Out of nowhere the line tightened and trout number two swam around in a circle for a while until it woke up and proceeded to charge around like a lunatic.

I got that one too, landing it in identical fashion as the first one. The goldhead had claimed a second victim. While I was playing that fish another couple of rainbows had risen in the near vicinity but by the time I was back in action they had moved off. I took this to be a sign the fish were moving in small pods which can be a good thing as more fish are likely to see your flies and also there may be an element of competition between the individuals in the pod.

The chap with the bubble float down the shore from me continued to haul out fish after fish but things had gone quiet for the wormers on my right. One of them packed in but the other lad stuck it out, only moving to a new spot after an hour or so. I could not make out any fly life at all on the surface on in the air but that is not surprising at this altitude.

Regardless, I was tempted to switch to a dry daddy but the mist came down even heavier so I decided to just stick to my current set up. Trout number three showed up with a hefty pull but it turned out to be the smallest of the day. Lightly hooked, it swam off strongly when I released it. I rate rainbows very highly when it comes to the fight, they give 100% every time, even small specimens like this one.

With pressure to land a fish now off me, I could relax and enjoy my surroundings. This was a lovely spot, the water framed by rugged hills on the far side. The air tasted fresh and clean, scented with heather and peat. Many anglers were fishing along the shore but I was the only one using a fly rod. I am not a snob and can see the attraction of worming but any trout on the fly is more enjoyable than one reeled in on heavy spinning gear in my opinion. With reasonably good fly gear available at low cost these days, I wish more anglers would at least try fly fishing. Unlike when I grew up, there are so many different ways of learning how to fly fish it is easy to get started.

Fish number four smashed into the fly and leapt twice, huge, acrobatic jumps I could do nothing to control. The hook held and that one too came to hand, the goldhead once again far down his throat. That one too went into the bag. After that it went quiet and reluctantly I concluded the road home would be a better idea than staying on here for another while. It would be a long road filled with holiday traffic so the sooner I started the journey the better. Solemnly I wound in the line and parked the tail fly safely in the keeper ring.

At least, I was travelling light and had no great encumbrance in the form gear (or a net). Getting up hills is easier for me than descending them and I got back to the car quickly and without mishap, three shining rainbow trout in my salmon bass as that was the only bag I had in my jacket pocket.

Breaking down the rod I took one last look at Barfinnihy as the mist rolled across the hills and a lapwing cried in the distance. The lake had been kind to me and fishing had been thoroughly enjoyable, I just wish I had longer there to explore it a bit more. The extreme western end is a jumble of large boulders and it looked exceedingly 'fishy' to me. I could easily picture myself picking my way through the confusion of rocks and casting into the water to waiting 'bows. Instead I drove off and joined the holiday traffic.

Every fish had taken the ubiquitous black goldhead, just showing what an excellent searching pattern it can be for stocked fish. The dressing is in another chapter and I urge you to tie a few up, it can pull out a trout when nothing else will. On reflection, I should have tried a dry fly but then hindsight is an exact science.

With Kerry completed, I find that I have only five counties left to conquer, a position which I would hardly have believed six weeks ago. Realistically, I will be lucky to do one per month this summer but that would mean by the end of this autumn, if I am spared that long, my goal of catching a fish in every Irish county will have been completed.

Chapter 28
Tipperary

County number 28

Wednesday, 29th June 2022
    Swift and Suir

Confession time, I love Excel. I have relied on it for years at work and all that 'right click in the box' has spilled over into my fishing, helping me to keep track of plans, trips and records of catches. Updating the 32 project master spreadsheet on my laptop one evening I was a bit taken aback to see it was coming up for two years since I had started this project. 6th August 2020 when I fished lough Talt in Sligo to be exact. Since then there have been long periods of inactivity interspersed with bursts of frenetic angling trips.

The merry month of May this year saw a big change for me. I took the whole month off work, one of the few luxuries of my then employment. While there were numerous other commitments, I still had time to undertake more of the 32 project, bagging 6 more counties during those four weeks. Now a free Monday in June presented another opportunity for me, so I saved my brownie points through the week and persuaded my long suffering other half that I simply had to go fishing again.

2022 has been some year so far. Ireland, like every other European country, is filling up with our friends from Ukraine. Lord knows what they make of the cost of living here. The price of everything has shot through the roof so allowances have to be made on all fronts and savings ring fenced in readiness for the next stage of the financial onslaught.

For me and this project, it has meant earlier starts and longer days as I reduce my speed appreciably to try and conserve fuel. It does make a small difference but it is still very expensive to travel far from home. Why not buy an electric car? Here in Ireland electric vehicles are for rich people, not for the likes of me.

All the talk about going green in the transport sector is pure hogwash, just politicians in Dublin talking utter crap and totally out of touch with the real world here in rural Ireland. The best I can do for now is just ease off on the pedal and hum along slowly, letting other drivers whiz by.

While I am on about driving, I will give you an update on the wee black Renault, my ride for the past 7 months. Since acquiring it I have driven about 8,000 kilometres and during that time there have been the odd little technical glitch but it has not let me down so far. Various things don't work at all (sunroof, heater fan etc) while other things work on occasion. Some sort of Gallic poltergeist seems to reside in the cars electrical circuits as some days the wipers work, sometimes they don't and quite often they just please themselves what speed they decide operate at.

The same malicious spirit (or a very close relation) lives in the electric window systems meaning the everyday task of opening a window is laced with a certain apprehension. The car starts, it runs and it stops efficiently so anything above that admittedly low base line is a bonus on an old French car. The bodywork is pretty tatty (much like my own chassis) but that doesn't matter to me as I spend my life driving down narrow, pot-holed roads adding to the tally of scratches and bumps on a near daily basis. My main gripe is the lack of space but I knew that when I bought the car so I just need to get on with it. At the end of the day, the elderly tin can on wheels is doing what I ask of it so I am relatively happy.

It is not such a long way to Tipperary, not for me at any rate. This south-central county butts up against Galway among others and while a good few miles must be travelled it is all along good roads so it is easily accessible for me. 'Tipperary' is colloquially known as simply 'Tipp' here in Ireland and I fully intend to use that term in this post. A hurling county which sits in the middle of Ireland, its rich farmlands roll across the face of the land, interspersed with low hills and busy country towns. And the rivers, there are miles and miles of lovely rivers to fish. Tipp boasts some wonderful trout fishing and it was my full intention to avail of this sport in my latest effort to catch a fish from each of Ireland's 32 counties.

An early summer morning dawned and found me loading the gear into the back of the car once again. I know I mention this in every post but it really is an important part of the day for me. With the combination of a small car and numerous different forms of fishing, I need to remove and reload gear nearly every time I set off.

Today the outboard, fuel tank and all the lough fishing stuff had to come out and be stowed away before the river gear found a billet in the back of the Renault. Here in lies the opportunity to forget some vital piece of equipment and over the years many's the slip twixt cup and lip has occurred. The idea of preparing lists of what I need for each type of fishing has crossed my mind but I have taken that no further (yet). With every passing season, my memory gets worse and worse so perhaps committing my requirements to paper is not such a bad idea.

No need for an early start today as any activity was unlikely to start much before 11am. The rear of the car housed a couple of light fly rods, a spare reel and chest waders. The rest of my equipment was stowed in the maze of pockets on my waistcoat. Who knows what treasures live in some of these pockets, many of them have not been opened for years! I made sure to check my dry flies were there though, I was really hoping for some surface action today. And one of those expensive little bottles of Gink. How many times have I forgotten that over the years!

I digress. Down in the south of the county lies the village of Golden, an anglicised corruption of the Irish, An Gabhlaine. There, around an island with a ruined castle on it, on the edge of the village flows the river Suir. By the time the Suir reaches the salt water at Waterford, it is a substantial river but that is many miles downstream. Here, it is 30 or 40 yards wide and flows swiftly over gravel and weed beds, a trout fishers delight. Along with its tributaries the Suir boasts many miles of excellent trout fishing, drawing keen anglers from near and far to fish its clear waters.

To get there I drove down to Limerick then picked up the N24 to Tipperary Town. From there, the N74 took me due east for a few pleasant miles. I was well down the country now. There is sometimes a dichotomy for me when I'm so far from home. Do I just enjoy the day at my chosen venue or do I push to fish a second county on the same day. Both have their attractions and my feelings shift between both options depending on a range of factors. It is hard to really enjoy the fishing when constantly thinking about the next venue.

Then again, when I am already 200 miles from home and the next county is only a 40 mile hop away the temptations are very real. Usually I prefer to just fish one county simply because it is tiring enough to do that let alone travel on once again. The last 32 trip to Cork and then Kerry left me tired for a couple of days afterwards. Today I had decided before departure I was not going to attempt two counties but rather enjoy a few hours on a new river to me.

The fishing at Golden is controlled by the local angling club and a visitor like me can buy a permit for the sum of €25. Much as I had tried I could not find out online where to buy a permit but this is Ireland and somebody in the village would know. I pulled up on the main street opposite a butchers shop. Parking outside, I stretched my stiff joints after the drive then strode inside where (for vegetarian me) the unusual smells of dead animals greeted me.

The butcher, a large and jolly man, appeared from the back of the shop and I sheepishly asked if he knew were I could but a fishing permit. "Sure, right here!" was his answer and he reached for clipboard and the form to be completed by me. Now folks, I have been around but this was the first time I have bought a fishing permit from a butcher.

When tackling a new river, I admit to being very conservative in my initial choice of flies. Not knowing a water means you are at a huge disadvantage but starting with some tried and trusted 'general' patterns is usually a sound approach. If there is no sign of surface activity, I like to commence operations with a team of spiders.

My logic is I can cover a lot of water quickly with the team of small wets, all the time looking for clues even if the flies are not getting a response. If that fails, I will swap to nymphing but will always keep my eyes open for any rising fish so I can switch to the dry fly. Some rivers respond well to searching with a dry fly even when there is no signs of surface activity and a well presented dry fly cast into likely looking lies can often bring a reward.

What waders to wear when visiting a new river is always a hard call. In general, I prefer chest waders so I can get in deep if required but they can be a liability if access is an issue. Barbed wire fences or thorn bushes can destroy a pair in no time. Today I had both options in the back of the car. From what I could see, there was a little path to the river and no immediate signs of lethal barbed wire to cross so I chanced the chesties. Setting up the faithful old Orvis with a floating line I tied on a leader with a size 18 black waterhen spider on the dropper and a size 16 goldhead PT nymph on the end.

With such clear water, I had dropped to a 3 pound leader, thoroughly degreased as much to take the glint off it as to making it sink. Car locked, through the gap in the low stone wall, I crossed the green sward to the river where it burbled happily under a road bridge.

Operations commenced on the downstream side of the island which is immaculately maintained. Pushing through the reeds I gained the water and waded in to the gin clear stream. Vast beds of bright green weeds clothed the gravel bottom and reeds poked up here and there, making fishing a bit tricky.

Throughout the morning I would be plagued by these reeds. Most were visible but some were just under the surface and it was these that my flies had a magnetic attraction too. I started to cast upstream, just short flicks so I could see the end of the line. A few casts in I had a pluck at one of the flies but missed it. Slowly I made my way down stream, hugging the bank to keep out of sight.

Maybe 20 minutes had elapsed when I struck into a trout. There was no take/pull/tweak, I just knew it was there. "Back up there now!" I can hear you all exclaim. "What is all this 'knowing' stuff?" Those of you who fish upstream wetfly know exactly what I am on about but for the rest of you this is going to very hard to explain. When fishing downstream with wets, there is generally a pull when the fish takes, sometimes accompanied with a splash or rise of some sorts.

When using a nymph set up, there is usually a tweak or at least some indication of a take such as the tip of the line or your indicator moving. Upstream wets are a whole different ball game and most of the takes are not visible. There is no rise, no splash, no pull or even a stoppage on the line. You just sense the fish is there and strike. It took me years of practice to develop this skill and still I suspect I miss far more fish than I hook. Anyway, I hooked this lad and brought him to hand.

A lovely little wild brownie who had fallen for the charms of the Black Waterhen Spider. A quick snap then he was set free, none the worse for wear. That was more than could be said for my leader which he had managed to tangle up during the fight so I had to sort it out before resuming. Near the end of the pool a second trout took in very similar fashion and this one too was quickly played and released. Not a bad start to the day!

A gap in the reeds where the island tapered to an end gave me access to the main stream and by wading out I could fish a line of seams where two different currents meet. This was an awkward spot with deep, fast water right in front of me, forcing me to mend furiously with each cast and high-sticking to keep control of the line. Two more trout were landed and a few lost as I worked hard under the grey clouds. Time flew past, such was my concentration. I love this type of fly fishing where each cast requires me to think in detail about how and where I am going place the line and fish the flies most effectively.

This really was lovely fishing. Once I felt I had covered all the water I could I headed up to the top of the island and started to cast into a deep, fishy looking pool. One more trout fell for the PT on the tail, a fish with the most amazing dorsal fin. I released that one and began to cast again, completely forgetting about the tree behind me. Sure enough I lost both flies on a high branch. I took the opportunity to tie a new leader and swapped on to the dry fly, a small Adams Spider being my choice.

There was no sign of any flies on the surface but I fancied fishing dry so I gave it a lash. One fish rose to the Adams but I missed it completely. An hour passed with me chucking small dries into the wind but the fish were seriously unimpressed. Time for a spot of lunch so I went back to the car and ate a sandwich before rebuilding the leader and going back on to wets.

This time I fished a size 18 red-ribbed black spider and a hare's ear nymph on a long leader. Back on the island once again I decided to run the wets through a streamy section which had defeated my efforts with the dry fly. Long casts across the stream and placing the flies as close as I dare to the reeds kept me on my toes and resulted in the best trout of the day leading me a merry dance before I netted him. The poor fish was exhausted so I popped it straight back into the water without adding to the stress by taking a photo. Afraid you will just need to take my word that it was a super fish of a bit over a pound in weight.

Once I had fished that section I decided to walk upriver. A path on the east bank looked promising so I started to walk through the summer grass and flowers, the river on my left through the trees and pasture on my right guarded by electric fences. I walked and walked, the water being universally deep and slow up here. Finally, I found a faint stream near a fallen tree and I fished it hard but without rising anything.

More walking and fishing ensued but all to no avail, I failed to catch any more fish at all during the afternoon. In the end, I turned and retraced my steps through the greens and yellows of the grasses. Grasshoppers, daddy-long-legs, butterflies and moths all fluttered and hopped around, an utter joy of insect life.

I thought about staying on for a while longer but I suspected it would be near dark before the river woke up and I was many miles from home. So I headed back to the car and broke down the gear, my day in and around the swift flowing river Suir was over all too quickly. It really is a lovely river to fish and I would recommend it to those of you who are experienced river anglers. For novices, it could be harder as the water is very clear and access requires agile wading in deep water in some places.

I had set off full of confidence in the morning and thoroughly enjoyed my day in Tipp. Most of the river can be accessed on local permits at reasonable cost so it is highly likely I will try another stretch of the Suir in the future. For now though, I can put a big black '**X**' through it on my list of counties to do. Excel is great, isn't it!

Chapter 29
Waterford

County number 29

Wednesday, 27th July 2022

Was there an element of exhaustion creeping in? A mental as well as physical tiredness seemed to be growing on me of late. The finishing line is so close but it felt like it would take a herculean effort to complete the next county on my '32' list. A second dose of Covid didn't help either, like the first time around it left me very tired and lacking energy. I was over it now though and it was time to pick up the baton once again. Waterford is so far away from Mayo and just like many other counties I knew so little about the fishing there.

Some of the Ulster counties are equally distant but up there I found fisheries which I felt confident I could tackle. Waterford was a different prospect all together. Nestling on the southern coast of the island, this county is probably best known in angling circles for the salmon fishing on the river Blackwater. I've fished that river once before in a raging flood and blanked. I didn't fancy repeating that process.

Night after night I had scoured the internet looking for angling options. There are no canals in Waterford so my 'go to' solution of float fishing some maggots for roach and perch was out of the question. Try as I might I could find no coarse fishing lakes either, not so much as a farm yard pond full of stunted rudd. Was there any trout fishing down there? Scrutinising the internet I eventually found a couple of stocked reservoirs which might just fit the bill. Knockaderry and Carrigavantry, which supply drinking water to the city, lie some distance apart to the south west of Waterford and the angling there is controlled by the Waterford City and County Trout Anglers Association. They put some brown and rainbow trout into both lakes every year.

With no other viable alternatives open to me, I made up my mind it was the stocked fish in Knockaderry that I would attempt to catch. These are fly only waters and the fishing is from boats which you can hire. The only engines allowed are electric ones and since I don't own an electric I would be using good old fashioned oars all day.

Getting there involved a trek from the north west to the south east of the country. Down to Limerick and then along the N24 for a bit to Carrick-on-Suir. It wasn't a particularly difficult journey, just very long. To make the best of the day I planned set off early, hitting the road at 5am in an effort to miss the worst of the commuter traffic. In practice, it was nearly an hour later than that before I set off after being up most of the night with a sickly cat.

Once on the move my sedate pace meant the journey was boring but I was trying to be frugal, what with diesel being so over-priced these days. Traffic in Tipperary Town and Carrick-on-Suir slowed me down even further but I always knew these choke points would add to my journey time. The whole concept of the 'bypass' has never really caught on with Irish road planners.

When I started out on this project, I thought I had a fair handle on this country. Work and relaxation had taken me to most corners, or so I thought. Turns out I had hardly scratched the surface and perhaps the travelling to get to the fishing in each county has been more of an education to me than expected. I wonder if there are still travelling salemen/women who criss-cross the country to make a living and know each county by heart? Or have they all been replaced by underpaid internet 'customer service' people who wouldn't know Skibbereen from Ardee?

I knew a fella once who sold farm machinery and I recall asking him what he enjoyed most about his job. He told me he could pullover and talk for ages to any farmer he met anywhere in Ireland, the pair of them chatting over a five bar gate about the land, the cattle or GAA. To him that was the perfect way of life. He possessed a seemingly inexhaustible litany of tales, some of which would make your hair stand on end, from all across old Ireland. My fleeting few hours as I dashed here and there were not going to afford me the same experiences but just these short visits whetted my appetite to get to know more about this land.

The first stop was the Centra shop in the little village of Kilmeaden where you buy your permits. €25 for the day permit then another €15 for the hire of a boat. I know that is not much really but it felt like a lot of money given that much of the project has taken me to free or ridiculously cheap venues up until now.

The money was handed over with as much grace as I could muster and in return I had my permit for the day ahead and a small key on a large fob. Back in the car again it was only a few more minutes behind the wheel until I reached the car park and my first glimpse of Knockaderry. A fine floating harbour is home to a number of small, sturdy boats. The lough stretches away to the right, the dam is to the left. Thinking of a whole day ahead on the oars I decided unless I had a very good reason I'd fish close to the harbour (that changed!).

I had brought along a couple of fly rods, my Leeda 7 weight 11 footer and an old Hardy 11 foot 6 weight for dries and as a spare one in case anything happened to the heavy rod. Boxes of flies, cases full of reels loaded with all manner of different lines and my drogue. This contraption hasn't been used in 25 years or so but it was an integral part of my rainbow trout fishing back in the UK all those years ago.

The ability to slow the drift of the boat to allow sinking lines to get down helped me to catch an awful lot of fish back then. Of course you can't use a drogue on the big limestone lakes, to do so would court disaster when the drogue catches on the rough bottom. Here though, on an unobstructed lake, I felt it might give me a small advantage if it was windy. It is a shame I lugged it all the way down there only to find it was flat calm! I recall the skinny line originally supplied with the drogue frayed badly after only a couple of outings so I fitted a length of thick yellow 'machine rope' pinched from the mill and it is still as strong as ever all these years later even if the colour has faded to off-white.

The 32 project has brought me back to fishing for rainbows, something I thought I had left behind me when I departed Scotland all those years ago. When I lived in the central belt, I haunted lochs like Leven and Fitty as well as some of the smaller venues. Double figure days were almost the norm back then and I employed just about every method, ranging from stripped lures through buzzers to drys. A well sunk Ace of Spades and Cats Whisker were my favourite lures and between just those two I must have landed hundreds of trout. If the going was tough today, I might have to resort to my old bad habits!

With some rainbows in the lake, my first thoughts were to fish a sinking line, just to try and get me one fish but that could all change if there were fish rising when I was afloat. A fast sinker or a slow one? My intuition told me to go for a slow sinker but in the end I set up with a DI7, a fast sinking 5 foot tip and a leader with three flies. With so little wind, I presumed the trout were likely to be down deep.

Just getting the flies in front of any fish was my biggest concern. I checked the time, it was 11am already and I was only now loading up the boat with my gear. After such a long journey, I was really feeling the pressure. July can be a tricky month, hot weather and low water can put the fish off the feed but I had made my choices and here I was, pulling on the oars and heading out into the lake.

So what flies to start with? My damsel was a good bet on the tail, its weight taking the leader down quickly and erratic action might wake up any lethargic fish. In the middle, I began with an Orange Montana. A what? This is something I tied up decades ago for fishing in warm water. It's the shape of a Montana Nymph but in hot orange instead of black.

The top fly would be something with a dash of tinsel in its make up so I opted for a Silver Invicta first. My logic here was there could be pin fry on the menu for the rainbows so small but flashy might be good. Having no idea how big (or small) the fish were in this place I made up a leader from six pound mono straight through. I had made it here and was set up in the boat, what would the day hold?

With steady pulls on the oars, I set off to find a likely looking spot to begin. I enjoy rowing. Apart from being good exercise there is also an element of skill in propelling the boat in roughly the right direction. A whole day on the oars is a hard work though so today was definitely going to a challenging one for me. On the plus side, there was little in the way of wind as I set off. Lacking any specific knowledge I had no preconceptions regarding the size of trout in the lough. Nothing I could find out while researching this spot gave any indication of big or small fish being stocked.

They could be ten inchers or three pounders for all I knew, so my six pound leader felt like it should be able to cope with anything 'normal'. Lakes which are stocked with ultra large trout tend to advertise the fact loudly to attract those anglers who value big fish. As always on these 32 jaunts size was of no importance to me and a solitary foot long spotted fish would send me home to Mayo a happy fisher. Here, just off the shore, looked like as good a place as any to start fishing.

The rod flexed like a living thing in my hand as the first casts of the day sang through the rings. It takes time for me to settle into the fishing after all the driving to get here. The concentration required when behind the wheel is very different to what I find I need when fishing. Being encased in a little tin can as you whizz along the tarmac dodging homicidal others road users takes one skill set while angling for fish on a new water most definitely requires a totally different set of mental and physical processes. I find it hard to instantly switch from one to the other.

Fly fishing from a boat on your own can be a bit tricky. The weight distribution is poor so the boat rarely travels directly down wind, tending instead to wander about depending on the whims of the capricious wind. Today though there would be none of those issues as there was no wind. The boats were smallish but just fine for a lough this size.

It soon became apparent this was going to be a tough day. Trout were leaping all around me, but not in a good way. The fish were not rising to feed on flies, they were just shooting vertically in the air then dropping back with an almighty splash. I hate to see fish doing that, They are preoccupied with something else other than food and are the devil's own work to catch. After a while I changed flies, the first of a seemingly endless series of changes which kept me busy the whole session. The deep water beside the dam was thoroughly searched with me counting the line down.

Ten seconds, then fifteen, twenty next and so on. That didn't work so I changed the flies again, then moved to different 'drifts' across the deep water.

No joy. Next I rowed to the other end of the lake and fished the shallower water there. A tiny ripple developed so I tried the dry fly but nothing was tempted by that so I went back to the fast sinker. Another change of flies and a new, finer leader on the sinker failed so I swapped to a fast glass. It was flat calm again now but I could see some movement over in a small bay so I rowed in there and chucked the kitchen sink at the fish leaping in there. Of course they refused to play. Back to the deeps then...

There were rainbows jumping all around me about 50 yards off the dam wall but try as I might I could not tempt one. A faint ripple got up as a breeze appeared so I set up a floating line on the six weight and started to cast. No response, not even after yet another change of flies. OK, I will try buzzers. A long leader with three heavy buzzers, then a washing line set up all proved to be useless. I changed to seven weight back to the fast sinking line and went through my lure box trying minkies, IPN's in different colours, damsels, cats whiskers in different hues and floating fry imitations. Not so much as a nibble.

Putting the sinking kit aside, I picked up the six weight and tied on three new flies, a size 12 Octopus on the bob, a similar sized Wickhams in the middle and a small Yellow Green Peter on the tail and fished them at different speeds. A pod of fish were jumping behind the boat now so I left the rod down with the flies still in the water while I pulled on the oars to take me 20 yards back up the wind.

The inevitable happened of course and after only a few strokes on the oars the reel screamed as a heavy fish latched on to the flies trailing behind me. Ten yards of line were gone in an instant before the leader snapped. I saw nothing of that fish but it sounded like a good one! Yet another new leader and different flies were soon attached and I started to cast once again amid the splashes of the jumping trout.

All this time I has been looking for any clues as to what might be going on with the fish. The water was low and warm, opaque grey in colour. I had seen some fry in the harbour but none out in the deep water at the dam. There was no fly life to be seen. In warm weather, lime green and orange lures often work but not today. By four pm, I had tried dozens of lures, wet flies, dries and buzzers, fished floating, intermediate, fast glass, slow sinking and fast sinking lines. Retrieves had varied from static to near-supersonic and the whole of the lake had by now received my attention. I had covered scores of fish, the only take being that one who savaged the flies as I was rowing. I was rapidly running out of ideas!

Pretty much becalmed, I put three new flies on the fast sinking line and went back to counting them down to fish the whole water column right down to the bottom. Each cast was a carbon copy of the last, blast the line out as far as I could, count it down then retrieve in short, sharp pulls until I rolled the line on to the surface for the next cast.

By now, there were only a handful of trout leaping and a little light rain began to fall. Then, out of nowhere, there was the faintest pluck at one of the flies. Not a proper take but a hopeful sign none-the-less. I cast again, muttered the seconds under my breath and started the retrieve. After a few pulls, the line miraculously tightened…

A lot of anglers hate sinking lines, with the action happening deep below there is none of the visual joys of a take. For me, there is something wonderful in that sensation of the fish 'appearing' on the end of a well sunk line. My line went tight and the slack line on the deck flew through the rings as the fish felt the hook. Two runs took me almost to the backing then he started to jump. Five or six times he took to the air but the hook held for me. Another run but this time much shorter. I got the net ready and played him out. Hooked on the bob fly, I drew him into the meshes at the first time of asking, a lovely fish of between three and four pounds. A photo, unhooking then I slipped the fish back into the grey water. It was all over in no time at all.

Why had that fish taken a fly when so many others had refuse to all day? I will never know and maybe that is part of why we going fishing, there are no certainties. For the next hour, I cast out and retrieved without so much as a touch so in the end I rowed back to the harbour and tied up. Gear transferred to the car, I filled in my catch on the permit and stuffed it in the box by the gate along with the key. Then it was back up that long road to Mayo, past the fresh cut golden fields and through busy rural towns of Waterford, Tipp and Limerick. Helen gave me that 'you are mad' look as I walked through the front door just before nine pm.

What fly did the trout take in the end? After chucking every lure know to mankind at the fish all day my only trout fell for a size 12 Octopus.

The drogue was never needed and it has been tucked away in the fishing den once again. I'll admit I fell in love again with my old Hardy six weight and intend to use it more often. So, Waterford has been stroked off the list after a difficult but hugely enjoyable day. I am edging ever closer to the finishing line.

Chapter 30
Wicklow

County number 30

Wednesday, 3rd August 2022

Hearing the name Wicklow always conjures up visions of the mountains for me. Rising like some mythical protector of the land, the Wicklow mountains guard the southern approaches to the capital, proud and ancient. These hills and glens are thronged with people every weekend as they escape the city for rest and relaxation—walking, biking and jogging on the miles of tracks and paths. Being situated so close to the capital Wicklow has become a natural commuter base for those who can afford to live there. Aside from the mountains there is some farmland and a string of towns along the coast.

Pretty, historical and easily accessible from the capital, Wicklow is a nice place to escape the hubbub of the city. From an angling perspective, Wicklow has a history of good sea fishing from the beaches where smoothhounds and flatties used to be caught in numbers. I am not sure the catches are still so good in these days of over fishing. A handful of rivers rush off the mountains to empty into the Irish Sea, home to small brownies and some sea trout.

Being so close to Dublin Wicklow is an obvious destination not just for locals but visitors and the county boasts all levels of accommodation and attractions. It can get awfully busy at times and the price of everything seems to be extortionate to someone from 'down the country' like me. There is lots to do and see and something for everyone here or so it seems.

Wicklow has been ravaged by wild fires this summer, decimating the wildlife and scarring vast chunks of the woodland. We can ill afford to lose any forest in Ireland, there is hardly any left now and the powers that be don't seem to care. The image we like to portray to the wider world is a rural ideal but the truth is a land blighted by intensive farming, over grazed uplands and barren seas. I try to be optimistic and look to the EU for greater environmental controls and some enlightenment regarding our fragile eco systems but it is not easy. These wild fires show us the climate does appear to be changing and we must adapt how we are living to cope in the future.

Initially I considered two very different fisheries but rejected them both in the end. The river Liffey which flows through Dublin city centre starts out as a lively hill stream in the Wicklow mountains and there is a bit of trout fishing to be had as it flows in a wide circle through the county. While this initially appealed greatly to me but I have been doing a lot of brown trout fishing so far this year so I wanted a change. I may fish the upper Liffey sometime in the future, it looks like a nice stream to fish up in the hills.

Then there was the river Aughrim which looked very inviting, small pools in heavily wooded glens just waiting to be explored. The only problem for me was at this time of year the water will be horribly low and the trout hard to fool. I will leave this lovely river for another time too. I find the process of selecting where to fish to be a bigger challenge than the actual fishing. By now, you will have gathered I spend a lot of time searching for the 'right' venue and by that I mean ones where I feel I have the best chance of catching a fish. There is always a sneaking suspicion I am missing out on somewhere nicer.

In the end, I plumped for the other option altogether, a small stocked fishery called Annamoe down near Laragh in the south of the county. Allegedly home to rainbow trout of up to twenty pounds it sounded like a nice spot for a few hours. Stocked fisheries have been good to me over the years so it was with a level of confidence that I laid my plans. Surely even I would manage at least one rainbow trout! At the back of my mind was the notion of hooking a big trout, one to put a real bend in the rod. I have been fortunate enough to land many fish over the past couple of years but nothing very big—so far.

Small stocked fisheries have actually made up a larger proportion of the fishing for the project than I had initially thought they would. I'll confess this turned out to be deliberate as the need to catch 'something' was so important. Days spent tackling difficult waters, while interesting and stimulating, would not propel me towards my goal if they ended up as blanks.

So stocked loughs and ponds offered me an advantage which generally worked out in my favour. For some purists, this might be seen as an easy option and none too sporting but I enjoy most forms of angling so a day chasing rainbows in a small lake can be enjoyable as well as productive. I guess I am spoiled by living in the west where I can fish the big loughs anytime I want!

Not much tackle was required for this trip, a couple of fly rods, some reels, two boxes of flies and a net was all I packed this time, a change from the normal mountain of tackle that litters my car on a '32' journey. With some big fish potentially swimming around in the lake, I double checked my leader butts and connections to the fly lines, giving them a good tug to see if they would hold under pressure.

Then I made up a couple of leaders using 9 pound Stroft which I find is both thin and strong. It knots well but you must use plenty of lubrication when pulling your knots tight. My huge salmon net came with me, partly in case I ran in to a big trout but more because it is the only large knotless net I own.

The obvious route to Wicklow for me is to drive to Dublin then around the M50 as it circumnavigates the city then down the M11 to Bray. This had all the appeal of a visit to the dentist so instead of sitting in endless queues of frustrated commuters on six lanes of tarmac I drove down to Athlone, Tullamore then across south Kildare and in through the back door of Wicklow on some minor roads. The fishery doesn't open until ten o'clock in the morning so there was no need for a stupidly early start to my day. That terribly nice weather lady on RTE the night before had promised a day of strong winds and showers for Wednesday and I went to bed with the windows rattling and the garden being well watered from above.

I wake a few minutes before the alarm after a night of tossing and turning in the humid darkness. Yer wan on the telly was right, the trees along our street are bent by the wind and puddles on the road testify to last night's downpours. Coffee, toast, one last check I have everything then I'm off. Wind buffets the car and the occasional heavy shower clatters down all the way to Athlone but it dries up after that. The roads in Wicklow are heaving with traffic and every pub, hotel or restaurant I passed look like they are wedged with tourists. I find the fishery without any problem and park beside another couple of cars.

A white haired man who looked to be about my own age greets me and we talk for a while. This is the owner and I could have spend the day just listening to him. With strong connections to Mayo, he had been in the car sales industry for many years before deciding to create the fishery here in Wicklow. I was shocked when he told me he would turn 81 this year, there must be something in the water in these parts as I swear he looked as if he was in the same class as me at school.

But I was here to fish so once I had paid my dues I set up with the six weight then made my way through the trees to the lake. Perfectly manicured grass, seating dotted around it and interestingly shaped, this is a visually stunning place to come fishing. As it is surrounded by mature woodlands the wind is quite light, just ruffling the surface and no more. I see a very occasional fish show as I thread a clear intermediate through the rings and tie up a leader complete with a black goldhead, a dark sedge and a green peter.

One of the other anglers has headed off into the distance but the other lad, introduces himself as Tommy and sets up a few yards along the bank from where I am. A pipe clamped between his teeth, he casts through a cloud of sweet smelling smoke. Stopping for a chat with him I notice the left leg of his spectacles is held in place by a safety pin. He is a regular here and I listen intently as he points out good spots to fish. Returning to my gear I get into my rhythm and casting is a joy with the light eleven footer. As I cast I'm watching for any clues as to what the trout are feeding on but there are no insects on the water surface.

The slow rise forms suggest buzzers to me but just as I am thinking of a change the line tightens and I am in to one. He moves off to my left, taking a little bit of line but after a few seconds everything goes slack and the fish has gone. Reeling in I check the hooks and all seems to be in order. I stick with the same flies for a while but there are no more offers so I change to a small goldhead damsel and a pair of buzzers. An hour later and many more changes of fly, I hook another trout but it too falls off after only a short run. I could see that fish had taken a goldhead damsel on the tail but the take had been very wishy-washy so it was no great surprise that one did not stay on the hook. I decide to walk along the bank.

Annamoe is small and intimate but there are only three of us fishing here today so there is plenty of space. A change to the floating line seems to be worth a try and then I fish around the far end with small lures. Cat's Whiskers, Viva, White IPN, Orange Montana and others all get a try. When none of them work, I decide it is time for changing to dries. A daddy with a dark coloured Bob's Bits above it looks good to me but the fish don't agree. Nothing works today!

Checking the time I see that I'm half way through my four hour session. Two hours left to catch a fish and to be honest I am running out of ideas. Sitting at a wooden bench, I eat my sandwiches and try to think this through. An odd fish is showing around me but with no hatch I decide to go back to the goldhead and a couple of nymphs. Tall fir trees are close to the water here and casting is tricky but I resume fishing and flick the line out from under the canopy then inch it back to me.

Every couple of casts I take a step along the bank so I am covering new water. I have been doing this for maybe fifteen minutes when miraculously there is a tap-tap-tap at the flies and I strip strike into a rainbow. Gingerly I play the hard fighting fish out and at the second time of asking I net my first ever county Wicklow fish. This is a fine trout of a couple of pounds and fully finned. I release him and start fishing again, vaguely aware of the stupid grin on my face.

I fish on and am rewarded when a trout grabs the goldhead just as it hits the water. It too come to me after a strong fight, a bit smaller than the first lad but still very welcome. By now, I am asking myself why I had taken the black goldhead off in the first place. I manage to tangle the tip of my rod in the tree branches as I draw the fish towards the net and am lucky to get away with untangling it and not lose the fish. Taking stock of where I am fishing and the difficulties in casting from under the trees here I look around for an alternative. The small island opposite looks to be easier to fish from than the bank I am on so I decamp and cross the timber bridge on to the island and start fishing there.

With less trees behind me, I can make longer casts and this soon pays off handsomely. A heavier fish grabs the goldhead and puts up a tremendous fight, nearly taking all the fly line off the reel twice before I subdue him. During the fight I try to take some photos of the action but with limited success.

After that, it goes quiet again and for the next thirty minutes there are no more offers. Happy with three trout, I take a break and change all the flies again to see if I can catch on something other than the black goldhead. A black fritz goes on the tail, a sort of stick fly in the middle berth and an old favourite of mine, an Iven's Brown and Green Nymph on the top. I'm in to the last hour of the session so these flies do not have long to prove themselves.

The next fish grabs the Ivens and turns cartwheels after a long run but the hook holds and number four comes to the net. A fish shows just within casting range so I chance a few long casts in his direction. Sure enough I hook a fish on the stickfly out there. This one does take me to the backing but that is not as spectacular as it sounds as the trout had the fly at about 25 yards distance so a quick dash away from me was all it had to do to pull the joint in the line out of the rings.

That period of activity comes to an end as things go quiet but just before I pack up one last trout falls for the Ivens, a final seal of approval for the old pattern. All the trout had been swiftly released and swam off slowly once unhooked. It is very warm and the air feels oppressively heavy so just before three o'clock I call it a day. Back across the bridge I trudge, suddenly aware that my left ankle is sore.

Funny how I only feel this once I stop fishing! I chat with the other two lads on my way to the car and like me they caught nothing until after lunch. Tommy, still puffing his pipe, has landed a couple but is grateful for a black goldhead I pass on to him. I have used or given away almost my entire stock of black goldheads over the past few weeks so they are at the top of the list for tying more this winter.

I am hot and sweaty by the time I reach the car and am glad to divest myself of the fishing jacket and boots before taking the rod apart. That old familiar weariness descends on me now the fishing is over. I didn't feel tired at all during the action earlier this afternoon but now it is a different story and I could lie down for a nap on the grass verge. I double check that all the gear is in the car before setting off. I once left a much loved rod on the roof of my estate car and drove off, only recalling what I had done as I was driving along one of the main roads in Aberdeen. Screeching to a halt, I retraced my journey and found the remains of the rod squashed into the tarmac. A sobering lesson learned the hard way!

The drive home was uneventful but slow as there was heavy traffic and I took a wrong turning somewhere in Kildare, ending up crossing the Curragh before picking up the motorway. A thoroughly enjoyable day had been had and I like to think I will return and fish Annamoe again someday. While the fish were obviously the stars the lovely surroundings made just being there, a total joy. Thirty counties, that is how many I have successfully fished now. I don't want to count my chickens but surely I will see the project through to it's end?

I find that I am physically very tired the next day after a long trip like this one and so the driving and fishing are obviously taking a lot out of me. Balanced against that there is the undoubted mental health benefits of fishing these far off waters. I will take the tired limbs and sore ankles any time if I get to enjoy days like today.

Dressing of the Iven's Brown and Green Nymph

Hook: sizes 6 to 10, heavy wet fly hook (you can tie it on long shank hooks too)

Tying silk: black, 8/0

Back and tail: about 5 strands of peacock herl.

Rib: finest gold wire or oval gold tinsel on larger sizes.

Body: one strand of green ostrich herl and one of brown wound together. Pull the peacock herl over the wound body and tie down, leaving space for the head.

Head: a few turns of peacock herl.

You can vary this dressing slightly by replacing the green herl with an olive one. I tie these flies in both weighted and unweighted versions.

My take on the Stickfly is very simple. Stickfly patterns used to be very popular back in the '70s and '80s but they have largely fallen out of favour nowadays. That's a shame as these are excellent flies for both rainbows and browns.

Hook: a size 12 long shank (you can go bigger or smaller)

Underbody (optional): some lead or copper wire wound around the shank. Having a few of different weights is handy to deal with different depths.

Rib: fine copper wire.

Abdomen: peacock herl covering two thirds of the hook shank.

Thorax: Pearl Litebrite.

Hackle: a couple of turns of black hen.

Chapter 31
Limerick

County number 31

Monday, 8th August 2022

Here's the craic, Limerick (along with Louth) kept slipping down my list of counties to fish for the better part of two years. My research kept coming up short on options for both of these counties so I put them on the long finger for ages. Louth was completed some time ago though, so it was now well past time to get to grips with the Treaty county. The tributaries which flow across the flat lands into the Shannon from the south seemed to be obvious choices but the cream of the brown trout fishing was over for this season. The Maigue, Mulclair, Feale, Morning Star and the rest all were past their peak, gripped by low water and chocking with weeds. How about trying for some coarse fish on the main river itself?

This county is of course dominated by the city of the same name. 100,000 souls abide in the conurbation, some in luxurious manors, others in dismal, drug ridden estates. St. Johns Castle on the Shannon is many peoples picture of the city, a testament to a more violent past when the Normans arrived and overthrew the local chiefs.

Beyond the city lie green fields full of cows as this is primarily dairy country. Not being a lover of either cities or cows there has been little to draw me to Limerick in the past but it would be nice to spend a day there for a change. Recently I have passed through it many times as I visited other counties but on this occasion I would be stopping and wafting a fishing rod about.

After a dip in my enthusiasm earlier this year, there is a tangible excitement around each of these last two upcoming '32' jaunts. They have a very different feel to those I undertook last year when the list ahead of me felt endless and sometimes insurmountable. Like a runner coming off the final bend and seeing the line for the first time I have found that extra spurt of energy to complete the task I set myself two years ago.

Only Limerick and Donegal remain unconquered and today I would pit my wits against the fish in the Shannon. My luck has held so far this year with fish landed on the first attempt on each trip but surely that could not continue. Failure would be hard to stomach. I had come damn close on my recent trip to Waterford and I was taking nothing for granted this time around.

Today was going to be a relatively short journey and one which was none too taxing from a driving perspective as there is motorway for a lot of the way to Limerick. The 'new' stretch of the M18 from Tuam to Gort makes a huge difference in travel time, bypassing the dreaded bottlenecks of Claregalway, Oranmore and Kilcolgan. I know I moan a lot about the state of Irish roads but the M18 is an excellent piece of infrastructure. My trips in this direction when I went to Cork and Kerry felt like an odyssey, but this time once I had turned off the motorway and passed Tulla I was only a short way from my destination.

The old car is running a bit better after it was serviced the other week. Parts were horrendously expensive and, being a Renault, half of the car had to be dismantled to reach the fuel filter, which appeared to have been the same one in it when it left the factory in Douai all those years ago. A leaky air hose was also replaced at the same time and the little diesel engine now runs a lot smoother as a result.

So it would be the Shannon. I had shied away from this mighty waterway for most of the 32 project but I felt my best chance for a fish in the horrid sunshine would be in the deep, cool waters of the lower river instead of casting for trout on a lough. In the end, I had plumped for a stretch at O'Brien's Bridge to the north of the city. There was plenty of information about the north bank of the river at this point, the only problem with that being the north bank is in county Clare! I could see nothing regarding the south bank but working on the assumption the fish cared not a jot for county boundaries I expected the same species were likely to be swimming around on the Limerick side. Would my optimism be rewarded?

Roach, Bream and hybrids of the two were the expected species with maybe the odd small perch hanging around as well. Pike would be in there too and I figured if I could not do anything with maggot or worm I would be forced to spin for jacks. After a few recent outings fishing for rainbow trout, it would be nice to get back to some coarse fishing. For various reasons, I have done very little with float and feeder so far in 2022 and I have missed my quiet, contemplative days.

Fog greeted me when I opened the curtains just after five in the morning so I went back to bed for a while. Creeping slowly along the road virtually blind did not appeal to me so I postponed my departure for a bit longer. The mist would burn off as the sun rose making the journey much more pleasant. And so I whittled away another couple of hours dozing and reading before raising myself, showering and packing the last few bits into the car. The heat was building as I set off in what had turned to a thin mist, it would be a scorcher today.

The roads were busy but moving after I passed all the roadworks around Castlebar. The only interruption was some cows crossing the road at O'Callaghan's Mills, sure milking time waits for no man. A gorgeous male sparrowhawk flew across the road in front of me at one point, such pretty birds but the scourge of the little song birds.

East Clare looked well under the summer sun. Banks of silvery mist came and went all the way down to the Shannon but clear blues skies greeted me as I drove over the old bridge from Clare into Limerick. Once across the river I found a quiet spot to park up close to the bridge. The first thing that struck me was the wide reed beds which seemed to go on as far as the eye could see.

Car parked, I lugged my heavy load of gear along a faint path in the oppressive heat. I had more weights and groundbait than normal as well as an extra rod and the whole lot felt like it weighed a ton. At least, I didn't require my thick waterproof coat for a change. Summer had arrived at last and the hot weather is due to last all week. I trudged across a couple of fields, the second one full of inquisitive horses. From there, a faint path led me to the boundary wall of an old cemetery where I stopped gather my breath and my bearings.

Looking upstream I could discern a thinner spot in the reeds beside some trees. Maybe I had found myself a spot to fish from. The only issue would be getting across a barbed wire fence atop a bit of a drop. It took me a few minutes to crawl under the wires and push through tall nettles and brambles but I made it but was badly stung in the process and thick brambles torn at my hands.

The river is a bit complicated here thanks to the ESB, Ireland's state electricity supplier. In the 1920s, they built a dam across the river here and installed turbines to produce hydro power. I fully appreciate that the new country badly needed this infrastructure as most parts of the state had no access to electricity back then. These days I firmly believe we should dismantle the dams and allow the Shannon to flow freely, but that is an argument for another day.

From where I was on the south bank, I was looking out at an island and further upstream Purteen Weir held back the flow. With no stands to fish from, I would be fishing from the bank into pretty deep water. The flow was placid but if I moved upstream the pace would quicken. It looked to me like a swimfeeder sort of a place.

My spot consisted of maybe ten feet of fairly open area in front of me where the reeds only stretched 5 yards out into the water. I could see more underwater growth through the clear water beyond but after that it was deep and slow moving. Trees to my right and slightly behind me made casting a bit tricky but manageable. A nice little white fibreglass boat was tied up to a hurdle in the trees.

This would do just fine so I set up the seatbox on the thick mud where animals had been coming down to drink. A quick check on my bait showed my worms were in fine fettle but the maggots that had been in the fridge for a week were now rapidly turning hard and there might not be enough to last the whole session. I could use the casters as loose feed.

The big feeder rod was made for this kind of fishing so it was the first one I set up with ten pound running line to a heavy feeder and a twizzled boom to a six pound bottom about a foot long. Ground bait consisting of brown crumb, oats, corn, hemp and Sensas 3000 made into balls. Some dead maggots also found their way into the mix as well as some of those casters. Normally I suspect I am a bit mean when mixing it but for once I made up a large batch of groundbait, figuring my big challenge might be attracting fish into my chosen swim. Four balls went in for a start and I made six casts with the feeder to lay some groundbait out from that too. Here fishy, fishy, fishy…

Next I set up the other feeder rod, this time a much lighter rig with six pound line on the reel and a four pound bottom. This one was much shorter at only six inches or so. My plan was to try different rigs and see what, if anything, worked. Maggots which I impaled on a size 12 hook were soon on the bottom of the Shannon.

Hot and dirty already what with lugging all the gear to the swim then mixing the groundbait, I felt I had earned a drink of water and a bite to eat under the intense sunshine. The trees did provide a modicum of shelter from the rays but it was clear today would be a hot, sticky one. The red tipped rods were fixed by my steely gaze as I settled back to see what the day would bring.

There must have been a path on the far side of the river as I could just make out people walking through the trees over there. In the stillness, I could hear their conversations, loudly at times then fading as they headed into the village. Two women were in a deep conversation, totally unaware I could hear them from across the Shannon. I won't go into detail but some poor fella was in awful bother when he got home that night!

I won't bore you with the details of the next two hours of cast/wait/retrieve, suffice to say there was no action. I fed my original swim and a new one over to my left. I changed hook bait frequently, dropped down in hook size on the light rod and tried a worm kebab on a hair rig on the heavy rod. All of this was to no avail and not a single nibble came my way.

There was more action in that old graveyard I had passed on my way here! By now I was hot and bothered, running out of ideas and cursing my decision to try this part of the river. Capricious confidence floated away on the rivers smooth current.

A slight rustle behind me caused me to turn around, only to be confronted by a huge hairy black head with two horns sprouting from it not three feet away.

Initial alarm this was a bull was quickly dispelled when a small calf poked its head out from behind it's mam. After a couple of minutes gazing intently at me, the pair of them wandered off. I expect they normally came down to this spot to drink from the river and were very surprised to find me there.

Away over to my right I thought I could see some fish rising. Hard to define for a start, I watched for many minutes trying to figure out what I was seeing. Just some tiny Rudd I mused, but I kept watching and decided they were coming slightly closer to where I was set up. There was a float rod in the quiver, should I try to catch a Rudd?

Almost imperceptibly the rises edged ever closer. Was it too big a risk to dismantle one of the leger rods? A decision was required quickly before the fish moved off again. Right, that's it! I will make up the float gear.

Taking down the light leger rod I soon had the reel transferred on to the old thirteen footer and I set a loaded crystal waggler at five feet. A number 4 shot at the loop to loop connection was all I needed to allow the single maggot on a size 18 hook to fall gently down. By now, there were some rises in front of me so I cast out. Nothing the first cast but on the second one my float dipped and I lifted into a fish. It was a roach! So much for my fish spotting skills but I'll admit to being unfeasibly happy with that small fish. The maggot was well chewed so I re-baited and cast out again. My worries that I would run out of maggots diminished and I would manage to fish the whole session with the scant few left wriggling in the box.

The next roach was a tad bigger than the first one and the third was larger again but none of them were massive. Bites were simply a very slow sinking of the float, nothing dramatic. I missed a number of what looked to be perfectly good bites for no obvious reason but at least there was some action to keep me entertained.

Sure enough, a tiny Rudd turned up next then I was back into roach. Three more had come to hand when the float gave a slight wobble and I lifted into something a bit better. Winding in, I didn't pay any real attention to the fish, just thinking it might be a pounder this time. The rod bent as I applied a little pressure to lift the fish up when it got near to the weeds but just then it turned and shot off with stunning power and speed, snapping the four pound line like it was sewing thread.

This sort of thing happens far too often to me, I get complacent when the silvers are biting and am never ready when a big fish comes along. So what could that large, strong fish have been? I dearly wish I could say I saw it but I didn't, so I am left guessing. Being so high in the water I doubt it was a tench leading me to think it was a big trout but I'll never know for sure.

Tying on a new tippet I moved up to a size 16 hook and went on to double maggot for bait. My motivation for this change was to try and find another better class of roach. This very quickly got me a small perch instead. Things went quiet and less fish were rising now. Then, out of the blue, about 20 minutes later my last roach inhaled the twin maggots. After that, it went completely dead. Under a fierce sun I stuck it out for a while longer to see if the roach would come back but it was stifling hot and felt like the river had gone to sleep. I decided to call it a day some four hours after starting to feed the swim.

In total, I had landed a meagre 7 small roach, a perch and one tiny rudd, hardly a session to remember but I can now state without fear of contradiction that I have now caught fish in county Limerick. While that was the whole point of the day, it also opened my eyes to the Shannon and fired up a desire to get to know more about the fishing along its length. The famous Mudflats section of the river is but an hours drive from home for me but I have yet to try it out. Maybe this autumn I will address that glaring omission.

Retracing my steps to the car was slow in the oppressive heat. If the green fields had been sand, I could have been mistaken for John Mills in 'ice cold in Alex'. Covid has left me with a deep exhaustion which is hard to shake but I finally crossed the last stile. Between the muddy bank, groundbait and sweat I was a right sight (and smell I dare say) but given the difficult conditions I was happy enough with my day's work. County number thirty one had been completed.

The sun still beat down as I disrobed and packed the car. Above, on a telephone wire a lone swallow sat, an occasional chirp giving away its presence. We regarded each other, me a sunburnt human and the swallow, a couple of ounces of feathers and courage. Soon it will be off on an unimaginable journey across Europe and the Sahara to spend the winter feasting on flies near the equator. I could hardly find my way across a couple of fields in Limerick but he would wander the skies then return here, to this very spot next April.

As I drove home I was thinking about what the future holds and how unlikely it was that others will emulate this project by driving all over the country to go fishing. The expense is one thing but the use of cars is going to have to decline in light of our over consumption of fossil fuels. Maybe electric or hydrogen powered cars are the way forward but nothing is certain. I judge myself extremely lucky to have been able to attempt this project before the era of personal transport changes forever. Maybe the next fella who does it will be on a push bike!

Chapter 32
Donegal

County number 32

Wednesday, 17th August 2022

Thirty one done, only one to go. Donegal was in my crosshairs as for the last time I would take to Eire's highways and byways on my wee project. The rugged lands of the far north west of Ireland have captured the hearts and minds of many who have travelled there. This is picture postcard Ireland, white washed thatched cottages set amid forty shades of green, deserted golden beaches backed by purple cloaked mountains. For those who enjoy the great outdoors, Donegal has an awful lot to offer. The geography is a bit complicated with salt water inlets biting deep into the coast, shallow tidal lagoons and even new lakes created by storms but it begs to be explored and enjoyed. The people are wonderfully friendly and hospitable. They are all stone mad of course but in a likable kind of way. I always felt very much at home in this county and cherish any time spent there.

Donegal was another of those counties where the only problem was deciding which one of hundreds of venues to visit. It is hard to get your head around the seemingly endless options this county presents to an angler. There is some great trout fishing on numerous loughs, large and small. Being one of the few places in Ireland where sea trout are still relatively common it is worth a trip just to fish for these enigmatic wanderers.

Salmon fishing on the river Finn can be very good after a spate and permits are easily available. There are lots of productive spate rivers too where grilse and sea trout run during the summer if there is a bit of rain. I could go on and on but there is a lot of information out there on the angling in Donegal to help you find some memorable fishing.

In truth, I have caught many, many fish in Donegal over the years as I used to work up there. After a day's work, I often wandered off to chuck a fly in a small stream or hill lough for an hour. This almost always yielded a few small trout before the midges drove me back to the pub for a swift pint before bed. For the purposes of this project though I would assume a clean slate and try my luck on a lough I have not fished before.

I made a list of potential venues but that burgeoned to a point where it became unmanageable. Some clarity of thought was required so I decided I wanted to fish from a boat for the day, thus ruling out the vast majority of the loughs. Once I had narrowed my options down things became a lot clearer and I decided to try Lough Anure, somewhere I read about, driven past scores of times, but never fished.

I feel very 'comfortable' fishing from small boats on Irish loughs, like it is my natural habitat. No doubt the fact I have spent a huge chunk of my adult life messing about on them is the main reason but for me there is a spiritual side to being out on the vastness of the loughs, a oneness with the elemental forces if you will. The ways of the wind, waves, weather and fauna endlessly fascinate me. Out there I feel like a child full of innocent wonder instead of an old, world weary man.

Handling the boat in all weathers, be that purring along on the engine or straining on the oars just adds to the enjoyment and all of this is before I even cast a line for those beautiful evasive fish. It was fitting that the thirty second county should feature a day spent in a boat on a lough. It felt 'right' somehow.

Sitting to the north of the famous Rosses fisheries, Lough Anure is a medium sized, shallow lake on the river Crolly system. The rugged shoreline and numerous islands should make for an interesting day I figured. The largest of the islands, Trairagh, is inhabited and a causeway links it to the eastern shore. A few salmon still make it into the lake along with some sea trout but this is mainly a brown trout fishery. An active club has boats for hire on the lough and so I brought along my engine and all the rest of my fly gear to try a few drifts.

The internet provided me with lots of photos and even videos of the presentation ceremonies the local club held after various competitions on the lough. This was all well and good but I really wanted a bit more in the way of technical information such as what are the flies which catch most of the trout or where are the shallow reefs where said trout might be lurking.

The little I was able to glean about the fishing on this lake suggested most of it was very shallow, there were lots of rocks to be wary of and it held a good stock of small, free rising trout. At this time of the year, I might be lucky enough to contact a sea trout or even a salmon. As for what flies to try it seemed to be a case of 'the usual' so I almost certainly had a few in the box that would work.

Petrol tank filled (a traumatic experience these days) and engine tucked in the boot, I hit the road at 8 am on a dull mid-August morning. There was hardly a breath of wind to stir the trees in the garden, not the best of conditions for lough style fishing but I hoped there would be a breeze up in Donegal. Sligo was busy of course as I passed through just after nine but the roads were fairly quiet after that.

On to the Donegal Town bypass but after that, the day began to take a turn for the worse. The turn off up the R262 was blocked and a sign proclaimed the road to be shut to traffic. OK, I could carry on the N56 instead so adding a few extra miles I made for the village of Glenties. What I did not know was the road beyond Glenties is under major reconstruction and I spent a frustrating 20 minutes stuck at traffic lights there.

Donegal is in every respect the forgotten county when it comes to transport. The government in far off Dublin could not care less about this part of Ireland. There is no rail connection nor direct main road to links the county with the capital. The English seriously considered taking Donegal as part of Northern Ireland when they partitioned the island and you have to wonder how that would have worked out.

The journey north gave me plenty time for reflection on what the last day of my project meant to me. What had started off as a vague notion that it would be nice to catch a fish in every county grew like Topsy and was about to culminate today (hopefully). Thousands of miles driven, fishing in all weathers for all kinds of fish and the highs as well as the lows had created a wonderful experience for me. As long as the trout played ball today it would come to an end, consigned to history.

That felt sad, like something was going to be stolen away from me. I guess the more effort you put into something the greater the sense of loss will be when it is over. Would the project have felt the same if I had imposed a different criteria on myself and instead of catching a fish in each county I just had to go fishing there? Mulling this over I decided that the catching was important and added a massive challenge to each day out. Stretching myself to land at least one fish really got me thinking and made me focus much more than I usually do on a 'normal' fishing day.

My first stop was in the village of Dungloe and the centre for all things angling in the area, Charlie Bonner's shop. Here I could buy a permit and sort out the hire of a boat for the day. Parked up, I strode to the door of the shop only to find it closed. A hand written sign on it declared 'back at 10.30' but as it was already 10.45 I assumed there had been a further delay in opening up. I went for a walk along the mean streets of Dungloe and returned just as the shop was opening.

A permit was quickly secured and I was off on the last leg of my journey. The village of Dungloe is a great spot to base yourself if you come to the county for an angling holiday as it sits in the middle of the Rosses fisheries. If yours is an outdoorsie sort of family, there is plenty for the non-angling members to enjoy too.

From there, it was only a few more miles to the lough. Turning off on to the track next to the petrol station I found the car park by the water's edge. There was no sign of the boat I had just hired! A phone call soon identified the problem—the boat I had hired was kept at the other end of the lough. Back in the car and off down narrow roads. I got lost once but finally found the boat at the bottom end of a field by a ruined cottage. I parked under a twisted mountain ash and took in the vista before me.

My hire boat for the day was a nice Burke's Anglers Fancy, built across the road from where I used to live in Ballinrobe. It seemed to take me ages to get the engine and gear sorted out and push out through the thick bed of reeds into open water. One minute past midday said my phone as I pulled the cord and the Honda burst into life. I was fishing at last!

The old six weight rod and a floating line would do to start with and I tied on a five pound leader, more than strong enough for the small trout in here. The wild brown trout of the Donegal loughs tend not to grow too big. A half pounder is a decent fish and one reaching a full 16 ounces is an exceptional trout on most loughs. The peat makes the water acidic which in turn limits the food supply for the fish, hence their relatively small size. I am perfectly happy fishing for the small lads and so Lough Anure was the ideal spot for me. It is set amid wild bog land with peat hags on the shore in some places and large boulders scattered around both in the water and on the land around it. I love fishing wild places.

What flies to try? A size 12 Green Peter is always a good starting option for the bob and since I was here I tied on a size 10 Donegal Hopper in the middle. On the tail, I tied a Silver Daddy. I suspect many of you will not be familiar with the Donegal Hopper so here is the dressing:

Hook: a size 10 or 12.

Tying Silk: Black, red or blue, you pick! (I prefer blue)

Tag: I add a wee tag of holographic red tinsel, just 2 or 3 turns.

Body: Medium blue seals fur. I pepper mine with some chopped Globrite no.14 floss.

Rib: Medium flat silver tinsel, 3 or 4 turns.

Legs: Paired pheasant tail fibres, knotted and dyed black. I use 4 pairs but you can add more or less as you desire.

Hackle: Black hen, long in fibre.

Today would be all about traditional style wet fly fishing from a drifting boat. Like so many anglers from across the world I absolutely love fishing in this style. Not knowing the lough meant I would spend the day crawling along at a snails pace constantly on the lookout for shallows or sneaky rocks just below the surface which could wreak the engine.

A few scrapes on the bottom of the boat are just part and parcel of lough fishing but trashing the bottom end of an outboard is an altogether more serious matter so I take great care when I don't know a lake. When it looked like I was in very shallow territory, I lifted the engine and resorted to using the oars. It was to be a day of bumps and scuffs as the lough showed me where her stones were. Some people get a bit spooked by these underwater reminders but the sudden stops followed by vigorous shoves with the oars are all part of the days fun for me.

It was evident right from the start I was in for a tough day. The surface of the lough was like a mirror and the sun beat down from on high. A couple of drifts near where I had launched were unproductive so I moved further up the lough and fished three more shortish drifts. These took a long time as there was no wind to move the boat, meaning I resorted to using the oars to give me some movement.

The faintest of breezes got up from the west and I manged a drift into a small bay where a trout plucked at the flies but failed to stick. I changed all three flies and tried to fish that drift again but the faint wind had died and I was becalmed. I used the time to move again, this time into the largest piece of open water to the north of the big island. More drifts (if you could call them that) and more changes of fly. No good.

With the lack of wind, I decided to try the dry fly, so making up a new leader I tied on a daddy and a small sedge. The better part of an hour later and nothing had even had a sniff of the dries so took off the floater and went on to a slow sinking line and another three new flies. Still the lack of wind was my concern, wild brownies hate a flat calm and today was providing me with ample proof. Different parts of the bay were explored but without any signs of fish.

The day was slipping by quickly and I was making a very poor show of it so far. By now it was after 4pm, time for something else, but what? I changed back to the floater and put on a Claret Hopper, a Connemara Black Dabbler and a Butcher before motoring back up to just outside the harbour. As I reached my destination the wind miraculously began to blow. It wasn't much but there was enough to ruffle the surface a bit.

Casts were flying out in all directions as I frantically searched for a trout before the wind died again. The boat was being slowly pushed to the north and I kept her within casting distance of the western shore with strokes from one oar. Maybe 100 yards past the harbour I heard a trout rise behind me but when I turned around there was no sign of where the fish had broken surface.

I was sure I had not imagined it, so taking three swift pulls on the oars to push me further out I switched the line from my left to right, depositing it off the bow of the boat. Feeling sure that rise was further to my right I recast, landing the flies another 3 or 4 yards further away. A few pulls of the line then splash, he was on. I won't attempt to detail the struggles of a half pounder, suffice to say it was quickly in the boat with me, a handsome little chap who had fallen for the charms of my Connemara in the middle.

Photographed and briefly admired, I popped the little lad back over the side and with a flick of his tail he was gone. The dropper was tangled so out came the scissors and I re-tied it before starting again. There was a small island ahead of me which looked interesting and as I drifted past it I rose four small fish in quick succession but none of them felt the hook. None of them were of any consequence. Even as I turned the boat to go back over that drift again the wind died on me and I was back to a flat calm. I took the opportunity to make more changes and with three new flies on the leader, I headed back up the lough's eastern shore, hunting for a ripple.

Up there, close to the rocky shore a fitful wind blew, then died, then blew a little more, making for a frustrating evening. On the verge of packing up, the breeze appeared again and as if by magic a small trout grabbed my leggy Bibio on the bob only feet from the shoreline of another small island. I had number two for the day. Rowing (because the water was very shallow) I made my way along the other side of the big island and found some wind which allowed me to drift once again. Three more fish rose to the flies but I failed to hook any of them. I moved on again.

By now, I am sure you are getting as frustrated as I was! When the wind blew the fish responded but as soon as the lough became calm the trout vanished, it was as simple as that. Dodging as close to the rocks as I dared, flicking flies into each small space between the boulders, I worked the shorelines as the wind allowed. At the end of a drift, just as the water became shallow a fish rose and this time I set the hook.

It was another typical hill lough trout of less than half-a-pound but on a day like today it was very welcome. I fished on some more but in the end I grew tired and turned the boat back towards where I had found her. At 7pm, the keel ground on to the gravel and I disembarked. Not only was today over but the whole 32 project had now come to a conclusion. Exhausted, unloading the boat and tying her up took me far longer than usual, I had run out of energy completely. The engine, near empty fuel tank and my tackle bag all felt as if they were cast from lead as I dragged them up to the car but in the end everything was safely stowed away.

As I opened the driver's door I spotted the tail feather from a Hooded Crow lying there on the short grass. Where had that come from? It certainly was not lying there when I parked the car. I picked it up and took it home with me, a small reminder of my day in Donegal. The engine spluttered into life then I wound my way along the narrow, grassy track to a decrepit gate where I did the old familiar "stop, get out and open the gate, get back in the car and drive through, stop the car, get out and close the gate, get back in the car" dance. It was late by now but finally I was back on the road home to Mayo. Avoiding those awful roadworks at Glenties I instead cut over by Fintown to Ballybofey then down the good road to Sligo.

And so it was over, I had achieved my goal and caught a fish in every one of the thirty two counties on the island of Ireland. I suppose not many anglers can claim to have done the same thing but that was never the point, it was not some sort of competition. If not, then what was it? For me it was trying something new, be that new venues, new methods or even seeing new places on the road. Instead of one big goal it became a collection of tiny events, sights and feelings which lifted me out of my angling lethargy which I had been gradually sinking into.

As much as the project was about new things it was equally a celebration of endings. Most of these I grant you were in my head but are real to me. I had just turned 60 years old when I fished the first county, Sligo, back in 2019, today I am 63 and a third (to use a Harry Potter-ism). In that space of time, the world has degenerated significantly and we all feel less secure and more uncertain about the future. I know I have changed so much over the time of the 32 and now lead a very different life having retired from full time employment.

In many ways, trotting across the country has helped me to transition into retirement. It gave me space to think about what I was doing and what I really wanted for the future. Long hours behind the wheel, a normal feature of my working life, now assumed a different feel.

We get so set in our ways, don't we? Take things for granted, believe we know it all and are in charge of our lives when in fact the opposite is true. The world spins in space, loved one pass away and our wrinkles deepen. The careless optimism of youth dissipates and we realise what we thought we knew was just smoke and mirrors. Only a lucky few like me have family and friends, enjoy reasonable health and live in peace. The 32 project was an extension of my good fortune. Not many people have been able to visit every Irish county with a rod and line and to stretch themselves outside their comfort zone amid the greenery of the Irish countryside.

I doubt if many will follow in my footsteps and undertake a similar journey, simply because the use of a car for motoring long distances purely for pleasure is about to come to a shuddering halt. My old cars were frugal and my driving style meant I was almost always returning more than 60 miles to the gallon on the open road. Compared to the super-rich who use personal jets to hop from one city to the next I did little damage to the environment but even that will become unacceptable in the very near future. My own feelings are mixed about cars and personal driving. We motorists are being blamed for an awful lot when in fact governments and large companies could have done so much more to develop new technologies and transport infrastructure. It is always easy to blame the little guy!

Much as I enjoyed Loughanure, the day's angling was veiled in melancholy as my project wound down to the last cast on the final day. It had been a stop-start sort of affair with long periods of inactivity interspersed with frantic bursts of rushing across rural Ireland. I felt genuinely sad it was all over but for now county Donegal had given me a wonderful day out and even if the fish were scarce. In the end, I had indeed caught a fish in every single Irish county.

Reflections

I would like to be able to state that each trip was carefully considered and slotted into the grand plan with military precision. That would be a lie of gigantic proportions though and the reality is I selected the running order on an ad hoc basis. While it sort of worked out in the end, I had stupidly left most of the distant counties until last, making for a tiring end to the project. It took over two years for the task to be completed, a timeframe I would have scarcely believed when I started out. Eventually though, I did manage to catch a fish from each county albeit Dublin took me two attempts.

Now it is over I have taken the time to review and tabulate the results of my 32 counties project. As with all statistics the truth is mangled and twisted but here is how it all ended according to my spreadsheets.

Most of my trips took place during the periods May to September over 2020 to 2022. This pretty closely shadows the best angling times here. The outliers were undertaken simply due to the easing of Covid-19 travel restrictions when I had been cooped up for months and was unsure if /when further restrictions would be imposed.

I could and undoubtedly should have caught many more fish. Sometimes I packed up while the fish were still biting because the long journey home was still ahead of me. The newly stocked trout in Fermanagh stand out of course and if I had stuck it out there I would have landed many more of those hapless fish. But to what end? Then there was the voracious shoals of skimmers in Monaghan who were biting at every cast. At some point, you have to ask yourself if simply hauling out fish after fish is really why you go fishing.

Long ago I figured out that while catching something was important, catching huge numbers of fish was not. If I compare that day on lough Keenaghan when I caught all those stockies to my final trip to Loughanure in Donegal on a day of flat calm and I struggled to catch three fish I have to say I enjoyed Loughanure more. I know that sounds wrong but in truth overcoming the challenges are more stimulating to me than just winding in large numbers of fish.

Despite my profligacy, I still landed 290 fish in total (an average of 9.06 per county), a number I am very happy with and much more than I had anticipated when I embarked on the project. A better angler would have caught more, of that I have no doubt, but the sum total of the experiences were of greater value than the actual catch.

In terms of the catch, predictably Brown Trout were my most numerous fish landed with Skimmers a close second. Perch and Roach of course turned up in good numbers. I surprised myself how often I fished for Rainbow Trout, given there is not an overabundance of fisheries with them. In all, I landed 13 species of freshwater fish:

68 x Brown Trout, all caught on the fly.
58 x Roach, mainly on the float but a few fell to the feeder.
53 x Skimmer, almost all on the feeder and most of them on one day in Monaghan.
40 x Rudd, a surprisingly large number I thought.
36 x Perch, at the outset I thought I would catch many more than this.
21 x Rainbow Trout, all on the fly.
6 x Hybrids, a mix of roach/rudd and roach/bream.
2 x Carp, both from the commercial fishery in Wexford.
2 x Bream, no slabs and a disappointing low number.
1 x Salmon, God bless Carrowmore Lake!
1 x Sea trout, also from Carrowmore.
1 x Pike, a fluke.
1 x Dace, who said these were easy to catch?

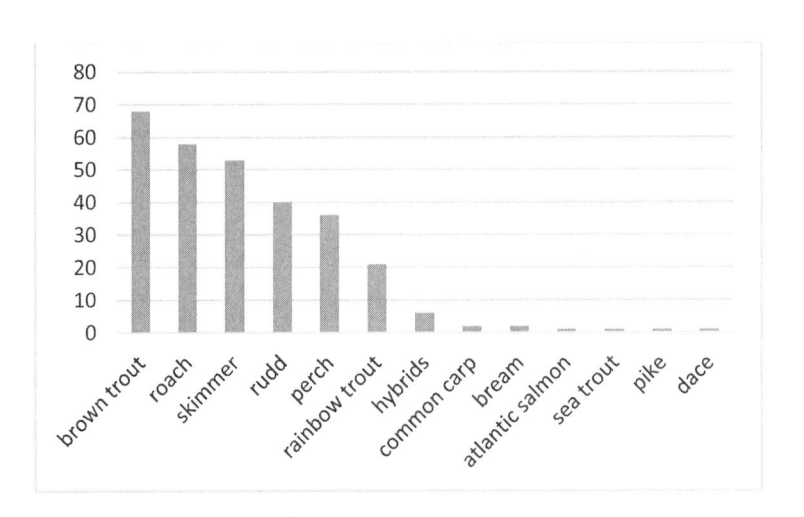

Together, brownies, roach, skimmers and rudd accounted for three-quarters of the total catch. There were no monsters among them and indeed, some days saw me land only tiddlers. The best fish was a ten pound Salmon, not the biggest fish ever but in these days of diminishing runs any salmon is good one. At the other end of the scale, a single small Dace was all I could muster in Carlow and those tiny Rudd hardly put a bend in my rod in Clare but that, as they say, is fishing.

From the outset, I wanted to document the realities of angling here in Ireland and that was bound to include blanks and poor days. I could have done things differently and had much greater success. For example, I could have pre-baited a lough and had a much better chance of a bag of large bream but I wanted to reflect the reality of just turning up on a bank and trying to catch something (anything!).

You will have noticed that I returned to two counties long after my initial and frankly unconvincing visits. I suspect a good psychiatrist would be able to put a name on this behaviour but it felt to me like I had something to prove to myself. Cloonahee in Roscommon was so early on in my coarse fishing career that I was pretty much clueless and only by the utter fluke of a pike happening upon my sweetcorn did I avoid a blank.

One year on and a second visit saw me haul out fish as I confidently tackled the same water with better bait and much improved tactics. Similarly, I struggled terribly on Cloondorney in county Clare but the water was filthy on that day, probably due to run-off from the nearby roadworks. Again, when I re-visited this lovely lake I quickly started to catch fish on a day when the water was fresh and clear.

At the same time as I was fishing all the counties, my own life was changing in very fundamental ways. I found that my approach to work seismically shifted over a relatively short period of time and the idea of retiring germinated and flourished in the rich compost of lockdown. Like many other people I began to question why I was working so hard? What was the point working until you drop?

A health scare in the spring of 2022 brought an end to the job I was doing then, further advancing the pace of change. Once you start down that road it is hard to turn back and as momentum for changing my lifestyle grew so outline plans for the future were made. Even now in late 2022 I have yet to nail down the details of my retirement from the workforce but it is time for this old codger to pass the baton to the younger generation and leave the field.

I had not figured on changing the car and to be honest I miss that old wreck of a Golf. It swallowed all my tackle with ease and was a nice car to drive. Its replacement lacks space, is noisy and the electrical systems vary from erratic to defunct. On the plus side, it is very fuel efficient so I can't complain too much.

How much did all this charging around Ireland cost me then? I kept a note of all expenditure and in the end it came to a grand total of €1,086, give or take a few bob. Exactly three-quarters of that went of fuel. Between both cars I covered a total of 10,644 kilometres meaning the trips averaged out at roughly 333km each.

Other odd facts include:

Number of rods broken—1, number of sandwiches consumed—63, number of times I forgot my net—2, number of cars towed off to the scrapyard—1.

OK, so that is the numbers, what did the project feel like? How has it affected this old angler? At the very beginning I was a total novice when it came to coarse fishing and I very reluctantly took up that branch of the sport solely to fulfil the needs of the 32 project. My life long held preconceptions about coarse fishing were very negative, to the point of being dismissive of the whole genre. This ignorance on my part meant I was ill prepared for the steep learning curve I embarked on back in 2020.

My ridiculously amateur efforts to start with were rewarded with a lack of success they so richly deserved and I found myself struggling badly for many weeks. Yet the frequent disappointments on the bank spurred me on to learn and become semi-proficient with float and leger.

Frustration slowly and painfully morphed into understanding and enjoyment as each failure increased my knowledge a little more. For the purposes of the project, I landed a total of 199 coarse fish, a number that experts would consider to be an average catch for a couple of sessions I suppose. But that equates to nearly 70% of all the fish I caught, showing how important coarse angling is in this country.

The coarse fishing has taken me to peaceful places and taught me so much about this type of angling. I fear that I will never be a particularly good coarse angler, and certainly would not consider entering a competition but give me a reed fringed lough with some roach or bream (and ideally a few tench) and I'll be very happy. Quite a turnaround for someone who thought coarse fishing was crap until now. Not only did I learn how to fish for coarse species but I found I actually thoroughly enjoyed this branch of the sport. In doing so, I also learned more about my own shortcomings and began to question many more of my more dogmatic beliefs. I guess I was not as 'well rounded' as I had imagined but then none of us are perfect.

While no expert, I am reasonably proficient with the fly rod and thought at the start of the '32' I had not much more to do than just roll out my 'usual' tactics and all would be well. Trout across the country had other ideas and they made me work very hard on some days. That was a good thing, it has woken me from an angling somnolence and invigorated me once again to learn more about fly fishing.

As a fly tyer the project brought me back some patterns I had almost forgotten about and I am plotting a huge change to the stocks of flies in my various boxes over the coming winter. I had become lazy and lacked the desire to push myself at the vice but my head is now bursting with ideas that I have to translate into new dressings.

The enigma which is Northern Ireland has frustrated, terrified and delighted those who have visited there for centuries and I am no different. This project has ignited a desire to fish the six counties more often and I want to sample more of the province in future. I had grown apathetic towards the travel across the border but in truth I can be in Enniskillen in just a couple of hours so no excuses can be accepted for not going there more often.

Final days are always bitter-sweet but Donegal was on another level for me. I love the county and discovered that I miss it very much. Driving back from my day on Loughanure along oft travelled roads brought a lump to my throat as memories flooded back of people and places from my past. I am very happy in Mayo but if you told me I had to move to one other county it would unequivocally be Donegal. So I will be making plans to fish up there more often in the future.

To say that I enjoyed every minute of every day would be a falsehood. Some days I got soaked to the skin which is never pleasant. Other days I was bedevilled with lack of bait or some other frustration that had me cursing into the wind. For all those problems, though there were so many more magical times in beautiful places. 32 different journeys and each was a unique experience for me. My eyes were opened to endless angling opportunities, to meeting interesting people and enjoying the great Irish countryside one again. All in all it had been worth the effort.

To summarise the whole experience—I saw places I had never been, caught fish on methods that were totally new to me and learned a lot about myself. Physically tiring at times, I found the whole experience intellectually and spiritually uplifting and it proved to be something I will never forget. Those hours of research on the laptop, fretting over where to buy a pint of maggots and long, lonely miles on every conceivable type of highway are now in the past but I will long remember the highs and lows of my time fishing every one of Ireland's unique counties. I hope you enjoyed coming along with me.